Peter W. Vik
760 South 19th St.
Pocatello, ID
83201

"I Tremble for My Country"

SOUTHERN DISSENT

UNIVERSITY PRESS OF FLORIDA

Florida A&M University, Tallahassee
Florida Atlantic University, Boca Raton
Florida Gulf Coast University, Ft. Myers
Florida International University, Miami
Florida State University, Tallahassee
University of Central Florida, Orlando
University of Florida, Gainesville
University of North Florida, Jacksonville
University of South Florida, Tampa
University of West Florida, Pensacola

SOUTHERN DISSENT

Edited by Stanley Harrold and Randall M. Miller

"I Tremble for My Country"

THOMAS JEFFERSON AND THE VIRGINIA GENTRY

Ronald L. Hatzenbuehler

Foreword by Stanley Harrold and Randall M. Miller

UNIVERSITY PRESS OF FLORIDA

Gainesville Tallahassee Tampa Boca Raton
Pensacola Orlando Miami Jacksonville Ft. Myers

A record of cataloging-in-publication data is available from the
Library of Congress.
ISBN 0-8130-3007-2

The University Press of Florida is the scholarly publishing agency
for the State University System of Florida, comprising Florida A&M
University, Florida Atlantic University, Florida Gulf Coast University,
Florida International University, Florida State University, University
of Central Florida, University of Florida, University of North Florida,
University of South Florida, and University of West Florida.

University Press of Florida
15 Northwest 15th Street
Gainesville, FL 32611-2079
http://www.upf.com

To John and Stephanie, Lindsay, and Patrick

Contents

Illustrations

Figures

Tables

Foreword

Thomas Jefferson is an American icon: author of the Declaration of Independence, third president of the United States, advocate of democracy and religious freedom, architect, naturalist, and purchaser of the vast Louisiana Territory. Jefferson is also an "American sphinx," a riddle composed of contradictions that historians have not solved. During recent years his reputation has suffered because of his apparent hypocrisy concerning slavery and race. An early opponent of slavery, he never freed his slaves, and grew increasingly opposed to abolition. An advocate of black physical and mental inferiority, he had children with a slave woman on his plantation.

For good or ill, Jefferson was a national figure almost from the start of the American Revolution in 1775 until his retirement from the presidency in 1809, and he remained one, even in retirement at Monticello, where he received numerous visitors from home and abroad, experimented in agriculture, laid out plans for a university, and wrote on national affairs. He served as a delegate to the Continental Congress, as ambassador to France during the 1780s, as secretary of state in George Washington's first presidential administration, as a creator of the first American party system, and as a two-term president. His vision of the United States as a decentralized agrarian republic retained political and intellectual force well into the nineteenth century, and his warnings against overexpansive government remain watchwords for many Americans today.

Although Jefferson increased central government power by purchasing Louisiana from France in 1803, he hoped that westward expansion into that territory and beyond would perpetuate a society dominated by planters and farmers. He believed their economic self-sufficiency encouraged republican virtue and discouraged centralized political despotism linked to corrupting business interests. Aside from the opening words of the Declaration of Independence, Jefferson's most famous statement is perhaps "that government governs best which governs least." Jefferson insisted that local government, tied to the interests of farming classes, must predominate in a republic. As it turned out, this traditionalist agrarian vision fell before a modernizing American economy as a market-oriented, progressive, cosmopolitan, and increasingly egalitarian North crushed the South and slavery during the Civil War.

In *"I Tremble for My Country": Thomas Jefferson and the Virginia Gentry*, Ronald L. Hatzenbuehler addresses forthrightly the contradiction inherent in Jefferson as a national figure who advocated localism. For nearly two centuries, historians have placed Jefferson in a national context. Hatzenbuehler does not neglect that context. But he goes beyond it to reveal Jefferson the Virginian, a man who defined himself from his boyhood as a member of the local gentry, retained that orientation throughout his career, and took pleasure in it during his long retirement. Hatzenbuehler portrays Jefferson as a slaveholding aristocrat shaped by the rhythms of a traditional agricultural society, who nevertheless dissented from that society in his early opposition to slavery, his promotion of agricultural reform, his campaign for religious toleration, his advocacy of public education, and his argument for a new state constitution to enfranchise westerners. He shows that Jefferson's time away from Virginia helped him realize that aspects of its society could serve as the basis for building a republic in America. In trembling for his "country," Jefferson assumed a skepticism about the received order that encouraged new thought drawn from local experience and experiment.

In all this, Hatzenbuehler reveals the tension at the center of Jefferson's personality. He was a national figure who preferred life on his plantation, an advocate of emancipation who could not escape the interests of the slaveholding class, a president whose outlook was shaped more by Virginia's interests than by national and international developments. In the end, Hatzenbuehler suggests, Jefferson could not escape the local culture into which he had been born, and in fact did not choose to do so. This extensively researched, carefully argued study is a welcome addition to the Southern Dissent Series.

Stanley Harrold and Randall M. Miller, Series Editors

Introduction and Acknowledgments

In late June 1826, as Thomas Jefferson neared death, he received complimentary letters inviting him to attend celebrations marking the fiftieth anniversary of the nation he had helped to create. For Jefferson, the approaching celebration stimulated both nationalistic sentiments and pride in his role in the founding. In one of the last of his thousands of letters, Jefferson said that he would have enjoyed exchanging "congratulations personally with the small band, the remnant of that host of worthies, who joined with us that day, in the bold and doubtful election we were to make for our country." Then he broadened the significance of the nation's independence by placing the document in a universal context:

> May it be for the world, what I believe it will be, (to some parts sooner, to others later, but finally to all), the signal of arousing men to burst the chains under which monkish ignorance and superstition had persuaded them to bind themselves, and to assume the blessings and security of self-government. . . . All eyes are opened, or opening, to the rights of man. . . . For ourselves, let the annual return of this day forever refresh our recollections of these rights, and an undiminished devotion to them.[1]

Although Jefferson was unable to receive the accolades of the celebrants in July 1826, with this letter he succeeded in shaping the view that continues to dominate interpretations of his life. As primary author of the Declaration of Independence, he established the United States' hopes and chose words that inspire people to achieve lofty principles.

Two distinguished past presidents of the leading professional associations of historians in the United States—the American Historical Association and the Organization of American Historians—have recently made just this case. For Bernard Bailyn, Jefferson embodies the provincialism inherent in the architects of the United States that allowed them to distance themselves from the past and to "[seek] to achieve a profound transformation of government and politics." "[H]e remained throughout his long career the clear voice of America's Revolutionary ideology, its purest conscience, its most brilliant expositor, while struggling to deal with the intractable mass of the developing nation's everyday problems." Despite disappointment and knowledge that neither he nor the nation succeeded in accomplishing the full measure of the possibilities the American Revolution promised, Jefferson continued until his death to hope "that the common sense of the people and their innate idealism would overcome the obstacles and somehow resolve the ambiguities, and that America would fulfill its destiny" to lead all people to overcome tyranny.[2] Joyce Appleby agrees. Jefferson devoted his public career to purging his nation of colonial, aristocratic traditions that blocked achievement of a "psychology of democracy." "He imagined a different kind of social world, and the peculiarities of time and place gave him a historic opportunity to act on that vision. . . . Thomas Jefferson jump-started democracy in the United States and, by extension, the world."[3]

Both Bailyn and Appleby acknowledge that the story is more complicated than this—that Jefferson's words cannot erase the fact that his commitment to equality and rights outstripped his capabilities to accomplish the full measure of what independence promised, that his contributions extended primarily just to white males, and that an expanded vision of equality remains elusive for the nation he helped to establish. This theme resonates in recent Jefferson scholarship, especially in the wake of the 1998 DNA study published in *Nature* magazine confirming that a Jefferson male fathered Sally Hemings's last known child.[4]

I join this debate by shifting its focus from a national and international perspective to a local one in order to assess Jefferson's legacy. I take my cue from Jefferson's writings, in which he most commonly called Virginia, rather than the United States, his "country." A case in point centers on a passage in *Notes on the State of Virginia* in which Jefferson said that Virginia's culture in the Revolutionary era made him "tremble for my country." I argue that his life was remarkable not only because he saw so clearly what Virginians were capable of accomplishing but also because he expressed such strong disappointment in their failures to live up to the possibilities for change.

In order to demonstrate how these themes inform his life, I proceed chronologically while simultaneously arguing that Jefferson's commitment to reform was periodic. Chapter 1 locates Jefferson within the gentry culture of Virginia at the time of the American Revolution. Based upon his status as a tobacco planter, he worried about the negative effects of that plant on the society that by 1620 had been single-mindedly devoted to its production. He was not the first to express these concerns. The theme of declension that Jefferson identified also troubled Virginia's earliest chroniclers, including its first historian, John

Smith. It led them to question whether Virginians were capable of realizing the promise of human renewal that the New World offered. The early writers also provided Jefferson with a rich literature of how mercantilism—the economic system based on the nation-state's control of gold—had stifled Virginia's development (Chapter 2). Drawing on this corpus of writings, Jefferson became one of the primary spokesmen for Virginia's economic and political rights in the face of British controls, especially after 1774.

The justification that he devised for the commonwealth's break with England also relied heavily on works of his contemporaries, most notably George Mason, a fellow tobacco planter and opponent of British mercantilist policies. Whereas Mason focused his attention on delineating how the British had historically denied Virginians their constitutional rights, Jefferson broadened Mason's ideas by rooting them in nature rather than history. Mason also inadvertently influenced Jefferson's draft copy of the Declaration of Independence because as Jefferson was writing the preamble for that document, he copied from Mason's Virginia Declaration of Rights (Chapter 3). Longing to be with Mason and the other burgesses who were creating a government for their country, Jefferson, in Philadelphia, wrote a draft constitution that he felt would not only break the political ties that bound the colony to the mother country but also begin a revolution to change the nature of Virginian society. When his peers rejected his draft constitution, Jefferson worked for two years beginning in the fall of 1776 in the Virginia Assembly to change the laws of his country. In 1779, he accepted an offer to become Virginia's governor, and in 1781, he suffered along with the state during the British invasion of Virginia that nearly cost him his freedom, if not his life.

When offered another seat in the Virginia legislature at the end of his term as governor, he declined due to his wife's failing health and because of allegations of cowardice in the face of the enemy's attacks—a charge that haunted him long after he was officially absolved of the charges of misconduct. Rather, in the winter of 1783–1784 he devoted himself to revising *Notes on the State of Virginia*, the book that he had begun in exile from the governorship (Chapter 4). In *Notes*, he touted Virginia's climate, flora and fauna, and devotion to agriculture (although he urged shifting attention from tobacco to grains). Primarily, however, he renewed his attack on the Virginia constitution, especially the state's support for the Anglican Church; the lack of a system of universal, public education; and the inability to amend the constitution in order to extend political participation to those white male Virginians who lived in western areas of the state. He also launched an attack on the institution of slavery in his country by noting fears that bound labor was destroying virtue among slave owners who were relying too heavily on the hard work of others. Further, he expressed concerns about the effect slavery was having on the children of slave owners and used religion to try to jolt the gentry from their ways by proposing the possibility of divine intervention to punish Virginians for squandering the opportunity the Revolution offered to reform their society.

Accepting an appointment as minister to France gave him an opportunity to view Virginia's affairs from abroad (Chapter 5), and in France his devotion to change his country's society dissipated. Jefferson's years in Paris confirmed a devotion to his native state, especially as he learned of problems in the United States during the 1780s. As the French moved toward revolution, Jefferson fixed his attention on Shays's Rebellion in Massachusetts and warned Virginia's leaders about problems he believed the Constitution presented to his country's autonomy. When he returned from Paris and learned of George Washington's offer for him to become the first secretary of state, Jefferson's interactions with James Madison (positively) and Alexander Hamilton (negatively) further confirmed conclusions that he had developed in *Notes* regarding political economy. Commerce should serve agriculture, manufacturing should be left to Europeans, government should be small and frugal, and the young nation should use its alliance with France to break British dominance of American trade.

His election as president in 1801 offered him the opportunity to implement these ideas, and in his inaugural address he vowed to reverse the effects of Hamilton's program on the nation (Chapter 6). As president, he strove to save the nation from Hamilton's domestic financial program that benefited bankers and manufacturers at the expense of farmers and laborers. He also reversed the treasury secretary's foreign policy that Jefferson felt endangered the nation's independence by making it subservient to Great Britain's international interests. But acquiring the Louisiana Territory and the continuing warfare between the British and the French dashed Jefferson's hopes for retiring the national debt and threatened the nation's security.

In the summer of 1807, Jefferson concluded that a war with Great Britain was necessary in order to thwart British plans to destroy the new nation, but he could not convince his party's congressmen that belligerence would best protect national honor and ensure prosperity. That same summer, Eston Hemings's conception confirmed the president's primary orientation toward Virginian society. Following his retirement as president in 1809, Jefferson welcomed a return to Monticello and its comforts and concentrated on local concerns.

Home in Virginia, Jefferson quickly became caught up in the routine of life on his plantations and nearly forgot about reforming Virginian society (Chapter 7). When an 1814 letter from Edward Coles reminded him of his earlier attempts to end the practice of slavery, he devoted his last years not to accomplishing that goal but rather to creating a new state university, designing its buildings, and establishing its curriculum. In building the University of Virginia, however, Jefferson experienced once again the full measure of his peers' reluctance to change. As he had earlier in his life, he bowed to their wishes and abandoned his plan for universal education that he had outlined in *Notes*.

While working for his countrymen's sons, he also built a country retreat that he hoped would provide financial security for one of his grandsons, but in so doing, he further compromised the financial security of his larger estate. Personally bankrupt, he balanced his emotional ledger with the accolades from the nation as it approached its fiftieth anniversary and used his epitaph to flout the gentry's reluctance to reform.

Following his death, Jefferson's grandson Thomas Jefferson Randolph and University of Virginia professor George Tucker worked for different reasons to shift attention from "Jefferson the Virginian" to "Jefferson the American" (Conclusion). Neither would have appreciated the fact that their work provoked a scathing attack from an émigré son of Virginia on the eve of the Civil War, but Henry Stephens Randall's three-volume biography secured their national emphasis on Jefferson's life. Today, they could take satisfaction in the fact that the nation has embraced Jefferson as one of its heroes. "It has been said," Merrill Peterson writes, that Americans "venerate Washington, love Lincoln, and remember Jefferson."[5]

In pursuing the interpretation that Jefferson is best understood as an uneasy member of the Virginia gentry, I am sensitive to several criticisms that I have received at conference presentations and from prior publications. First, *any* single interpretation of Jefferson's life risks failing to capture the richness and complexities (some will say, in addition, the evasions and deceptions) of the man. In his 1975 book review of Fawn Brodie's *Thomas Jefferson: An Intimate History*, Winthrop Jordan offered the following assessment: "If we regard biographers as in some measure standing in an adversarial relationship with their subjects, Jefferson wins hands down."[6] When in 1981 Dumas Malone finished the sixth volume of his magisterial *Jefferson and His Time*, he wrote that he "could not hope to have done justice to a virtually inexhaustible subject."[7] Jefferson himself, in *Notes*, cautioned against those who would "[i]ntroduce the bed of Procrustes . . . and . . . make us all of a [single] size."[8]

For all of the variety of his interests and accomplishments, Jefferson repeated key themes across his long life, and scholars frequently have found themselves dealing with similar themes, irrespective of their intended topics. Human beings in society; natural rights, human rights, and God-given rights; republican government and the ideal political economy—these issues dominate his writings. These interests, I believe, stem directly from Virginian influences on Jefferson that were deeper and longer lasting than previous scholars have appreciated. As will become apparent throughout the book but especially in Chapter 6, I argue that Jefferson never fully devoted himself to national issues, in contrast to the other early presidents from Virginia—George Washington, James Madison, and James Monroe. In short, there is an important distinction to be drawn between Jefferson as an "American" and Jefferson as a "Virginian"; the two identities are not synonymous.

Second, as many of Jefferson's students have noted, it is possible that Jefferson's commitment to forge fundamental change in his society was more show than go, that he postured but would not produce.[9] In 1989, Professor Douglas Egerton of LeMoyne College and I discussed this point at the meeting of the Society for Historians of the Early American Republic at the University of Virginia. In my paper, I chided Jefferson's gentry peers for failure to attend more closely to his warnings to mend their ways. "Given the opposition of the gentry to his ideas for constitutional reform," I concluded, "it is remarkable that . . . he kept trying to reform their lives and rescue his 'country' from decline. Instead of obstructing his ideas, they should have taken his advice." In his comments on my paper, Egerton took a different tack. In *Gabriel's Rebellion*, Egerton demonstrates that fears of Toussaint-Louverture's rebellion in Saint Domingue and Jefferson's reluctance to free slaves who plotted escape in Virginia turned him, as president, away from plans for a gradual emancipation of slavery.[10] At the conference, Egerton underscored the point that by the end of his life Jefferson had given up on efforts to reform his society and was protecting "the Southern racial order and . . . slavery." "Perhaps," Egerton surmised, "it was not that the gentry listened to him too little, but rather that he listened to them too much."[11] Based on this perceptive comment, I changed my conclusion in the published version of the paper to read that "as an individual Thomas Jefferson might have done more to reform his society . . . [, but] as a group the gentry could hardly have done less."[12] In other words, if it is true that Jefferson's devotion to change flowed and ebbed, it is also true that his countrymen consistently protected their privileged position in their society and forced him to retreat in several areas.

A final point of concern relates to the methods I use to reach my conclusions. Because all students of Jefferson read the same materials, the primary difference in their conclusions becomes context: his writings offer numerous answers, as witnessed by the fact that biographies of the man continue to emerge. As Robert Booth Fowler observes, "Jefferson's political ideas do not deserve dismissal as mishmash, [but] they hardly constitute a tight, consistent philosophy that somehow a correct reading of Jefferson, his texts, and their audiences can reveal."[13] I have attempted throughout the book to measure Jefferson's behavior against his words, to study his actions as well as his thoughts.

I concede that Jefferson's niche in Virginia's gentry class is not perfect. He lived west of the tidewater area on land cleared by his father; he built his home on a hill instead of next to a river; he planted crops other than tobacco along the contours of hills and rotated them; he traveled to Europe and gained acceptance there for his political accomplishments and scientific interests; he helped to create a national political party; and he served the United States as president for two terms. Without the frame of reference provided by his peers, however, his life is much less understandable. He was a man of cosmopolitan tastes but Virginia habits. French wine always tasted best at Monticello where he diluted it with water fetched by his slaves.

I gratefully acknowledge permission to reprint portions of my writings that were originally published elsewhere, including "Thomas Jefferson," in *Popular Images of American Presidents,* edited by William C. Spragens (Westport, Conn.: Greenwood Press, 1988); "Thomas Jefferson and the American Revolution," in *The American Revolution, 1775–1783,* edited by Richard L. Blanco (New York: Garland Publishing, 1993), reproduced by permission of Routledge, Inc., part of the Taylor and Francis Group; "'Growing Weary in Well-Doing': Thomas Jefferson's Life among the Virginia Gentry," *Virginia Magazine of History and Biography* 101 (Jan. 1993): 5–36; "'Refreshing the Tree of Liberty with the Blood of Patriots and Tyrants': Thomas Jefferson and the Origins of the U.S. Constitution," in *Essays on Liberty and Federalism: The Shaping of the U.S. Constitution,* edited by David E. Narrett and Joyce S. Goldberg (College Station: Texas A&M University Press, 1988); and "'Answering the Call': The First Inaugural Addresses of Thomas Jefferson and William Jefferson Clinton," in *The Romance of History: Essays in Honor of Lawrence S. Kaplan,* edited by Scott L. Bills and E. Timothy Smith (Kent: Kent State University Press, 1997). In addition, I am deeply grateful to Mr. Norman J. W. Thrower, Emeritus Professor of Geography at UCLA, and the University Press of Virginia for permission to reprint the map of "The Jefferson Country" that originally appeared as endpapers for *Thomas Jefferson's Farm Book, with Commentary and Relevant Extracts from Other Writings,* edited by Edwin Morris Betts (Princeton: Princeton University Press, 1953).

Many of these essays (and others in this book, not heretofore published) began as conference papers or roundtable discussions at the Southern Historical Association, the Society for Historians of the Early American Republic, the Social Science History Association, the Intellectual History Seminar at Notre Dame University, and the Meeting of Pacific Northwest Early American Historians. At these meetings, numerous individuals gave me the benefit of their comments, particularly Dan Jordan, Nelson Lankford, Sara Bearss, Joan

Gunderson, Jacquelyn Miller, Mike Zuckerman, James Turner, and Richard R. Johnson. Travis C. McDonald, Director of Architectural Restoration at Thomas Jefferson's Poplar Forest, graciously conferred with me about changes that Jefferson made to the sleeping arrangements there. Jeff Saunders, Curator and Chair of the Geology Section at the Illinois State Museum, helped me locate an image of the *Mammuthus jeffersonii* and clarified problems of nomenclature.

Grant Number 803 from the Faculty Research Council at Idaho State University supported my work on Chapter 4. Colleagues in my own department and others graciously read drafts of chapters and listened to my ideas, especially JoAnn Ruckman, Merwin Swanson, Peter Boag, David Gray Adler and Stephen Adkison. The research of graduate student Fred Jacobi was especially helpful in unraveling the structural complexity of *Notes on the State of Virginia*.

Throughout my work on this book, I have benefited greatly from the friendship and suggestions from members of the Front Range Early American Consortium. Notably, Jack and Gloria Main, Ann Little, Jack Marietta, Jenny Pulsipher, and Gail Rowe helped me sharpen my focus in a number of areas. Other FREACs who deserve my special thanks include Harry Fritz, Ken Lockridge, Mick Nicholls, and Billy Smith. Harry read a version of Chapter 6 over two decades ago and gave me the encouragement that I needed to embark on an extended investigation of Jefferson's life: "It may not be fresh, but it seems so." Ken set aside other projects in order to read an early draft of the manuscript and offered valuable suggestions both for revisions and for specific word choices; readers who spot infelicitous phrasings in the text will wish I had taken more of his advice. Mick shared his extensive knowledge of early Virginia with me on numerous car trips across Wyoming on the way to Jack and Gloria's house in Boulder as well as insightful comments on Chapter 4 (including the subtitle). Billy invited me to Bozeman on a couple of occasions, where I was able to work out the logic of parts of several chapters.

Two people who also deserve special mention for their encouragement are Larry Kaplan and Doug Egerton. I have often dreamed that a book of mine on Jefferson might sit close to Larry's *Jefferson and France* on library shelves. His wisdom, his keen reading of Jefferson's texts, and his suggestions for alternative ways of viewing Jefferson's life have been both a support and an inspiration. Doug and I have shared thoughts and questions with each other since we first met in 1989; I admire both his acumen and his professional engagement.

Finally, I want to acknowledge my editors at the University Press of Florida —Stan Harrold and Randall Miller for their careful readings of drafts, and Meredith Morris-Babb and Derek Krissoff for not giving up on the project. I am delighted that it will be part of the Southern Dissent Series. Two anonymous readers for the Press also helped me to bring the book to its final form.

On a personal note, I thank my family for supporting this undertaking. I'm dedicating the book to our children because they kept me going over the years by gently asking how it was coming. Well, guys, it's finally done.

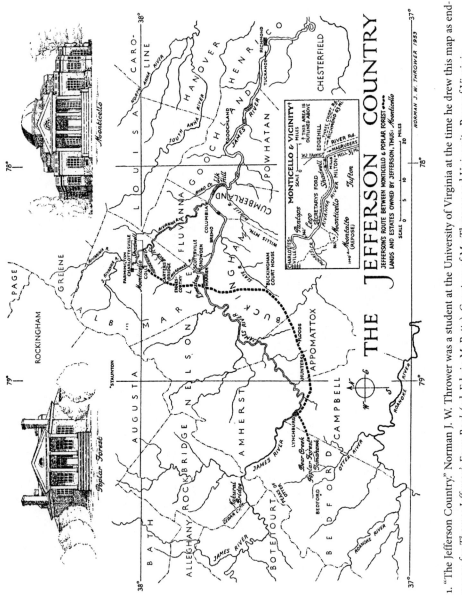

1. "The Jefferson Country." Norman J. W. Thrower was a student at the University of Virginia at the time he drew this map as end-papers for *Thomas Jefferson's Farm Book* (ed. Edwin M. Betts). Courtesy of Mr. Thrower and University Press of Virginia.

1

"Sowed a Bed of Peas"

Observing and Criticizing Virginia's Gentry Culture

In seeking to reduce the complexities of Thomas Jefferson's life to a pattern, most of his biographers have focused on his words, perhaps because he offered posterity so many of them. Further, because his words—in letters, speeches, and official state papers—were so thoughtful and well-crafted, scholars have emphasized that he formed his ideas based upon his intensive study of the books in his extensive library. As Merrill Peterson observes, "One is struck, first of all, by . . . Jefferson's intellectuality. He was pre-eminently a student, strenuous in the pursuit of knowledge. . . . [F]ar more than most men, he was dependent on books and inclined to take his knowledge from them rather than from direct acquaintance." In Peterson's reckoning, Jefferson (along with Benjamin Franklin) best represented in America "the intellectual movement, [the] temper of mind, [and] the climate of opinion" associated with the Enlightenment and its emphasis on scientific rationalism.[1]

Although the Enlightenment—like most broad historical movements—cannot be succinctly characterized, its leading writers agreed that observations formed the basis of human learning, and actions counted more than beliefs or opinions. As Jefferson put it (altering the wording of René Descartes), "I feel: therefore I exist. . . . On the basis of sensation, of matter and motion, we may erect the fabric of all the certainties we can have or need. . . . When once we quit the basis of sensation, all is in the wind."[2] In other words, Jefferson believed that human beings encounter the world empirically, through the senses. Then, their minds organize what they have experienced. "I can conceive of thought," he wrote, "to be an action of a particular organisation of matter."[3]

As Jefferson observed the endless variety and glorious detail of life in Virginia—both natural and human—what caught his eye most often were the agricultural rhythms of life on his and nearby plantations. "[T]hose ideas were significant [to Jefferson]," Adrienne Koch noted, "which related to the needs, the sweat, and the labor of the human life. He never quite lost the farmer's sense that the products of the orchard, the garden, and the fields are born of arduous labor."[4] But as T. H. Breen reminds us, a tremendous gulf separated Jefferson and those like him who planted tobacco and those who eked out an existence growing corn or raising livestock. Because the crop required attention throughout the year, tobacco planters like Jefferson honed their powers of observation in order to "master" the land and the labor necessary for a successful harvest. They kept one eye on nature's seasons of sowing, growing, and harvesting and the other eye on each other as they competed to produce the best crop.[5]

This chapter seeks first to establish the fact that Thomas Jefferson belonged to Virginia's gentry culture on the eve of the American Revolution. Although he never mentioned in his writings a gentry class, much less that he was a member of it, Jefferson's behavior conforms in the main to that of other tobacco planters. But as he observed his peers' devotion to producing the annual tobacco crop, he warned them about the effects of the staple on their lives and tried to get them to change their ways. In criticizing his associates' behaviors, he continued the efforts of a distinguished, though small, group of Virginians who preceded him, and this discussion forms the second portion of the chapter.

In *Notes on the State of Virginia* (1786), the only book he ever wrote, Jefferson listed four histories of Virginia that he admired: John Smith's (1624); Robert Beverley's (1705); William Stith's (1747); and Sir William Keith's (1738).[6] These books contain at least one common feature: they praised Virginia's climate and soils but criticized the fact that humans abused nature's gifts. As did Jefferson, these historians railed against the production of tobacco in Virginia. Although Jefferson never wrote a history of the Old Dominion, in his writings he joined a select number of Virginians who were both adherents of and dissenters from the behavioral norms that their society embraced. As these men drew lessons from the life they observed, they challenged Virginians to reform their lives and live up to the possibilities of life in a paradise.

I

Almost without exception, scholars emphasize Jefferson's education at the College of William and Mary, especially his course work under the guidance of the Scottish teacher Dr. William Small, as kindling his interest in systematic observation and scientific inquiry. For all of the reputed effect of Small's teaching, however, book learning does not appear to have been high on Jefferson's list of reasons for deciding to attend the college at Williamsburg.[7] "By going to . . . College," he wrote in 1760 to one of his guardians (his father having died two years earlier), "I shall get a more universal Acquaintance, which may hereafter be serviceable to me; and I suppose I can pursue my Studies in the Greek and

Latin as well there as here, and likewise learn something of the Mathematics."[8] His letters from 1762 through 1769 clearly certify success in the first goal—gaining "a more universal acquaintance"—as gossip about his classmates and wishful thinking about prospective mates dominated his correspondence, and he included Latin phrases in many of these missives.

Evidence of the third goal—learning "something of the Mathematics"—cannot be found in his papers, nor can proof of his early interest in any other academic scientific inquiry. Whatever Small may have taught Jefferson and his friends in the classroom, Jefferson benefited greatly from Small's tutelage because of the company that the two men kept. Small introduced his pupil to many important people, including George Wythe (the man who became Jefferson's mentor in studying law) and the accommodating royal governor of Virginia, Francis Fauquier. These men exposed Jefferson to the world of Virginia's gentry class and helped him make connections within it, as his letters so clearly indicate.[9]

Following college, Jefferson began his academic study of law under Wythe's guidance, but the lifelong relationship Jefferson developed with his mentor makes his formal training in the law pale in comparison. "I do wish the Devil had Old Cooke [Sir Edward Coke]," he wrote in December 1762, "for I am sure I never was so tired of an old dull scoundrel in my life. What! are there so few inquietudes tacked to this momentary life of ours that we must need be loading ourselves with a thousand more? . . . But the old-fellows say we must read to gain knowledge; and gain knowledge to make us happy and be admired. Mere jargon!"[10] Indeed, his few surviving legal pleadings are best characterized as discursive rather than legally rigorous.

Jefferson struggled with "Old Cooke" and Wythe's law office until 1766. Perhaps to celebrate the end of his apprenticeship he traveled to Maryland, Pennsylvania, and New York. Aside from one letter comparing the Maryland legislature to the Virginia House of Burgesses, he did not record his impressions of what he saw.[11] This first trip outside of the Old Dominion may have caused him to want to know more about his home. In any case, with the end of his indenture to Wythe, he was free at age twenty-three to chart a new direction, to be the master of his fate.

The first evidence in Jefferson's writings of an interest in systematic observation appears neither in his recollections of his studies with Small nor in his letters to classmates or friends, but rather in his *Garden Book*. There, on February 20, 1767, he wrote: "sowed [at Shadwell] a bed of forwardest and a bed of middling peas. 500. of these peas weighed 3^{oz}.- 18^{dwt}. about 2,500 fill a pint." In 1768, there are four entries for February and March, each of them concerning planting and observing the progress of his peas.[12] Then, there is a two-year gap in the record, perhaps a result of his establishing and trying to build his legal practice.

In 1770, his father's house, Shadwell, burned (along with all of his books and personal papers), and Jefferson began to build his own mansion, which he named Monticello.[13] From 1771 until his death in 1826, whenever he was home to supervise his garden at Monticello, he dutifully noted the dates when his peas entered the ground, emerged and bloomed, and came to table. When extracted and arranged by date from the *Garden Book*, the data he compiled appear as in Table 1.1.

It can be argued that there is nothing exceptional about the contents of this table. After all, Jefferson kept extensive records of the other vegetables in his garden as well as recording other phenomena, including when he heard the first frogs croaking or birds singing, saw flowers blooming, or noticed the availability of produce at markets. It is possible, however, that there is an important lesson to be learned about the man from the charting of his peas.

Perhaps he was the quintessential Enlightenment farmer hoping to learn something about the world based upon observations.[14] The epitome of his systematic record keeping centers on his observations of the weather. At Williamsburg, for example, from 1772 to 1777, he noted the rainfall, wind direction, and maximum and minimum temperatures. After leaving the presidency, from 1810 to 1817 he made 3,905 recordings of the temperature at Monticello just before sunrise and between three and four o'clock in the afternoon.[15]

From this documentation, he hoped to be able to reach a definitive conclusion regarding how human beings might be changing the natural environment of their country. It was the opinion of many, he stated in *Notes*, that the climate of Virginia had moderated since settlement. Sensibly, it felt warmer—snows did not accumulate as deep or last as long, winds seemed more powerful without trees to block them, and the danger of late frosts moderated.[16] Based upon his charts, however, he was forced to reserve judgment. All he could do was "hope that the methods invented in later times for measuring with accuracy the degrees of heat and cold, and the observations which have been and will be made and preserved, will at length ascertain this curious fact in physical history."[17]

Another practical reason for these accounts might have been a hope that he could become more efficient and economical. Sometimes, his devotion to improvement meant that he tried to relive the experience by writing about it in order to establish the best procedure. In 1795, for example, he theoretically rearranged the placement of his slaves during the harvest just completed. "Were the harvest to go over again with the same force," he wrote, ". . . the whole machine would move in exact equilibria no part of the force would be lessened without retarding the whole, nor increased without a waste of force. this force would cut, bring in, & shock 54. a[cre]s. a day, and complete my harvest of 320. a[cre]s. in 6 days." Unhappily, due to weather, illnesses, and mechanical breakdowns he

Table 1. Chart of Jefferson's Table Peas

	Shadwell				Monticello		
Year	Date Planted	Up	To Table	Year	Date Planted	Up	To Table
1767	Feb. 20	Mar. 9	Apr. 24	1814	Feb. 8	Feb. 22	May 9
	Mar. 17	Apr. 1	May 28		Feb. 21	Mar. 19	May 13
1768	Feb. 24	Mar. 14		1815	Mar. 3	Mar. 11	May 15
				1816	Feb. 3	Mar. 1	May 22
Monticello					Feb. 16	Mar. 1	May 22
1771	Mar. 6	Mar. 25	May 30		Mar. 1	Mar. 16	May 23
1772	Mar. 30			1817	Feb. 19		May 25
					Mar. 1		May 25
1773	Mar. 12	Apr. 1	May 22		Mar. 10		May 30
1774	Mar. 10	Mar. 21	May 16	1818	Feb. 27	Mar. 13	May 24
	Mar. 10	Mar. 21	May 26		Mar. 9	May 24	June 5
	Mar. 24	Apr. 1	June 5				
				1819	Jan. 27	Mar. 3	May 13
1775	Feb. 25				Jan. 27	Mar. 4	May 25
					Feb. 24	Mar. 8	June 4
1777	Mar. 10	Apr. 21	June 4		Mar. 3	Mar. 15	June 13
1778	Feb. 26	Mar. 14		1820	Feb. 14	Feb. 25	May 9
					Feb. 14	Feb. 28	May 19
1794	Mar. 1	Mar. 16	May 19		Mar. 1		May 25
	Aug. 12		Sep. 15				
				1821	Feb. 8	Mar. 1	FROST
1809	Mar. 23		May 25		Feb. 9	Mar. 19	June 2
	Mar. 27		June 5		Mar. 1	Mar. 26	June 2
	May 5		July 10	1822	Feb. 25	Mar. 9	
	May 16		July 26		Feb. 25	Mar. 10	
1811	Mar. 1		May 11	1823	Feb. 22		May 11
	Mar. 9		May 23		Feb. 22		May 20
	Mar. 25		June 4		Feb. 22		May 21
	Apr. 23		July 2		Mar. 1		June 1
1812	Feb. 15	Mar. 6	May 22*				
	Mar. 6	Mar. 23	May 22*	1824	Feb. 19		May 24
	Mar. 6		June 5		Feb. 20		May 28
	Mar. 6		June 12				
1813	Mar. 1	Mar. 16	May 18				
	Mar. 29		June 5				
	Mar. 29		June 14				

* Notes that he was away from home when they matured and they "might have been used some days sooner."

never realized such an efficient harvest. In 1796, it took ten days to harvest 300 acres. In 1799 it was even worse, requiring seven days to harvest 167.5 acres.[18]

In spite of these failures, he persisted in his record keeping. If a valued observer gave advice about crops or animals, he cataloged it. If he read about or heard of a plant that promised greater yield or quality, he tested it.[19] Throughout his life, Jefferson was constantly on the lookout for plants that would improve the lot of farmers. He acquired rice, olives, corn, and strawberries from Italy; sesame from Africa; kale from Germany and France; Siberian barley; Jerusalem wheat; South American pumpkins; Jamaican lima beans; potatoes from Liverpool; and the Tahitian mulberry.[20]

With most of these crops, he judged the success of his agricultural experimentation quantitatively by carefully measuring the number of bushels, pints, pecks, or pounds that could be produced over the longest growing period at the least cost. As Jefferson put it, "The spontaneous energies of the earth are a gift of nature, but they require the labor of man to direct their operation. And the question is so to husband his labor as to turn the greatest quantity of this useful action of the earth to his benefit. . . . The plough is to the farmer what the wand is to the sorcerer."[21] Thus, he planted strawberries that "on the average bear 20. strawberries each"; pumpkins that grew to "127. lb," and "cauliflower of 25. to 30. lb."[22] One can sense the euphoria he must have felt in 1825 when he acquired seeds from cucumbers that had reportedly grown to "2½ f. and 3 f. in length."[23]

On a negative note, in 1794 he complained that he was discouraged because his potatoes "made [not] more than 60 or 70 bushels to the acre." In 1808 he wistfully reported that the French were producing 10,000 pounds of Jerusalem artichokes per acre, "which they say is three times as much as they generally make of the potatoes."[24]

Jefferson's interest in the progress of his peas, however, cannot be explained by reducing his observations to a system. Every year, he planted them as early as he felt they would germinate and survive the unpredictable weather on his little mountain, but he never succeeded in bringing his crop to table any faster. As Table 1.1 indicates, irrespective of when the seeds entered the ground, if his peas lived through the inevitable late frost they invariably matured no earlier than May 9 and usually after May 20. In some years (like 1816, 1817, and 1823), peas planted in different locations and at different times all were picked on the same day.

Because it appears that Jefferson learned nothing from charting his peas, another explanation for his fascination with chronicling them must be sought than that of the Enlightenment farmer intent on increasing yield. Perhaps practicality, in this area, was secondary to Jefferson's lifelong belief that discipline produced good of itself. Regimen ordered his life, and recording observations may have been part of the way in which he structured his behavior. Writing at least in part rhetorically to his daughter Martha in 1787, he advised her that "[of] all the cankers of human happiness, none corrodes it with so silent, yet so baneful a tooth, as indolence. . . . No laborious person was ever yet hysterical. Exercise and application produce order in our affairs, health of body, [and] chearfulness of mind."[25]

An alternative, more romantic explanation would be that peas were the first produce of his beloved garden in the spring, symbolic of nature's renewal and energy. Despite Jefferson's belief that the climate of Virginia was superior to that of New York or other states farther north,[26] winters were harsh at Monticello. Legend has it that he brought his bride there through three feet of snow in late January 1772. On May 5, 1774, he recorded that a frost had "destroyed . . . at Monticello near half the fruit of every kind." In the succeeding March, he wrote, "[T]here came very cold weather and frosts every night for a week, which killed every peach at Monticello. . . . [T]his was the first instance since Monticello was seated of the fruit being totally killed." In 1779, he found the weather remarkably mild from "about the 8th of Feb . . . till the middle of March. . . . [T]hen it set in cold. . . . This killed all the fruits which had blossomed forward."[27]

These extremes persisted into later years as well, suggestive of why he remained dubious about whether the climate was moderating. In November 1796, he complained that it was 12°; "the ink freezing on the point of my pen renders it difficult to write." In 1809, peas and snaps were killed by an early frost on October 23; in 1815, tomatoes and okra froze on May 9; on February 18, 1817, "the whole of our winter lettuce and endive [died] though well covered"; on March 31, 1820, his peas were prostrated by cold "and snow which continued until April 30." In 1821, peas planted on February 8 were "compleatly killed. thermom. 20° on March 19."[28]

Most pertinent of all the possibilities in explaining Jefferson's devotion to growing his garden peas centers on Dumas Malone's suggestion that the local gentry in Albemarle County played a game each year among themselves to produce the first crop.[29] That Jefferson competed with his peers in this ritual of rural life surprises. The farmer engaged in one-upmanship is not an image that Jefferson's biographers have emphasized, nor is it one that Jefferson cultivated. Equally intriguing is the fact that he does not appear to have tired of the game even after he must have realized that George Divers's peas always beat his to table.[30]

Seen in this light, the trip he made at the end of his apprenticeship to Wythe in 1766 and the systematic entries into his garden book beginning with the planting of his peas in February 1767 mark Jefferson's rite of passage from youth to adult in the gentry class. By the next fall, he had won election to the House of Burgesses, where he claimed his seat in May 1769. In early 1771, he asked a

friend to inquire in England if his family had a coat of arms, and he spent most
of the fall of that year courting the eldest daughter of John Wayles, a prominent
tidewater planter and lawyer.[31]

At the time of his father-in-law's unexpected death in 1773, Jefferson owned
more than 10,000 acres of land and about 100 slaves, using the land and his
slaves' labor primarily to produce tobacco.[32] Study at the College of William and
Mary, legal training, connection with Virginia's prominent families, service in
Burgesses, ownership of property and slaves, and cultivation of garden peas for
amusement and tobacco for export all place Jefferson firmly within the ruling
elite of Virginia on the eve of the American Revolution.

II

Although Jefferson's behaviors establish his membership in the gentry class
of Virginia, in the enormity of his writings he acknowledged neither the existence of this group nor his connection to it. The closest he came was in a
letter to John Adams in late October 1813, in which he wrote about a "natural
aristocracy among men . . . [comprised] of virtue and talents" that he jux-
taposed with "an artificial aristocracy founded on wealth and birth, without
either virtue or talents." Jefferson taunted his friend that, since colonial days
in Massachusetts and Connecticut, a "strict alliance of church and state" had
elevated some families over others and had resulted in "hereditary succession
to office. . . . In Virginia we have nothing of this." Prior to the American Revolution, Jefferson acknowledged, "the English law of entails" had allowed a few
wealthy families to dominate "the king's council . . . ; and they Philipised in all
collisions between the king and people." Bills, however, that Jefferson introduced during "the first session of [the Virginia assembly] after the Declaration
of Independence" abolished entails and primogeniture by "dividing the lands
of intestates equally among all their children, or other representatives." These
laws, he claimed, "laid the axe to the root of [aristocracy based on wealth]."
Also, the Virginia constitution forced former "pseudo-aristocrats" to gain their
political power through frequent elections. Jefferson believed that white men
"[i]n general . . . elect the real good and wise. In some instances, wealth may
corrupt, and birth blind [the voters]; but not in sufficient degree to endanger
the society."[33]

In his response, Adams challenged Jefferson's distinction between "natural"
and "artificial" aristocrats on every point. "No romance would be more amus-
ing," Adams responded, "than the History of your Virginian and our New England families. Yet even in Rhode Island, where there has been no Clergy, no
Church, and I had almost said, no State, and some People say no religion, there
has been a constant respect for certain old Families. . . . You suppose a differ-

ence of Opinion between You and me, on the Subject of Aristocracy. I can find none." The only disagreement between them, Adams concluded, centered on the best means each man could devise for controlling the aristocrats—Adams through isolation in hereditary positions, Jefferson (erroneously, in Adams's mind) through elections.[34]

When Jefferson answered Adams's letter on January 24, 1814, he did not rejoin the debate over natural and artificial aristocracy beyond a curt rebuff and a history lesson. "[T]he strength of family distinction still existing in [Massachusetts]," he wrote, "[w]ith us is so totally extinguished that not a spark of it is to be found but lurking in the hearts of some of our old tories. . . . Here youth, beauty mind and manners are more valued than a pedigree."[35] The research of a number of prominent historians in recent years, however, has proved that Jefferson's recollections about his country's history in the eighteenth century are wrong. By 1720 and continuing through the American Revolution, a gentry class (numbering 2 to 5 percent of the colony's inhabitants) controlled Virginia's economic, social, political, and religious affairs.[36]

The evolution of this class followed a circuitous route consisting of three main factors: constant immigration throughout the seventeenth century, a high death rate of those immigrants, and the vagaries of the international market for tobacco. Without a constant stream of immigrants across the seventeenth century, there would have been no English culture in the Chesapeake Bay region. White or black, poor or rich, female or male, English or non-English, until about the 1680s there was a net population decline in both Virginia and Maryland.[37] Because the factor of death disrupted the normal course of English life and because of a constant imbalance in the sexes that reversed age-old trends in European society, many cultural changes were necessary. The premature death of one or both spouses severely weakened parental and male authority and rendered conventional ideas about family life obsolete. Extended families, rather than nuclear ones as in England or New England, were the rule.[38]

Until the late seventeenth century, those four in ten transplanted Englishmen in Virginia who lived through their period of indenture and got the land and labor necessary to plant tobacco could expect to make money. After 1680, however, there was a downturn in the tobacco economy due to European wars and glutted markets.[39] In addition, planters faced increased production costs because arable lands along the rivers had been taken, and it became necessary to move into the Piedmont area to find new fertile lands. Eventually, these lands proved more fertile than those in the tidewater, and tobacco production doubled in Virginia between 1700 and 1800. But the substantial costs associated with clearing the land and preparing it to grow tobacco depressed income.[40]

As labor needs increased in order to clear and prepare the heavily wooded lands, the pool of indentured servants in England that had allowed tobacco to flourish dried up, and planters had to find a new source of labor. By enslaving people from Africa, they hit upon a more profitable, and also more exploitable, source of labor.[41] In T. H. Breen's words, the apparent political tranquillity that existed in Virginia by the time of the American Revolution "grew not out of a sense of community or new value-orientations, but [out] of more effective forms of human exploitation."[42]

Kenneth Lockridge goes further. He notes that following Bacon's Rebellion in 1676, as slaves supplanted indentured servants on the tobacco plantations, an emerging gentility replaced the fractious insecurity of earlier decades among Virginia's elite. At Williamsburg, these newly minted gentlemen joined with the royal governors to create rituals that depicted "an elaborate courtesy . . . [of] bowing and scrapings, polite addresses, and gallant replies." Some men, like William Byrd, sent their sons "to England to learn how to do it right. They returned laundered of dirt, dressed in lace, and sporting the proper legalisms. Such men could serve as acolytes in the ceremonies presided over by a royal governor without the fear that they might miss a cue."[43]

As the tobacco culture spread into frontier regions, enterprising men took these values with them. Those like Thomas Jefferson's father Peter, who gained the new fertile lands and had the capital to make the transition from the labor of indentured servants to slaves, joined the ranks of the older gentry by marrying the daughters of the older tidewater gentry scions. These new men and their new lands rejuvenated the production of tobacco in Virginia and perpetuated gentry domination of Virginia society.[44]

The evolution of this class was hidden in the complexities of immigration lists, death rates, fluctuating tobacco prices, and shifting economies of scale. Its unwritten history became lost in obscurity. Those people who came to prominence as members of the gentry reckoned time from 1700, not 1607. As Mechal Sobel writes, Virginia's planters "saved few records [and] looked back to no great forefathers. . . . They were presentists with hopes for the future."[45] Neither were the Virginia gentry introspective about what they viewed as a natural development within a society lacking the extreme divisions in class dividing the peasantry and the aristocracy that so characterized European civilization. Like Jefferson, they were action-oriented. Because their tobacco crops demanded year-round attention, Virginia's "natural aristocrats" lived on their plantations in order to care for and manage them, except for the periodic trips to Williamsburg to attend sessions of the House of Burgesses.

In 1959, historian Jack Greene drew a composite portrait of the gentry in Virginia based upon the 110 men from 1720 to 1776 who, like Jefferson, sat on committees in the House of Burgesses. Of the committeemen, 75 percent owned at least 10,000 acres of land and many of these were also land surveyors (like Peter Jefferson) on the lookout for fertile lands; 90 percent were tobacco farmers who worked their plantations using slave labor; 40 percent practiced the law in order to guard their investments in land and labor; over 50 percent were related to a dozen prominent families; and 100 percent were Anglican in religious preference. These self-conscious men ran their parishes by serving as vestrymen and their counties by serving (80 percent of them) as justices of the peace.[46]

The recent archaeological research of Susan Kern confirms that men like Jefferson's father transplanted tidewater ideals into the newly settled Piedmont region. The house that Peter Jefferson built for himself and his wife Jane Randolph Jefferson—Shadwell—was hardly a frontier dwelling. In Kern's words, "[T]he Jeffersons clearly accommodated, in their house, landscape, material goods, and behaviors, the most up-to-date social expectations of Virginia's elite tidewater culture. . . . The tobacco economy extended into this part of Virginia, and with it, tobacco culture." Whatever else Thomas Jefferson may have learned from his father and mother, he most certainly acquired "the recognizable idioms of the gentry in a very conscious material display that advertised [the family's] own standing and enforced social ritual within the plantation and beyond it."[47]

In this agrarian society based on producing tobacco, speculative thought counted for little. Life centered on "broad acres, black labor, and a weed."[48] But by 1773, Virginia's "tobacco culture" was encountering hard times. Several factors, including overworked soil and escalating debts among the planter elite, threatened tobacco's preeminent status among the gentry. In spite of rising export figures and total value of the tobacco crop, members of the gentry class expressed doubts about the future of tobacco in their colony, and many shifted from *planting* tobacco to *farming* grains.[49] Although Jefferson lived in the heart of the new tobacco-growing region, he criticized the region's economic dependence on the crop. In *Notes*, he described tobacco as

> a culture productive of infinite wretchedness. Those employed in it are in a continued state of exertion beyond the powers of nature to support. Little food of any kind is raised by them; so that the men and animals on these farms are badly fed, and the earth is rapidly impoverished. The cultivation of wheat is the reverse in every circumstance. Besides cloathing the earth with herbage, and preserving its fertility, it feeds the labourers plentifully, requires from them only a moderate toil, except in the season of harvest, raises great numbers of animals for food and service, and diffuses plenty and happiness among the whole. . . . Besides [wheat] there will be other valuable substitutes when the cultivation of tobacco shall be discontinued, such as cotton in the eastern part of the state, and hemp and flax in the western.[50]

Jefferson mentions at the end of this passage that many Virginians experimented with hemp as a possible alternative to tobacco. As Charles Royster notes, in 1727 William Byrd tried to break his colony's overreliance on tobacco production by taking advantage of the Royal Navy's need for cordage. He hoped that producing *Cannabis sativa* would also attract investors because most of the product the navy used came from Russia, thereby draining the nation's gold reserves, especially in wartime when demand drove up prices. Unfortunately, Byrd found that the crop was not profitable because its production was too costly. Russian peasants could produce it for one-fifth of what it cost for Virginian slaves to produce it, and transportation costs from Russia to England were one-third of those from the colonies. In 1761, Charles Carter also advocated switching from tobacco to hemp (especially due to Carter's admonition against "the great Proportion of poysonous Quality contained in [the] Narcotick Plant"), but his plans also came to nothing. At the end of the decade, George Washington revived plans for hemp production in the Dismal Swamp, located between Virginia and North Carolina. As with Byrd and Carter, however, Washington's plans never materialized. Rice, hardwoods, and shingles outstripped hemp as exports from the area.[51]

Although he never devoted much attention to growing hemp, Jefferson did experiment with various crops, including wheat, but he could never break his dependence on tobacco because he always needed the cash that the sale of this crop brought him. The debts he inherited from his father-in-law, his absence from Monticello throughout most of the 1780s and much of the 1790s, and the unpredictable international economy resulting from the wars of Europe during his presidency further increased his dependence on tobacco. When he returned to Monticello in 1809, he devised elaborate plans to diversify his crops there by rotating his fields among grains and clover.[52] The War of 1812, however, led him to a nearly complete abandonment of these crops, and by June 1815, he was planting tobacco again, primarily on his lands in Bedford County. In 1822, he confessed to creditors that he derived his annual income "from the culture of tobacco and wheat," and he continued to plant tobacco until his death.[53]

III

Jefferson's harsh statements against the planting of tobacco and his criticisms of his peers' nearly exclusive devotion to its production that appear in *Notes* bear closer scrutiny. Written in response to a general request of François, marquis de Barbé-Marbois (referred to by Americans simply as Marbois), a member of the French legation in 1780, for information about the United States, Jefferson's answers extended far beyond the Frenchman's questions and led him to reorder Marbois's topics (Chapter 4). As point five on his list of twenty-two questions, Marbois requested "The History of the State," and Jefferson might have used this prompt as an opportunity to reverse the gentry class's presentist orientation by

undertaking a history of the state from its founding. Instead, Jefferson d
address the topic until query 23 (a number he added to Marbois's list), "
ries, Memorials, and State-Papers."[54]

Reflecting the attitudes of most of the members of his class, Jefferson had a
low opinion of the utility of history. Writing to his future brother-in-law Robert Skipwith with suggestions for building a library, Jefferson included some
volumes of history in his list of suggestions, but he also expressed doubts about
history's value "to fix us in the principles and practice of virtue. . . . Considering
history as a moral exercise, her lessons would be too unfrequent if confined to
real life. Of those recorded by historians few incidents have been attended with
such circumstances as to excite in any high degree this sympathetic emotion of
virtue."[55]

Reading history could also be dangerous if people supposed that the past
provided a certain guide to the future. To Samuel Kercheval in 1816, Jefferson
complained, "Some men look at constitutions with sanctimonious reverence,
and deem them like the ark of the covenant, too sacred to be touched. They as-
cribe to the men of the preceding age a wisdom more than human, and suppose
what they did to be beyond amendment. . . . [L]aws and institutions must go
hand in hand with the progress of the human mind. As that becomes more developed, more enlightened, as new discoveries are made, new truths disclosed,
and manners and opinions change with the change of circumstances, institutions must advance also, and keep pace with the times."[56]

Perhaps reflective of these biases, Jefferson advised readers of *Notes* that
there would be little to be gained from looking at the four histories of Virginia
that are listed at the start of this chapter. In turn, he dismissed each of these
works as flawed in one way or another.

Of John Smith, Jefferson noted that he was "honest, sensible, and well informed" and provided "almost the only source from which we derive any knowledge of the infancy of our state." As for Smith's style, however, Jefferson termed
it "barbarous and uncouth." Robert Beverley's history extended Smith's to the
year 1700, but Jefferson found little to say about it except that Beverley overly
compressed the time period. At the other extreme from Beverley's conciseness,
the history written by William Stith (described by Jefferson as a "reverend . . . a
native of Virginia and president of its college . . . [and] a man of classical learning") was deemed "inelegant" by Jefferson because it covered the same time
period as Beverley's but contained "details too minute to be tolerable, even to a
native of the country."

Regarding the final history, Jefferson described William Keith's book that
extended the colony's story to 1725 as "agreeable . . . in style" compared to Stith's
since it "passes over events of little importance." And because it was short, he
said it "would be preferred by a foreigner."[57] Easily missed, based upon Jeffer-

son's depictions of these histories, is the fact that these earlier chronicles of life in Virginia shared one important similarity with Jefferson's *Notes*. Each of the authors chided Virginians for failing to diversify their agriculture beyond planting tobacco.

The first report of an Englishman's use of tobacco grown in Virginia came from Thomas Hariot (1586), one of the Roanoke Island settlers. According to Hariot, the Indians inhabiting the island used tobacco for ceremonial purposes, by making "hallowed fires & cast[ing] some of the pouder therin for a sacrifice." Other times, "being in a storme uppon the waters, to pacifie their gods, they cast some up into the aire and into the water. . . . Also after an escape of danger, they cast some into the aire likewise." Their chief use for the plant, however, was personal. Having dried and crushed the leaves,

> they use to take the fume or smoke therof by sucking it through pipes made of claie into their stomacke and heade; from whence it purgeth superfluous fleame & other grosse humors, openeth all the pores & passages of the body: by which means the use thereof, not only preserveth the body from obstructions; but also if any be, so that they have not beene of too long continuance, in short time breaketh them: wherby their bodies are notably preserved in health, & know not many greevous diseases where withall wee in England are oftentimes afflicted.

Due to these supposedly beneficial qualities of tobacco, Hariot reported that the English "used to suck it after their maner, as also since our returne, & have found maine raire and wonderful experiments of the vertues thereof; of which the relation woulde require a volume by it selfe: the use of it by so manie of late, men & women of great calling as else, and some learned Phisitions also, is sufficient witnes."[58]

Despite Hariot's enthusiasm for the beneficial use of tobacco, the earliest settlers of Jamestown did not immediately turn to its cultivation because they expected to find riches taken more easily in the form of gold. According to John Smith's account of the first years of the colony (1624), "[O]ur guilded refiners with their golden promises made all men their slaves in hope of recompences; there was no talke, no hope, no worke, but dig gold, wash gold, refine gold, loade gold, such a bruit of gold, that one mad fellow desired to be buried in the sands least they should by there art make gold of his bones."[59] As for the colony's other early settlers, "[A]ll the rest were poore Gentlemen, Tradsmen, Serving-men, libertines, and such like, ten times more fit to spoyle a Commonwealth, then either begin one, or but help to maintaine one. . . . [T]en good workemen would have done more substantiall worke in a day, then ten of them in a weeke."[60]

John Rolfe's experimentation in planting tobacco in 1612 eventually gave men a reason to work but also produced unexpected negative benefits. Despite the fact that the soil of Virginia supported the planting of not only corn but also beans, peas, and wheat plus the breeding of cattle, the earliest settlers stopped looking for alternative ways to make money once they began to grow tobacco. "[B]ecause Corne was [valued] at two shillings six pence the bushell, and Tobacco at three shillings the pound," Smith reports, everyone began to plant tobacco to the exclusion of other crops. By 1621, Smith wrote in horror, the desire to plant tobacco caused men to hire Indians "in hunting and fowling with our fowling peeces," so the settlers could "root . . . in the ground about Tobacco like Swine." "[F]aire promises of plentie of Iron, Silke, Wine, and many other good and rich commodities" were abandoned by 1622, and "all [that] Summer little was done, but securing themselves and planting Tobacco, which passes there as current Silver, and by [which] . . . some grow rich, but many poore."[61]

Archaeological evidence of the first houses of Virginians supports Smith's conclusions. James Deetz's studies of archaeological excavations in New England and the Chesapeake indicate that "earthfast construction"—wood framing on posts buried in the earth—was common only in the Chesapeake.[62] An exclusive reliance on the production of tobacco, it turns out, explains this preference for easily constructed, albeit impermanent, dwellings due to the time required for planting and overseeing the crop. Indeed, Deetz argues that more substantial houses became possible only with the development of mixed-crop agriculture; hence, the earthfast house far outlived the tobacco boom period and continued to be used well into the eighteenth century. "In the Chesapeake limited resources and the cost of tobacco production, a lucrative pursuit, precluded the construction of more permanent buildings, even by those who had the means to do so."[63]

Subsequent histories amplified and extended Smith's criticism of the colony's exclusive reliance on the production of tobacco. One of the most notable of these, written by Robert Beverley in London in 1703–4, appeared in 1705. Beverley, like Smith before him, was hardly a disinterested observer of life in Virginia.[64] Beverley's family was one of the first in the emerging gentry class of the last decades of the seventeenth century, and his father was a close friend and supporter of Sir William Berkeley, royal governor of the colony from 1642 until 1677.[65] Following a recapitulation of Smith's history (a tendency that Jefferson himself later followed), Beverley introduced several new elements that became a staple of later works, including that overproduction of tobacco was responsible for lowering the price it attained in England and blaming Virginia's continued reliance on tobacco on the emergence of the colony of Maryland and British mercantilism.[66]

According to Beverley, some planters realized that their only hope of limiting their dependence on the crop lay in decreasing production in order to increase value. However, whenever Virginians tried to "prohibit the Trash of that Commodity [tobacco], to help the Market," Marylanders poured into England all the tobacco they could produce, "both good and bad, without Distinction. This is very injurious to the other Colony, which had voluntarily suffer'd so great a Diminution in the Quantity to mend the Quality." Beverley detailed how the House of Burgesses in the 1660s tried to stave off this competition by attempting to raise the price of tobacco with a law "prohibiting the Planting of it for one Year; and during that idle Year to invite the People to enter upon Manufactures. But, *Maryland* not concurring in this Project, they were obliged in their own Defence to repeal the Act of Assembly again, and . . . so all People relaps'd again into the Disease of planting Tobacco."

Bacon's Rebellion (1676) marked another turning point in the colony's history, in Beverley's telling, because following that event Virginia planters envisioned using even more drastic measures to increase the price of their crops. Because of the lack of success in securing an agreement from Maryland growers to cut back on production, several tidewater planters "resolved a total Destruction of the Tobacco in that Country [Virginia], especially of the Sweet-scented; because that was planted no where else." Their plan involved destroying the young plants while they were "yet in the Beds, and after it was too late to sow more. Accordingly the Ring-leaders in this Project began with their own first, and then went to cut up the Plants of such of their Neighbours as were not willing to do it themselves. However, they had not Resolution enough to go through with their Work."[67] As will be apparent in Chapter 2, George Mason and others who wanted Virginians to adopt nonimportation as a scheme to force the British Parliament to repeal its taxes on American goods also had problems gaining cooperation among tobacco growers in later years.

A second theme that Beverley introduced into his history that influenced subsequent histories was his tendency to blame England's rulers for Virginia's problems. John Smith wrote his history in a deferential style designed, he hoped, to induce James I to send him back to Virginia with resources to punish the Indians for their attacks on the settlement.[68] Beverley, however, attacked Charles I for granting a charter for Maryland and Oliver Cromwell for "contriv[ing] a severe Act of Parliament, whereby he prohibited the Plantations from receiving or exporting any *European* Commodities, but what should be carried to them by *English* Men, and in *English* built Ships." "The strange Arbitrary Curbs [Cromwell] put upon the Plantations," Beverley wrote, "exceedingly afflicted the People. He had the Inhumanity to forbid them all manner of Trade and Correspondence with other Nations, at a Time when *England* it self was in Distraction; and could neither take off their Commodities, nor supply them sufficiently with its own. Neither had they ever been used to supply them with half the Commodities they expended, nor to take off above half the Tobacco they made."[69] Eventually, the restrictions imposed on trade by Navigation Acts, Beverley concluded, led directly to Bacon's Rebellion for three reasons: "The extream low Price of Tobacco, and the Ill Usage of the Planters in the Exchange of Goods for it, which the Country, with all their earnest Endeavours, could not remedy. . . . Thirdly, The heavy Restraints and Burdens laid upon their Trade by Act of Parliament in England."[70]

William Keith's history (1738) extended Beverley's attack on the colony of Maryland for not agreeing to restrict the production of tobacco and Beverley's attribution of blame to Charles I, Cromwell, and Charles II to include English governors for encouraging Virginians' dependence on the growing of tobacco for their livelihood.[71] According to Keith's history, in 1690 Governor Sir Francis Nicholson persuaded the House of Burgesses to enact legislation "for the Improvement of several Branches of Trade, and the Encouragement of Towns." Unfortunately, the governor later changed his mind and in the succeeding year "altogether disapproved of what had been done the year before, which proceeded (as it was supposed) from the Influence of the Tobacco-Factors or Merchants at *London*, whose Interest, no Doubt, it was, to keep the *Virginia* Planters from cohabiting together in Towns; which probably might have forced some Kind of Trade and Shipping, that in time would have enabled them to transport their Tobacco to Market themselves."[72]

Similarly, Keith blamed Governor Alexander Spotswood for initially favoring legislation whereby planters would have to take their tobacco to "convenient Landing-places in the several Rivers" where it would be inspected for its quality and stored in government warehouses for shipment to England. As payment for their tobacco, planters would receive scrip with which they "might go to a public Store or Shop, and buy any small Quantity of Goods he pleased with his Tobacco Notes; whereas before, [they] could not deal without selling at least one Hogshead. But this Law, which had an excellent Effect in the Country while it lasted, proved likewise disagreeable to the private Interest and partial Views of particular Men, who found Means to have it repealed."[73]

William Stith (1747) told essentially the same story as his predecessors with equal passion.[74] As early as 1620, according to Stith, Virginia's fate had been sealed by its exclusive dependence on "a stinking nauseous, and unpalatable Weed[; it] is certainly an odd Commodity, to make the Staple and Riches of a Country. It is neither of Necessity nor Ornament to human Life; but the Use of it depends upon Humour and Custom, and may be looked upon as one of the most singular and extraordinary Pieces of Luxury, that the Wantonness of Man hath yet invented or given into."[75] Stith also blamed the English kings for perpetuating the colony's dependence on tobacco, including Charles I's instructions to Sir William Berkeley "not to suffer men to build slight Cottages, as heretofore hath been there used."[76]

IV

Jefferson's depiction of these early histories as being written inelegantly is true enough, and it is commonplace to blame others for personal failures, as these men did. It is also true that men like Beverley wrote their books in order to grind more than a few private axes. Virginia historian Louis B. Wright described Beverley as "a stout individualist whose views frequently differed from those held by the ruling faction in the colony." In addition, Wright said that Beverley's "failure to conform to the normal pattern of the governing class" was inherited "from an overly obstreperous father."[77]

If these stinging indictments of Virginians and English leaders for neglecting to diversify their agriculture were the work of cranks, there would be little need to accord them much attention. Beneath their criticisms, however, is a larger issue which Virginia's earliest chroniclers often raised, literally, to biblical proportions—that in planting tobacco Virginians ruined a paradise. The actions of the tobacco planters, seen in this light, replicated those of Adam and Eve in the Garden of Eden.[78]

John Smith, writing of "the starving time" (1609), refused to blame the environment for his men's failings—"the occasion was our owne, for want of providence, industrie and government, and not the barrennesse and defect of the Countrie, as is generally supposed."[79] For all of his criticisms of imperial policies and British kings, Parliament, and royal governors who supported outside direction of Virginia's internal affairs, Beverley continued Smith's theme of human degradation of the environment in his history, with even more emphasis. Virginia's climate and resources were supreme, he reckoned, "since it is very near of the same Latitude with the Land of Promise. Besides, as *Judea* was full of Rivers, and Branches of Rivers; So is Virginia: As that was seated upon a great Bay and Sea, wherein were all the conveniences for Shipping and Trade; So is *Virginia*. Had that fertility of Soil? So has *Virginia*, equal to any Land in the known World. . . . In fine, if any one impartially considers all the Advantages of this Country, as Nature made it; he must allow it to be as fine a Place, as any in the Universe." Stith agreed with Beverley: "Within these Capes they found a Country, which, according to their own Description, might claim the Prerogative over the most pleasant Places in the known World. . . . So that Heaven and Earth seemed never to have agreed better, to frame a Place for Man's commodious and delightful Habitation, were it fully cultivated and inhabited by industrious People."[80]

But here was the rub: Virginians had not lived up to Nature's promise. "I confess I am asham'd to say any thing of its Improvements," Beverley wrote of his colony,

> because I must at the same time reproach my Country-Men with a Laziness that is unpardonable. If there be any excuse for them in this Matter, 'tis the exceeding plenty of good things, with which Nature has blest them; for where God Almighty is so Merciful as to work for People, they never work for themselves. . . . [B]ut the extraordinary pleasantness of the Weather, and the goodness of the Fruit, lead People into many Temptations. . . . They spunge upon the Blessings of a warm Sun, and a fruitful Soil, and almost grutch the Pains of gathering in the Bounties of the Earth. I should be asham'd to publish this slothful Indolence of my Countrymen, but that I hope it will rouse them out of their Lethargy, and excite them to make the most of all those happy Advantages which Nature has given them; and if it does this, I am sure they will have the Goodness to forgive me.[81]

As Judy Jo Small notes, Beverley's "Edenic metaphors" were especially powerful because of the "realistic detail" of the book overall, thereby heightening the book's moral force. "From the very start," she writes, "the English venture into Virginia is seen as deeply flawed, pretending to be a divine mission but actually extending Old World corruption into a new terrain."[82] Jack P. Greene agrees. Beverley's *History* "revolved around an elaborate exploration of this palpable and intractable puzzle"—how "a country rendered so fine by nature had turned out to be in so many ways a profound cultural disappointment."[83]

Thomas Jefferson also criticized his countrymen for not fulfilling the promise of life in Virginia, and in doing so went beyond Beverley's admonitions by introducing a criticism of slavery both into *Notes* and into others of his writings. Beverley acknowledged near the end of his book that he had heard the English criticize Virginians for overworking "their Servants and Slaves, . . . [above] what every common Freeman do's." Yet Beverley also claimed that "Slaves are not worked near so hard, nor so many Hours in a Day, as the Husbandman, and Day-Labourers in *England*."[84] Jefferson, conversely, in *Notes* offered the opinion that slavery introduced into Virginians' behavior (or "manners" as he called it in Query 18) "the most boisterous passions, the most unremitting despotism on the one part, and degrading submissions on the other. . . . The man must be a prodigy who can retain his manners and morals undepraved by such circumstances." Climate, Jefferson opined, also supported the institution of slavery, "For in a warm climate, no man will labour for himself who can make another labour for him. This is so true, that of the proprietors of slaves a very small proportion indeed are ever seen to labour."[85]

Writing to his daughter Martha from Lake Champlain during a trip from Pennsylvania through New York and the New England states in May 1791, Jefferson compared the climate of the northern with the southern states. "[T]he weather . . . has been as sultry hot thro' the whole as could be found I believe in Carolina or Georgia. . . . On the whole I find nothing anywhere else in point of climate which Virginia need envy to any part of the world. . . . When we consider how much climate contributes to the happiness of our condn, by the fine sensation it excites, and the productions it is the parent of, we have reason to value highly the accident of birth in such a one as that of Virginia."[86]

Ironically, however, Jefferson later found the tables turned when his granddaughter, Ellen Randolph Coolidge, traveled through the same country thirty-five years later. The journey, she wrote,

> has given me an idea of prosperity and improvement, such as I fear our Southern States cannot hope for, whilst the canker of slavery eats into their hearts, and diseases the whole body by this ulcer to the core. When I consider the immense advantages of soil and climate which we possess over these people, it grieves me to think that such great gifts of Nature should have failed to produce any thing like the wealth and improvement which the New-Englanders have wrung from the hard bosom of a stubborn and ungrateful land, and amid the gloom and desolation of their wintry skies. . . . The appearance of the people generally is much in their favor; the men seem sober, orderly, and industrious: I have seen but one drunken man since I entered New England, and he was a south carolinian!

Jefferson's answer to her was terse and defensive. "I have no doubt," he responded, "you will find . . . the state of society there more congenial with your mind, than the rustic scenes you have left: altho these do not want their points of endearment. Nay, one single circumstance changed [slavery], and their scale would hardly be the lightest. One fatal stain deforms what nature had bestowed on us of her fairest gifts."[87] Like Beverley, Keith, and Stith, Jefferson criticized the customs of his countrymen while sharing many of their behaviors. Therefore, when Ellen near the end of his life noted this disconnect between words and actions, he took offense.

This tension as a member of an elite group who saw that he and they were engaging in destructive actions best informs Jefferson's life among the Virginia gentry.[88] In the period preceding the American Revolution, he sensed that his countrymen might use the political turmoil with England to bring about fundamental changes in many aspects of their society. Toward this goal, he lent his support.

"The God Who Gave Us Life, Gave Us Liberty at the Same Time"

A Summary View of the Rights of British America

In 1774, Thomas Jefferson became the preeminent spokesperson for those Virginians who questioned and eventually rebelled against British authority. In his pamphlet *A Summary View of the Rights of British America*, Jefferson cited a few examples from other British colonies (primarily Massachusetts and New York) to establish the case regarding Parliamentary arrogance and royal negligence, but the inspiration and context for *Summary View* lay in Virginia.[1]

Unfortunately, Jefferson's *Papers* are not very helpful in determining the exact source for the ideas and examples he used in the document. A fire at Shadwell in 1770 destroyed his library and whatever papers that might have shed light on this issue. Also, the facts that he was beginning his law practice and supervising the building of Monticello help to explain why there are fewer than one hundred pages of documents in his published *Papers* between 1770 and 1774. His biographers generally credit, in varying degrees, the classics, Renaissance humanism, Enlightenment thought, and English political dissenters as providing the language for Jefferson's *Summary View*.

Following an overview of how Jefferson came to write the document, this chapter suggests that he relied primarily on local texts, especially the writings of George Mason, in composing his influential pamphlet. Because Mason's papers give a much clearer view of how he justified rebellion than Jefferson's do, it is possible to see how Mason also benefited from the histories previously examined in Chapter 1, especially William Keith's *History of the British Plantations in America* (1738) and William Stith's *The History of the First Discovery and Settlement of Virginia* (1747). These authors delineated how mercantilism developed in the British Empire without destroying the colonists' right to self-government and how the Parliament's earliest Navigation Acts made Virginian tobacco planters partners with British merchants in expanding the wealth of the nation.

Keith and Stith also noted, however, a change of circumstances by the late 1600s, whereby Parliament and the English kings conspired to destroy the mutually advantageous system of centralized trade and local political autonomy. Because Keith and Stith so carefully described British neglect and abuse, Mason was able to apply their conclusions to the practical purpose of rallying Virginians to boycott British products.

But in taking a closer look at Mason's language and that of the early histories of Virginia, we do more than simply establish the intellectual and social context within which Jefferson drafted his *Summary View*. The investigation also clarifies how Jefferson recast these arguments in order to develop his own, peculiar justification for revolution. First, Jefferson built on the foundation these previous writers laid by showing how the British Empire utilized a federal sharing of powers between a metropolitan center and a locally oriented populace. This system of federalism helps to explain many of Jefferson's criticisms of Alexander Hamilton's financial plans (Chapter 5) and the principles he outlined for his presidency (Chapter 6). Second, Jefferson did not conclude the logic of *Summary View* with federalism. He showed his countrymen how they might improve on the British system by recasting the entire purpose of government.

I

The farthest most of the Virginia gentry ever traveled from their plantations was to Williamsburg, as young men to attend the College of William and Mary and to be introduced into proper society, and as older men to direct their colony's affairs in the House of Burgesses. By the time of the American Revolution, representative government had become the hallmark of Virginia's society, but politics in the colony must be appreciated less for the laws that the body produced than for how it operated. What most distinguished the House of Burgesses by the mid-1700s, Jack Greene writes, was its "functional and pragmatic character" that placed a premium on "the man of action, the man with a capacity for business who addressed himself directly to the problems at hand." These men projected themselves as "disinterested patriots par excellence" who sought not praise but rather praiseworthiness. They were "vigorous public servants who stood for activity, energy, and resolution in times of crisis."[2] Therefore, it is not surprising that members of the House of Burgesses became the leaders of Virginia's opposition to the Parliament's attempts to enforce the Navigation Acts in 1763 following a century of "benign neglect" and to the Parliament's determination to make the colonists help pay the costs of the Seven Years' War (the French and Indian War to colonists).

Thomas Jefferson took his place in the House of Burgesses in May 1769 and quickly fell in with men from the Northern Neck (the area from the mouth of the James River northward—more on this later) who were moving faster than others toward a break with England.[3] Although Jefferson was a new member, he was named to the committee charged with composing the body's response to Governor Norborne Berkeley Botetourt's opening speech. That document pledged that "[Great Britain's] Interests, and Ours, are inseparably the same," but not everyone agreed with this deferential language. Jefferson quickly became caught up in the efforts of Richard Henry Lee, George Washington, Patrick Henry, and George Mason to organize opposition to the Parliament's efforts to increase its control over Virginia. When relations between the governor and that body soured, Botetourt dissolved the Burgesses on May 17, 1769, and the body subsequently reassembled unofficially "with the greatest Order and Decorum" in order to draft nonimportation resolutions.[4]

In late May, Jefferson again appeared in a leadership position when a small group of burgesses wrote and helped to pass a resolution calling for a day of fasting and prayer on June 1 to protest the Boston Port Bill. Now a new governor—John Murray, Earl of Dunmore—summarily dissolved the new Burgesses. Following this dissolution, yet another meeting organized a formal boycott of East India Company products and called for a meeting of delegates from all the colonies. Throughout the summer, local county meetings selected delegates to attend an August convention and drafted resolutions and instructions for the delegates. These elections generally returned burgesses whom the governor had ousted. The August meeting adopted complete nonimportation after November 1, 1774, and nonexportation after August 10, 1775, if imperial disputes were not settled.[5]

Jefferson was elected to this August meeting but was unable to attend due (he wrote later in his *Autobiography*) to a bout of dysentery. He did, however, send two draft copies of a document, later published as *A Summary View of the Rights of British America*, to the meeting.[6]

Jefferson began his pamphlet with a bold assertion of the theory of natural rights. The terminology Jefferson chose for his document, he told the king, was "divested of those expressions of servility which would persuade his majesty that we are asking for favors and not rights." At the end of the document, he repeated the idea but with slightly different wording, saying that he wrote the document with "that freedom of language and sentiment which becomes a free people, claiming their rights as derived from the laws of nature, and not as the gift of their chief magistrate. Let those flatter, who fear: it is not an American art."[7]

Jefferson commenced his argument that colonial natural rights were being compromised with the Saxons. In Jefferson's reading of history, the Saxons "left their native wilds and woods in the North of Europe" and chose England as a land in which to establish "that system of laws which has so long been the glory and protection of that country"—in short, to establish what became the English system of representative government. The Saxons were integral to Jefferson's story because he next stated that the people coming to America exercised a right similar to that of their ancestors, "of departing from the country in which chance, not choice has placed them. . . . America was conquered, and her settlements made and firmly established, at the expence of individuals, and not of the British public. Their own blood was spilt in acquiring lands for their settlement, their own fortunes expended in making that settlement effectual. For themselves they fought, for themselves they conquered, and for themselves alone they have a right to hold."[8]

These freedom-loving individuals established "that system of laws under which they had hitherto lived in the mother country," retaining only their attachments to the king. Their life became, however, a continual defense of their rights against arbitrary power exercised by both the Parliament (the Navigation Acts, taxation, and removal of trial by jury) and the king (allowing the Parliament unjustly to expand its authority over the colonies and arbitrarily and capriciously giving away land to his favorites).

The lion's share of Jefferson's wrath in *Summary View* fell on the Parliament because of his belief that by regulating the trade of the colonies the Parliament benefited English merchants at the expense of American planters. Jefferson acknowledged that the Parliament had helped the colonies on occasion, especially "against an enemy who would fain have drawn to herself the benefits of their commerce to the great aggrandisement of herself and danger to Great Britain." But he denied that accepting aid ever gave the Parliament the right to exercise absolute authority over the colonies. He likewise calculated that the money was amply repaid "by our giving to the inhabitants of Great Britain such exclusive privileges in trade as may be advantageous to them, and at the same time not too restrictive to ourselves." Further, in the middle of the document Jefferson acknowledged that some of the Parliament's acts had been "nugatory" (i.e., "trifling" or "inconsequential") and that colonists as a consequence did not sufficiently protest the acts' unconstitutionality.[9]

Beginning with the Navigation Acts in the 1650s, however, the Parliament tried fundamentally to change the relationship between itself and the colonies by denying "the exercise of a free trade with all parts of the world, possessed by the American colonists as of natural right, and which no law of their own had taken away or abridged." Later extensions of the acts curtailed "manufacturing for our own use the articles we raise on our own lands with our own labor" so that "an American subject is forbidden to make a hat for himself of the fur which he has taken perhaps on his own soil. An instance of despotism to which no parrallel can be produced in the most arbitrary ages of British history." Another act prohibited the production of iron and required that it be purchased in Great Britain "for the purpose of supporting, not men, but machines." These acts and decisions had, at length, begun to pile upon one another and stifle freedom. "The true ground on which we declare these acts void," Jefferson wrote, "is that the British parliament has no right to exercise authority over us." Not single acts in isolation from one another, the English government's actions were rather "a deliberate, systematical plan of reducing us to slavery. . . . One free and independent legislature hereby takes upon itself to suspend the powers of another, free and independent as itself, thus exhibiting an phaenomenon, unknown in nature, the creator and creature of it's own power."[10]

Were the acts of the Parliament to be supreme in the colonies, the electors of the Parliament (reckoned by Jefferson at 160,000) would have had more power over the colonists than their own representatives, "every [one] of whom is equal to every individual of them in virtue, in understanding, and in bodily strength. . . . [T]hese are the acts of power assumed by a body of men foreign to our constitutions and unacknowledged by our laws; against which we do . . . enter this our solemn and determined protest."

Not only had the Parliament acted unjustly, but also the king had violated the British constitution. First, in discussing problems arising in Boston from the Parliament's "imposing duties on teas to be paid in America, against which act the Americans had protested as inauthoritative," Jefferson faulted the king for supporting not only the tax legislation but also for accepting the responsibility of deciding when to reopen the port of Boston to trade. "This little exception [delegating the responsibility to the king] seems to have been thrown in for no other purpose than that of setting a precedent for investing his majesty with legislative powers. If the pulse of his people shall beat calmly under this experiment, another and another will be tried till the measure of despotism be filled up." Second, Jefferson accused the king of negating laws passed in the colonies and for upholding contrary laws passed by the Parliament. "His majesty . . . and his ancestors, conscious of the impropriety of opposing their single opinion to the united wisdom of two houses of parliament . . . for several ages past have modestly declined the exercise of this power in that part of his empire called Great Britain." Now, Jefferson urged the king to recognize that the unwarranted interference of "new, and sometimes opposite interests" in the British Empire was pitting groups against each other. Therefore, Jefferson asked the king to "resume the exercise of his negative power, and to prevent the passage of laws by any one legislature of the empire which might bear injuriously on the rights and interests of another." Thus had the king refused to allow an end to the slave trade, the necessary antecedent to the "abolition of domestic slavery" which Jefferson characterized as "the great object of desire in those colonies where it was unhappily introduced in their infant state." In addition, the king had interfered with Burgesses' control of land in the colony, including the right to form new counties and provide representation to the people settling the western lands. "[D]oes his majesty seriously wish, and publish to the world," Jefferson asked rhetorically, "that his subjects should give up the glorious right of representation . . . and submit themselves the absolute slaves of his sovereign will?"[11]

Even more dangerous in Jefferson's mind was the king's insistence on granting lands by royal prerogative, deriving from the rules of feudalism that William I had introduced into England. Unfortunately, some of the original settlers of Virginia took lands under the fiction that the lands belonged to the king, especially when they were offered "for small sums and on reasonable rents." But, Jefferson asserted, "America was not conquered by William the Norman, nor it's lands surrendered to him or any of his successors. . . . Our ancestors however, who migrated hither, were laborers, not lawyers." Whatever may have happened in the past, Jefferson argued, "It is time . . . for us to lay this matter before his majesty, and to declare that he has no right to grant lands of himself."[12]

The only defense against such usurpations of rights, Jefferson advanced, was the people's representative assemblies. Just as the Parliament reestablished "the British constitution at the Glorious Revolution on it's free and antient principles," so now Burgesses should declare that "[f]rom [the] nature of things, every society must at all times possess within itself the sovereign powers of legislation." While these bodies were in existence, "they alone possess and may exercise those powers." This power to pass laws for the benefit of the group might then be "delegated" to bodies formed for that purpose, but no other external authority—neither the king, the Parliament, nor some other legislative body—could appropriate this legislative prerogative. "When [legislative bodies] are dissolved," Jefferson wrote, ". . . the power [to legislate] reverts to the people, who may use it to unlimited extent, either assembling together in person, sending deputies, or in any other way they may think proper." If people gave up these rights, they would make themselves slaves of kingly or parliamentary authority.[13]

Although Jefferson crafted the address as a petition to the king, throughout the document he used language that demeaned the position of George III. References to him as "the chief magistrate" or "the chief magistrate of the British empire" or "the only mediatory power between the several states of the British empire" or "the . . . common sovereign, . . . the central link connecting the several parts of the empire" or the man "holding the executive powers of the laws of these states" may sound conciliatory to modern ears, but Jefferson's language circumscribed the king's powers.

Perhaps based on his experiences as a student at the College of William and Mary (Chapter 1), Jefferson came to view the English king as a royal governor who should have learned, like Francis Fauquier did, how to mediate differences between Virginians and London bureaucrats. However he reached his position that the king stood between Great Britain and the colonists rather than as a supporter of the Parliament's authority, Jefferson wrote early in the document that the king was "no more than the chief officer of the people, appointed by the laws, and circumscribed with definite powers, to assist in working the great machine of government erected for their use, and consequently subject to their superintendance." At the end of the essay, he made the point bluntly. "[K]ings are the servants, not the proprietors of the people. Open your breast Sire, to liberal and expanded thought. Let not the name of George the third be a blot on the page of history. . . . The whole art of government consists in the art of being honest. Only aim to do your duty, and mankind will give you credit where you fail." All that was required was for the king to affirm that "our properties within our own territories shall [not] be taxed or regulated by any power on earth but our own. . . . This, Sire, is our last, our determined resolution."[14]

II

It is not surprising that Jefferson's peers adopted his document as theirs in 1774; the language he used throughout the document captured the stridency and seriousness of their emerging opposition to British controls. Their approval of it may also have centered in the fact that they found Jefferson's arguments familiar. Jefferson scholars acknowledge the fact that when he went to Burgesses he followed the lead of Lee, Washington, and the other Northern Neck men, but they have not pursued the possibility that Jefferson worked very closely with one of these men—George Mason—and that Mason and his writings were instrumental in helping Jefferson to find the words he used in *Summary View*.[15]

George Mason—whom Peter Wallenstein describes as "learned and able, experienced and wise, committed, industrious, and incorruptible"[16]—took the lead among his peers in rallying support to block British attempts to tax the British colonies in America and further regulate their trade following the French and Indian War. Although he did not attend the College of William and Mary, "Mason's letters and public papers clearly reveal," in the words of Robert Rutland, "that he was familiar with the books which most educated men knew, from Lucretius to Locke." Also, what Mason lacked in the way of a formal education he compensated for by learning ably to reckon "the value of sandy loams and timbered backlands" for growing tobacco.[17]

In his private correspondence before he became a spokesperson for his peers, Mason emphasized his interest in expanding his tobacco acreage, and it may have been this desire to protect his land investments that drew him into a leadership position of protecting Virginians' rights.[18] As John Selby notes, the Northern Neck of Virginia was the area of the colony where landholding was most concentrated in the hands of the gentry class. Whereas landholders throughout Virginia numbered about half of the adult, white males, ownership of land in the Northern Neck was considerably smaller, the result of the fact that lands had been distributed early on as large, speculative tracts. Estimates suggest that in places as much as 70 percent of the lands were concentrated in the hands of the gentry—the highest figure in the colony—and "[75 percent] of the whites in the area were landless."[19]

In addition to worrying about his current and future land holdings, Mason also wrote in the mid-1760s about the deleterious effect that slavery was having on the colony, especially the fact that by his reckoning "one Half of our best Lands in most parts of the Country remain unsetled, & the other cultivated with Slaves." In lieu of importing slaves, Mason favored "encouraging the Importation of free people & discouraging that of Slaves." He also expressed concern about "the ill Effect such a Practice has upon the Morals & Manners of our People" and worried that Virginia was heading down the same road to "Decay" that doomed Rome to destruction.[20]

After 1765, as protests mounted against Parliamentary taxation, Mason objected to these acts based upon the distinction later raised by John Dickinson and others ("the greatest & wisest Men in the Nation," in Mason's words) between the Parliament's power to legislate for the colonies, including regulating trade and the power to tax. "We do not deny the supreme Authority of Great Britain over her Colonys," he wrote to a group of London merchants in 1766, "but it is a Power which a wise Legislature will exercise with extreme Tenderness & Caution." Colonists, according to Mason, were "descended from the same Stock" as Englishmen and "nurtured in the same principles of Freedom. . . . [I]n crossing the Atlantic Ocean, we have only changed our Climate, not our Minds. [O]ur Natures & Dispositions remain unaltered." Although Jefferson in *Summary View* changed Mason's historical telling to make the Saxons the repositories of English freedom, the point and its phrasing about people retaining rights when they migrate are the same.

Mason also established the logic and very nearly the language that Jefferson later employed when he argued that an equal trade between the colonies and Great Britain would bind the colonists to the mother country more tightly than legislation the Parliament devised to prevent manufacturing:

If by opening the Channels of Trade, you afford Us a ready Market for the produce of our Lands, and an Opportunity of purchasing cheap the Conveniences of Life, all our superfluous Gain will sink into Your Pockets, in Return for British Manufactures. . . . Until you lay Us under a necessity of shifting for ourselves, You need not be afraid of the Manufactures of America. . . . It is by Invitations & Indulgence, not by Compulsion, that the Market for British Manufactures is to be kept up, & increased in America. . . . Do you, does any sensible Man think that three or four Millions of People, not naturally defective in Genius, or in Courage, who have tasted the Sweets of Liberty in a Country that doubles it's Inhabitants every twenty Years, in a Country abounding in such Variety of Soil & Climate, capable of producing not only the Necessarys, but the Conveniencys & Delicacys of Life, will long submit to Oppression; if unhappily for yourselves, Oppression shou'd be offered them?

Then, these words:

> We readily own that these Colonys were first setled, not at the Expence, but under the Protection of the English Government; which Protection it has continued to afford them; and we own too, that Protection & Allegiance are reciprocal Dutys. If it is asked at whose Expence they were setled? The Answer is obvious at the Expence of the private Adventurers our Ancestors; the Fruit of whose Toil and Danger we now enjoy. We claim Nothing but the Liberty & Privileges of Englishmen, in the same Degree, as if we had still continued among our Brethren in Great Britain: these Rights have not been forfeited by any Act of ours, we can not be deprived of them, without our Consent, but by Violence & Injustice; We have received them from our Ancestors, and, with God's Leave, we will transmit them, unimpaired to our Posterity.[21]

As he later did with Mason's Declaration of Rights (Chapter 3), Jefferson improved the effect of Mason's logic and language ("America was conquered, and her settlements made and firmly established, at the expence of individuals, and not of the British public. Their own blood was spilt in acquiring lands for their settlement, their own fortunes expended in making that settlement effectual. For themselves they fought, for themselves they conquered, and for themselves alone they have a right to hold"), but the words are Mason's.

It was also at Mason's urging that Virginians' determination to resist the Parliament's (illegal) attempts to tax took the form of a vow not to import English goods. "We may retrench all Manner of Superfluitys, Finery of all Denominations, & confine ourselves to Linnens Woolens &c, not exceeding a certain Price," he wrote to Washington in early 1769.[22] In May, he drafted "The Virginia Nonimportation Resolutions," which Jefferson and eighty-eight other gentry planters signed. The document pledged the signers by their "Example . . . [to] induce the good People of this Colony to be frugal in the Use and Consumption of British Manufactures, and that the Merchants and Manufacturers of Great-Britain may, from Motives of Interest, Friendship, and Justice, be engaged to exert themselves to obtain for us a Redress of those Grievances, under which the Trade and Inhabitants of America at present labour."[23] Unfortunately for Mason

and his collaborators, efforts at nonimportation of British goods failed miser-
ably because few of the signers accepted it wholeheartedly.[24] Jefferson himself
showed little enthusiasm for its details, as can be seen in a letter in 1771 in which
he anticipated that the nonimportation pledge would be limited only to those
goods that were taxed.[25] Writing to a friend late in the year, Mason confided,
"The non-Importation Associations here are at present in a very languid State.
. . . One Year wou'd do the Business; & for one Year or two we cou'd do without
importing almost anything from Great Britain."[26]

Mason's efforts to rally his peers to stand against the Parliament's attempts
to tax them reached a climax in the summer of 1774. In July, he drafted the
Fairfax County Resolves (published on July 26), in which he reprised language
that he had earlier employed in private correspondence. This document set the
stage for Jefferson's pamphlet, especially the words Jefferson chose with which
to address the king. "[T]his Colony and Dominion of Virginia can not be considered as a conquered Country," Mason affirmed, "and if it was . . . the present
Inhabitants are the Descendants not of the Conquered but of the Conquerors . . .
setled [not] at the national Expence of England, but at the private Expence of
the Adventurers, our Ancestors, by solemn Compact with, and under the Auspices and Protection of the British Crown." Because of the king's support and
protection, the colonists of Virginia were "in every Respect as dependant, as the
People of Great Britain, and in the same Manner subject to all his Majesty's just,
legal, and constitutional Prerogatives." But none of these royal pronouncements
negated the other, ancient rights of Englishmen, including the English "Civil-
Constitution and Form of Government," and these rights had descended to the
current generation who "were by the Laws of Nature and Nations, entitled to all
it's Privileges, Immunities and Advantages; . . . and ought of Right to be as fully
enjoyed, as if we had still continued within the Realm of England." The Resolves
continued:

> Chief among the rights that the English enjoyed and upon which it's very
> Existence depends, is the fundamental Principle of the People's being gov-
> erned by no Laws, to which they have not given their Consent, by Repre-
> sentatives freely chosen by themselves; who are affected by the Laws they
> enact equally with their Constituents; to whom they are accountable, and
> whose Burthens they share; in which consists the Safety and Happiness
> of the Community: for if this Part of the Constitution was taken away, or
> materially altered, the Government must degenerate either into an abso-
> lute and despotic Monarchy, or a tyrannical Aristocracy, and the Freedom
> of the People be annihilated.[27]

Whenever the Parliament had passed Navigation Acts in order to regulate the
trade of the colonies for the mutual benefit of the colonies and the nation, "our

2. "The Fairfax Resolves." Had the editors of the *Jefferson Papers* included this document in Volume 1 of the series, it might have influenced scholars' views of the origins of Jefferson's *Summary View*. The George Washington Papers, Library of Congress Manuscript Division.

Ancestors submitted to *it*, . . . while the entire Regulation of our internal Policy, and giving and granting our own Money were preserved to our own provincial Legislatures." But the Parliament's claims to sovereignty over the colonies violated "the first principles of the [English] Constitution, and the original Compacts by which we are dependant upon the British Crown and Government; [and] is totally incompatible with the Privileges of a free People, and the natural Rights of Mankind." Such actions on the part of the Parliament would "render our own Legislatures merely nominal and nugatory, and [are] calculated to reduce us from a State of Freedom and Happiness to Slavery and Misery."[28]

Mason's use of the word "nugatory" here is instructive and provides a specific example of the method that Jefferson used to recast Mason's thoughts. Whereas Mason believed that Parliamentary legislation was rendering colonial legislatures "trifling" or "inconsequential," Jefferson reversed the burden of the argument to say that the Parliament's legislation—not the colonial legislatures—was "nugatory." Following this section, Mason and Jefferson both drafted phrases designed to undercut the Parliament's allegations to its authority over the House of Burgesses. In Mason's words, because the Parliament was composed of people "in whose Election we have no Share, on whose Determinations we can have no Influence, . . . [and] who in many Instances may have a separate, and in some an opposite Interest to ours," the legislative body was attempting to "establish the most grievous and intollerable Species of Tyranny and Oppression, that ever was inflicted upon Mankind. . . . [T]ho' we are it's Subjects, we will use every Means which Heaven hath given us to prevent our becoming it's Slaves." Jefferson wrote, more concisely and directly, that the Parliament's actions were part of "a deliberate, systematical plan of reducing us to slavery."[29]

Until the Parliament repealed its unconstitutional attempts to bind the colonies to its absolute will, the Resolves called upon "all the Gentlemen and Men of Fortune to set Examples of Temperance, Fortitude, Frugality and Industry" by cultivating flax, cotton, and other domestic manufactures, including wool, and by ceasing to import any "Goods or Merchandize whatsoever" from the British Isles. Also, "no Slaves ought to be imported into any of the British Colonies on this Continent; and we take this Opportunity of declaring our most earnest Wishes to see an entire Stop for ever put to such a wicked cruel and unnatural Trade." If the Parliament did not attend to these grievances, Virginians pledged not to "plant or cultivate any Tobacco, after the Crop now growing; provided the same Measure shall be adopted by the other Colonies on this Continent, as well those who have heretofore made Tobacco, as those who have n[o]t."

Finally, the document "recommended to the Deputies of the general Congress to draw up and transmit an humble and dutiful Petition and Remonstrance to his Majesty, asserting with decent Firmness our just and constitutional Rights and Privileg[es,] . . . declaring, in the strongest Terms, ou[r] Duty and Affection to his Majesty's Person, Family [an]d Government, and our Desire to continue our Dependance upon Great Bri[tai]n; and most humbly conjuring and beseeching his Majesty, not to reduce his faithful Subjects of America to a State of desperation, and to reflect, that from our Sovereign there can be but one Appeal."[30]

That Jefferson saw this document cannot be proved from searching his papers, but he must have. On the same day as the Resolves were published, a group of his neighbors met and elected him and John Walker to attend the meeting set for August 1 at Williamsburg, the House of Burgesses having been suspended on July 8 by the governor, Lord Dunmore.[31] And although Jefferson did not attend the meeting, his *Summary View* clearly fulfilled Resolution 23 of Resolves that the Burgesses "draw up and transmit an humble and dutiful Petition and Remonstrance to his Majesty, asserting with decent Firmness our just and constitutional Rights and Privileg[es]."[32]

III

Because Julian Boyd and his staff did not include the Fairfax County Resolves in Jefferson's *Papers*, Jefferson's biographers have addressed neither its possible influence on the timing of Jefferson's composition of *Summary View* nor the language he used in it. As will be developed more fully in Chapter 3, it was uncommon for writers in Jefferson's time to acknowledge that they copied from others, and he certainly was not the only one to rely heavily on others' words. It is possible that he caught the essence, and perhaps even the exact wording of the Resolves, from conversations with his friends, and many of Mason's ideas are to be found in documents produced in other colonies.

Although George Mason did not say where he got his views, similarity of language suggests that he likely borrowed from the same histories of Virginia that Jefferson read. As noted in Chapter 1, Robert Beverley's *History* (1705) criticized Virginians and the English crown for making tobacco the exclusive staple of the colony during the earliest days of settlement. Beverley also blamed Oliver Cromwell for beginning the Navigation Acts during the 1650s, legislation that prohibited the colonists from trading with European colonies except through English merchants with ships built by Englishmen. These "strange Arbitrary Curbs," in Beverley's words, "exceedingly afflicted the People" because they came at a time when "*England* it self was in Distraction; and could neither take off their Commodities, nor supply them sufficiently with its own. Neither had they ever been used to supply them with half the Commodities they expended, nor to take off above half the Tobacco they made." Subsequent acts, to Beverley's way of thinking, made the effect of the first act worse by granting to English merchants an exclusive right not only to sell Virginia's tobacco in Europe but also to raise the value of European goods shipped into the colony.[33]

William Keith extended Beverley's arguments in his history by criticizing the English kings and the Parliament for their enforcement of the Navigation Acts, but Keith drew a different meaning from the Acts because he saw them in a different context. Whereas Beverley's book dealt primarily with the founding of Virginia and stopped at 1700, Keith dealt more with its maturation during the early eighteenth century. Keith also ranged further afield than Beverley, noting in the first pages of his book his intention:

> 1. To inquire into the Nature of Trade in General, how and for what Purposes it has been carried on in the Course of Time, by the most powerful and flourishing States in the World, what Relation it has to Civil Government, and the intimate Connection that must always subsist between them. 2. To inquire into the first Discovery of *America*, and into the particular Views which induced the *European* Nations to send over great Numbers of their People to make large Settlements, and to plant Colonies in that Part of the World.[34]

Of particular notice in this passage is Keith's linking of trade to government and his suggestions that the two are symbiotic. Keith's book is important because it falls between mercantilism—where government's regulation of the economy increases the nation's wealth, measured in gold—and capitalism, where competition in an open market establishes prices rather than government. In anticipation of capitalism, Keith described trade as "a voluntary Exchange of Things we possess, for those in the Possession of others, either to supply the Necessaries and Conveniences of Life, or to secure . . . a certain profit to ourselves." But his debt to mercantilism is also apparent because he believed that societies came into existence not in order to apportion goods to some and withhold them from others (the establishment of monopolies under mercantilism) but so that the public good would triumph over individual self-interest. "[I]t is inconsistent with the Nature of Things to suppose," according to Keith, "that a Civil Government ought to permit, much less encourage, any Traffick or private Gain to be carried on, which evidently appears to be prejudicial to the public Interest and Prosperity of the Common-wealth; the last and greatest Object of every good Citizen's Care and Ambition."[35]

Colonization occurred, according to Keith, when European nations found that international trade disadvantaged one country "either by the Deficiency of a sufficient Quantity of [a] Product to be exported . . . , or . . . when by a greater Share of Industry we are outdone by Foreign States . . . whereby the Balance of Trade is turn'd against us." By colonizing distant areas, nations acquired new products, thereby restoring "the lost Balance of National Trade. And this be-

3. "Europe Supported by Africa and America." This illustration captures perfectly the view of the Virginia gentry that English prosperity rested on American exports (supported also by African slavery). From John G. Stedman, *Narrative of a Five Years' Expedition* (London, 1796), Plate LXXX. Courtesy of The British Library, Shelfmark Number S66L24.

ing the original Intention of, and the only justifiable Reason that can be given for the Practice within these last Two Centuries, of making Settlements and planting Colonies on the uninhabited vacant Lands of *America*, whose People are protected by, but made subservient to, and dependent on their respective Mother States in *Europe*."[36]

Thus, according to Keith, did the British establish colonies, taking care throughout "to preserve the Sovereignty and Allegiance due to the Crown of *Britain*, but likewise to restrain the People of the respective Colonies, from enacting amongst themselves any By-Laws or Ordinances whatsoever, repugnant to, or any ways inconsistent with, the Fundamental Laws and Constitution of the Mother State, to whose Legislative and Supreme Authority they most certainly are, and ought always to be subjected." These strictures meant in practice that colonials were to raise products which the British needed in exchange for British manufactures and in return "not only enjoyed the Advantage of the same Laws, and the sweet Comforts of *English* Liberty in all respects, but they were also sure of being protected from the Insults and Attacks of any foreign Enemy, by the Naval Force, and at the Public Expence of Great Britain."[37]

Integral to this beneficial connection, however, were the private relationships that developed between English merchants and American colonists, each expecting to make a profit from exchanging raw materials for finished goods. These profits not only benefited the planters and the merchants as individuals but also enriched Great Britain as merchants invested "such Overplus or Balance . . . in some of the Public Funds, or . . . on Land-Security in *Great Britain*, . . . [thereby remaining] a part of the National Wealth or Stock. In like Manner the Profits arising to *British* Subjects in *America* . . . must terminate in the Advantage of *Great Britain*." Trade, therefore, united all parties—the British government, British merchants, and British colonists in America—in a mutually beneficial arrangement for the public good. But then a warning:

> From this simple and plain, but true State of the Case, it is evident of what Importance it must be to the public Interest of *Great Britain*, to be exceedingly careful to point out and direct the Object of their Subjects Labour, in the several Colonies in *America*, by such gentle Encouragements as will gradually lead them into the Channels of mutual and public Advantage; for Trade is a Child of Liberty, which either may be reared and nourished by Indulgence, or depressed and sunk under the Awe of a too severe Restraint. . . . It is easy to talk of Penal Laws, Prohibitions, and such-like Severities, to be executed by the Force of Power; but . . . as long as the Generality of a People are truly sensible, that their Rulers and Governors have nothing so much at Heart as the public Good of the Society, and the Honour and Prosperity of the Commonwealth, there will be no Occasion to apprehend either Discontent, Insurrection or Rebellion.[38]

In Keith's telling, the earliest Navigation Acts were beneficial to both England and Virginia because they established a system of mutual dependence between Great Britain and its wealthiest North American colony. Referring to Cromwell as "a skilful and wise Governor," Keith described the 1651 act as "a just and good Law, calculated for the mutual Advantage of *Great Britain*, and her Plantations abroad." Likewise, the extension of the Acts in the 1660s under Charles II, Keith characterized as occurring "for just and wise Considerations" and "very reasonable" in their intentions.[39]

With subsequent acts, however, Keith found problems. The 1673 law that added "several Duties . . . on the Trade from one Colony to another, and appropriated to Uses quite foreign to the People, from whom they were raised" whether intentionally or inadvertently worked to the benefit of "the Merchants in *England*, who enjoy'd considerable Profits by being Factors for the Tobacco Planters in *Virginia* . . . [because] the Price of Tobacco then was so low, that the Balance due to the Planter on his Account of Sales from *England*, amounted to little or nothing, nay, often brought him in Debt to the Factor; so that they really had not wherewithal, out of their laborious Toil, to cloathe themselves, and their poor Families."[40] In the 1690s, Governor Francis Nicholson further privileged the London merchants by prohibiting "the *Virginia* Planters from cohabiting together in Towns; which probably might have forced some Kind of Trade and Shipping, that in time would have enabled them to transport their Tobacco to Market themselves." Thereafter, British policy favored merchants over planters consistently, and the merchants' "covetous Desire to over-reach and to grasp at an immoderate Gain" began to wreck the harmonious relationship that needed to exist in order to increase the public good.[41]

By the end of the book, Keith expressed pessimism regarding the future. In a section entitled "Remarks on the Trade and Government of Virginia," he wrote, "As it is impossible for an innocent and unprejudiced Mind, to separate the Idea of Government from the Good and Happiness of the People that are to be govern'd, so it is not to be expected, That Men who are born free, and have any just Notions of Liberty, can force their Affections and chearful Obedience to Governors who exercise their Power with Partiality and Caprice." Fully "two Thirds of the *Virginia* Planters at this time," Keith calculated, "may be consider'd only as so many working Slaves for the Benefit of their Factors in *Great-Britain*, without so much as a Prospect of being released from that Bondage."[42]

Less than ten years later, William Stith published his history. Whether because Keith had been so critical of British merchants or because Stith felt that Keith had attributed colonial problems improperly to them, the latter's book returned to Beverley's criticisms of British monarchs. Beginning with the introduction where Stith referred to James I as "that silly Monarch," Stith lambasted the British kings. "*A King's Character, whilst he lives, is, and ought to be sacred, because his Authority depends upon it. But when his Authority, the Reason of it's being sacred, determines, the Inviolableness of his Character is also at an End. . . . And as for King* James I. *I think and speak of him, with the same Freedom and Indifferency, that I would think and speak of any other Man, long since dead; and therefore I have no way restrained my Stile, in freely exposing his weak and injurious Proceedings.*"[43]

Stith chiefly faulted James I for capricious actions concerning the Virginia Company, which Stith considered to be contrary to English laws and precedents. In language that suggests that Jefferson may also have used Stith's book or recalled its language in drafting *Summary View*, Stith wrote about James I:

> I am no lawyer, and therefore shall . . . only transiently remark, that, notwithstanding the frequent Repetition of the Laws of *England*, and the Equity thereof, his Majesty seems, in some things, to have deviated grossly from them. He has certainly made sufficient Provision for his own despotic Authority; and has attributed an extravagant and illegal Power to the Presidents and Councils. For he has placed the whole Legislative Power solely in them, without any Representative of the People, contrary to a noted Maxim of the *English* Constitution; That all Freemen are to be governed by Laws, made with their own Consent, either in Person, or by their Representatives.[44]

In contrast to what he regarded as the king's misuse of governmental prerogative, Stith praised the London Company for creating the House of Burgesses in Virginia in 1619, where "by the Introduction of the *British* Form of Government, by Way of Parliament or Assembly, the People were again restored to their Birthright, the Enjoyment of *British* Liberty." He also asserted that by royal charter "and by all other Law and Reason, the *English*, transplanted hither, had a Right to all the Liberties and Privileges of *English* Subjects"; otherwise "no Person, in his Senses, would have left the Liberty of *England*, to come hither (in order to improve the Commerce, and increase the Riches of the Nation) to a State of Slavery."[45]

While Stith acknowledged that the settlers of Virginia whether "by the Necessity of the Times, by the ignorance of the People, and by the Oppression and Tyranny of Governors" allowed themselves to be deprived of their English rights, he wrote that after 1619 they had jealously guarded their "native Right." "From this Time therefore," Stith eloquently boasted, "we may most properly date the Original of our present Constitution, by Governor, Council, and Burgesses; which altho' defective perhaps in some material Points, yet comes so near to the excellent Model of the *English* Government, that it must be the hearty Prayer and Desire of all true Lovers of their Country, that it may long flourish among us and improve." Thus, a law passed either by the Company officials in London or the House of Burgesses in Virginia was each subject to review by the other, and "in all other things, they were commanded, to follow the Policy, Form of Government, Laws, Customs, Manner of Trial, and other Administration of Justice, used in *England*."[46]

Stith identified another problem stemming from the fact that the early settlers of Virginia were not more zealously dedicated to defending their rights: the colonists did not assert that it was their industry that had built the colonies rather than the efforts of the English, especially the English kings. Indeed, Stith insisted that "his Majesty's poor Subjects, had adventured their Lives and Fortunes thither" without the king's grant of "many goodly Privileges and Liberties, under the great Seal of *England*."[47] Only to create "a perpetual Memorial and permanent Honour to his Majesty and his Royal Issue" had the colonists "named their chief Towns, and other most remarkable Places, after the King and his Children." But as a result of this naming pattern, according to Stith, English kings came to believe that they owned the lands of Virginia rather than the colonists. In no way, Stith averred, had any laws or proclamations altered "the Property of inheritance in those Places, which his Majesty . . . had granted to the said Company, for and throughout all *Virginia*."[48]

IV

Although neither Beverley, Keith, nor Stith used the term "federal" to describe the system that the British devised to rule the empire, this concept of shared authority between centralized and local government best describes how they envisioned the proper relations between the Parliament and Virginians. As Bernard Bailyn points out, federalism evolved from the provincialism of the colonists' everyday experiences by formalizing "the de facto constitutional world that they, as British provincials ruled by both their local assemblies and the Parliament, had known for generations."[49] John Murrin follows the same path as Bailyn but with more depth. Although the British architects of the empire never conceived that they were establishing a federal system, in fact the central government had always limited itself in two primary ways. First, in requiring local colonies to cover their own local expenses of government, the Parliament and the king had to negotiate with these local governments over how the empire functioned. The day-to-day operations of government depended on working through local authorities—especially locally elected assemblies, like the House of Burgesses in Virginia—who became, over time, increasingly jealous of their powers. Second, because the Parliament channeled its relations with the colonies almost exclusively into overseeing colonial trade, the colonies never developed parallel political institutions. Royal colonies patterned on Virginia became the model for structuring the legal underpinnings of the system, but the operations of government functioned differently in each colony.[50]

Nowhere is this lack of uniformity more apparent than when comparing Massachusetts Bay and Virginia, both of which were royal colonies after 1696. In Massachusetts Bay, the government that most directly affected people's lives remained the town meeting, whose local authority had been a hallmark of the Puritan experience from the beginning. In Virginia, by way of contrast, Burgesses concentrated attention on land acquisition and distribution, establishing and monitoring fixed labor contracts of first indentured servants and then slaves, and creating de facto aristocratic rule by the gentry class. Local government rested in the counties, justices of the peace, and quid pro quo arrangements between the local tobacco planters and yeoman farmers.[51]

The Seven Years' War exposed both the strengths and weaknesses of this federal system. During the war, from Massachusetts Bay to Virginia Americans responded to British calls for men and supplies, in Murrin's words, "on an unprecedented scale and were quite proud of their role in the great imperial victory."[52] Inside the empire and looking outward, Americans idealized the shared responsibility that had developed between local and metropolitan authorities and believed that each entity was equal within its own purview. In the Parliament, however, members questioned the huge expenditures of funds that transferred British gold to colonial coffers to pay the cost of the distant war. As the national debt doubled during the war, the Parliament's leaders began to shift that body's interest from regulating trade to paying the expenses of the war and laid plans to tax Americans directly, thereby bypassing local assemblies.

In Virginia, Patrick Henry, Richard Henry Lee, and others vocalized what became the nucleus of revolutionary rhetoric, that Crown and Parliament were reversing history by returning England to the tyranny of unchecked absolutism. George Mason and Thomas Jefferson accomplished the same feat in their writings by not only using a common language but also reshaping and recasting old arguments first developed in Virginia's early histories.

Because Beverley, Keith, and Stith had discussed the historical origins of mercantilism, neither Mason nor Jefferson had to repeat familiar arguments. And because Keith and Stith established the bases of Virginian government—including the origins of the House of Burgesses and its separateness from Parliament as well as establishing a precedent for attacking the king as well as Parliament—Mason and Jefferson could dispense with a tedious recitation of English history.

Although Jefferson acknowledged in *Notes* that he read these histories, he never mentioned them in connection with his drafting of *Summary View*. Still, if we view Jefferson's document from this perspective and subtract the language in these books and Mason's writings from his famous pamphlet, what is left?

In contrast to the histories and the great majority of Mason's writings, Jefferson conceptualized the Parliament's threats to Virginians' liberties in terms of natural rights rather than English rights. Perhaps because Keith and Stith established the fact that the Parliament had so egregiously violated English rights and placed the colonists on the verge of being led into slavery, Jefferson could recast the argument in *Summary View*. And by viewing nature as the embodiment of a rational order in the world, Jefferson was also able to supersede Mason's arguments in important ways.

Although the full extent of Mason's opposition to slavery remains contested scholarly terrain, a consensus exists that he was not consistently antislavery. Rutland notes that Mason's large slaveholding interests "make it obvious that he held to a double standard on slavery. [He] condemned slavery on moral and economic grounds, but since others would not heed his advice (or predictions) about the baneful effects of slavery, he tended to disregard it himself as did his sons." Wallenstein similarly points out that Mason's opposition to the slave trade served to benefit Virginia's slaveholders by increasing the value of their property, and however strong his language about slavery became, he never acted on his statements: "Whatever his occasional rhetoric, George Mason was—if one must choose—proslavery, not antislavery." Stephen A. Schwartz likewise notes that whereas Mason wrote and spoke in opposition to slavery, he did not really know "what to do about [it]," especially at the end of his life. "In the end," Schwartz writes, "it may have been as simple as . . . [that] Mason was unwilling to bankrupt his children."[53]

However he came to feel about slavery, through the summer of 1774 Mason remained primarily critical of the slave trade because it was grounded in mercantilism. As Murrin observes, both Jefferson and Mason drew from the ideas and writings of both John Locke and James Harrington (even though the two men often viewed politics from opposite perspectives), but only Jefferson developed these arguments into moral sentiments. According to Murrin, Mason was the more consistently Lockean of the two because Mason was able to use Locke's "highly rationalistic argument" to argue that Virginians could not be viewed as "helpless subjects in the hands of an angry king." As Mason blamed the king for the continued existence of slavery in Virginia, he also argued based on Locke's writings that *white* Virginians had brought their English rights with them to America.[54]

In *Summary View*, however, Jefferson attacked the existence of slavery in Virginia because it was inconsistent with liberty. In this way, he not only built upon the work of others, but also departed from them in a significant way. At the close of the first sentence of *Summary View*, Jefferson wrote that Parliament was attempting to take away "rights which god and the laws have given equally and independently to all." Then, three sentences from the end of the document, Jefferson returned to the point by affirming in one of his most oft-quoted phrases: "The god who gave us life, gave us liberty at the same time: the hand of force may destroy, but cannot disjoin them."[55]

For Jefferson, it was not enough to say that Virginians had inherited or re-established the rights of the English in the New World; he traced the origins of rights back to the start—to creation. In moving to this argument, he was independently following the same progression that Jean Le Rond d'Alembert and Denis Diderot also constructed in the *Encyclopédie* (Chapter 4). According to French cultural historian Robert Darnton, Diderot and d'Alembert believed that knowledge began with the senses, followed by "reflection ('I feel, therefore I am')." Out of this reflection came knowledge of self, then

> knowledge of external objects, the experience of pleasure and pain, and thence to notions of morality [and] . . . how individuals formed societies. Once engaged in social life, they began to question the source of their newly acquired morality. It could not come from the physical world, so it must come from some spiritual principle dwelling within us, which had forced us to reflect on justice and injustice. We recognize two principles at work, mind and body [Descartes]; and in the act of recognition, we sense our imperfection, which implies a prior notion of perfection itself. *In the end, therefore, we arrive at a conception of God* [emphasis added].[56]

As Darnton admits, "It was an odd argument. . . . D'Alembert had taken a Lockean route to a Cartesian God . . . [because he] wrote at a time when scholastic, Cartesian, and Lockean language jostled one another in philosophic discourse. . . . Instead of laying out a rigorously consistent set of premises and proceeding deductively, he maintained, philosophers ought to take nature as they found it, reduce its phenomena down to their underlying principles, and then reconstruct those principles systematically."[57]

When at the end of *Summary View* Jefferson wrote, "The god who gave us life gave us liberty at the same time: the hand of force may destroy, but cannot disjoin them," he affirmed that rights came with life. No more quibbling over internal or external taxes, royal charters, mercantilist theory, or the ambiguities of the British constitution: Virginians had received the right to rule themselves from nature. With this insight, he could write the Declaration of Independence and begin in earnest his quest to challenge the Virginia gentry to use the American Revolution to undertake a wholesale reformation of their country.

"Rights Inherent & Inalienable"

The American Revolution in Virginia

Major controversies continue to swirl about Thomas Jefferson's role in drafting the Declaration of Independence and his importance as a leader of the American Revolution. This chapter investigates the circumstances surrounding Jefferson's writing of the document and undertakes a close analysis of its language. As he wrote the famous document, local, Virginian influences—including further reliance on the words of George Mason (Chapter 2)—played a stronger role than most Jeffersonian scholars have indicated. Most of the ideas expressed in the second paragraph of the Declaration of Independence were developed in *Summary View*, as were many of the charges that he leveled against the king. In addition, Jefferson wrote to friends that he would have preferred to have been in Williamsburg helping his peers to draft the Virginia constitution rather than in Philadelphia as part of the Second Continental Congress. He sent copies of the Declaration to members of the Virginia Assembly to show his sympathy with them, and he left Philadelphia to join them as soon as he could after independence had been declared.

The Declaration of Independence represents a fuller expression of Jefferson's developing ideas on natural rights than the *Summary View*. Whereas Jefferson placed God's granting of life and liberty last in *Summary View* (Chapter 2), he put rights first in the Declaration of Independence. According to his "Rough draught" of the document, at the time of creation men attained "rights inherent & inalienable, among which are the preservation of life, & liberty, & the pursuit of happiness."[1] Further, Jefferson explains that government—resting on the consent of the governed—existed in order to secure these rights and that whenever a government became abusive of these rights it was "the right of the people to alter or to abolish it, & to institute new government . . . as to them shall seem most likely to effect their safety & happiness."[2]

Next, the chapter details how determined Jefferson was when he returned home in August 1776 "to institute new government" in his country by reforming the state's old laws and writing a new constitution for the state. Unfortunately, his optimism quickly faded as in his mind his peers refused to secure fully their "inalienable rights." As governor of the state from 1779 to 1781, he experienced the full measure of both his countrymen's resistance to change and their capacity for vindictiveness. By the end of the American Revolution, Jefferson had lost faith in the ability of his peers to change Virginian society because they had not seized the opportunity that independence from Great Britain offered.

I

In tracing scholarly interpretations of the context surrounding Jefferson's writing of the Declaration of Independence, one finds at least three major lines of argument, each of which gives credit to different sources for Jefferson's ideas—English Enlightenment thinker John Locke, Scottish philosophers, and Virginian George Mason.[3] Other scholars have dismissed the importance of specifying the origins of Jefferson's wording altogether. In 1945, Julian Boyd traced the evolution of the Declaration of Independence through its various drafts. Although he concluded that Locke provided the primary stimulus for most of Jefferson's language, Boyd downplayed any specific source for the Revolutionary generation's ideas. "The fact is that these broad concepts, familiar to any reader of Locke or [Jean-Jacques] Burlamaqui or [Emmerich de] Vattel, were so much a part of the air breathed by the patriots of 1776 that Jefferson could not have escaped using them and their more or less fixed phraseology even if he had desired to do so."[4] Three years later, Dumas Malone similarly emphasized the influence of Locke and other English writers on Jefferson's wording. He also acknowledged that Jefferson's words in the Declaration of Independence are "similar in parts" to Mason's "and may reflect [his] influence." Malone concluded, however, "the ideas were in [Jefferson's] mind already. . . . [T]hey were the property of all mankind. Certainly they were the property of the American Patriots, whose mind he was trying to express, and it really made no difference where they came from."[5]

Pauline Maier extends Malone's findings based upon her investigation of state declarations of independence and the editing of Jefferson's "Rough draught" by the members of the Second Continental Congress. Maier concludes that the Declaration "restated what virtually all Americans . . . thought and said in other words in other places." Also, as a statement of political philosophy, she believes that the text was "purposely unexceptional." Designed primarily for internal purposes, including its ability to be read at public gatherings, the Declaration of Independence was—as Jefferson later emphasized—"a public document, an authenticated expression of the American mind."[6] Maier also stresses the similarities with Mason's Declaration of Rights. Specifically, she compares the wording of the second paragraph of the Declaration of Independence and Mason's first three clauses. She even credits Jefferson for compressing Mason's language into "a more memorable statement of the same content. Less was more."[7]

In Maier's view, however, Jefferson owed less to Mason than to the English Declaration of Rights (1689), which she views as the chief inspiration for Mason's work. Noting that Jefferson was working on a draft of a constitution for Virginia at the same time as he composed the Declaration of Independence, Maier shows how the accusations against the king in both documents are nearly identical and asserts that both take the same form as the English Declaration of Rights. Finally, Maier underscores the fact that the first eight of the charges are in the same order and worded similarly to the way they appeared in *Summary View*. "He was no Moses receiving the Ten Commandments from the hand of God," she affirms, "but a man who had to prepare a written text with little time to waste, and who, like others in similar circumstances, drew on earlier documents of his own and other people's creation."[8]

Not surprisingly, the first person to raise the issue that George Mason influenced Jefferson's wording of the Declaration of Independence was one of Mason's descendants, Kate Mason Rowland, in her 1892 biography. According to Rowland, the Declaration of Independence "repeated [the] cardinal maxims, and adopted many of [the] phrases" of Mason's Virginia Declaration of Rights.[9] In 1924, John C. Fitzpatrick extended Rowland's argument, labeling the Declaration of Independence "a Virginia product" because it melded Jefferson's charges against George III, which he prepared for the Virginia Constitutional Convention (more on this later), with George Mason's Declaration of Rights and Richard Henry Lee's resolution for independence. Fitzpatrick found noteworthy the similarity in Mason's words in the first three articles of the Declaration of Rights and Jefferson's in the second paragraph of the Declaration of Independence. "While at work in committee upon the revision of the Preamble . . . a copy of the Virginia Bill of Rights, as adopted, reached Jefferson through the public prints. The clarion note of liberty in its first three sections found sympathetic echo in his brain; he seized upon them and, with the artist's perfect judgment, commenced the Declaration with the trumpet blast of their bold principles." Fitzpatrick credited Jefferson's "genius, and . . . high literary skill" in "fusing together" the three Virginia documents to produce the Declaration of Independence.[10]

Fitzpatrick's linking of the Declaration of Independence with Mason's Declaration of Rights attracted extended comparison, most notably by Gilbert Chinard. In his 1939 biography of Jefferson, Chinard extended Fitzpatrick's treatment of Mason by reprinting the first three of Mason's "Rights" in their entirety (as amended by the Convention). Chinard contended that "it is no longer a question of analogy, or similarity of thought—the very words are identical."

Because Jefferson quoted directly from the Virginia Declaration of Rights, Chinard noted that Jefferson should have acknowledged Mason's contribution. But his contemporaries, and particularly the Virginians, could not fail to recognize in the national document the spirit and expression of the state's document. "Jefferson had expressed . . . the mind of his fellow Virginians." Chinard further absolved Jefferson of plagiarism by saying that "*l'arrangement*" of Mason's words was new and hence original.[11]

Based upon the examination in Chapter 2 of Jefferson's borrowing of Mason's words in writing *Summary View*, it is not surprising that he should have done so again in drafting the Declaration of Independence. Still, in order to establish the full measure of Jefferson's reliance on Mason, it is necessary to reconstruct Jefferson's activities from mid-May through early July 1776, beginning with a closer examination of when and in what form he may have seen the Declaration of Rights.

Without exception, those scholars who stress Mason's influence on Jefferson base their arguments on the belief that Jefferson saw Virginia's Declaration of Rights in Philadelphia newspapers some time after June 6.[12] Mason, however, finished his draft on May 24, and a copy of his report likely reached Jefferson in Philadelphia a week or more earlier than is commonly believed. A stage left Williamsburg for Philadelphia on May 25 and probably contained a copy of Mason's draft in letters from Edmund Pendleton to George Wythe, or other Virginia delegates in Philadelphia.[13] Mason's draft copy of the Declaration of Rights reads:

> . . . That all Men are born equally free and independant, and have certain inherent natural Rights, of which they can not by any Compact, deprive or divest their Posterity; among which are the Enjoyment of Life and Liberty, with the Means of acquiring and possessing Property, and pursueing and obtaining Happiness and Safety.
>
> That Power is, by God and Nature, vested in, and consequently derived from the People; that Magistrates are their Trustees and Servants, and at all times amenable to them.
>
> That Government is, or ought to be, instituted for the common Benefit and Security of the People, Nation, or Community. . . . And that whenever any Government shall be found inadequate, or contrary to these Purposes, a Majority of the Community hath an indubitable, inalianable and indefeasible Right to reform, alter or abolish it, in such Manner as shall be judged most conducive to the Public Weal.[14]

As with *Summary View*, the spelling and arrangement of certain words in both Mason's and Jefferson's drafts suggest that Mason influenced Jefferson's word choices in the Declaration of Independence. For example, considerable speculation exists surrounding Jefferson's spelling of the word "inalienable" in his "Rough draught" compared to "unalienable" in the final copy, including the possibility that the final change came at the printer's office.[15] Notably, Mason spelled the word "inaliable" in his draft of the Declaration of Rights, the word being changed to "unalienable" in the final copy. Common spelling of the word "independant" also links the two documents, the word also being changed in both final copies to "independent."

More substantively, the case for Jefferson's reliance on Mason's wording is strengthened by comparing the Declaration of Rights and phraseology contained in the first three pages of Pennsylvanian James Wilson's pamphlet, *Considerations on the Nature and Extent of the Legislative Authority of the British Parliament* (1774):

> All men are, by nature, equal and free: no one has a right to any authority over another without his consent: all lawful government is founded on the consent of those who are subject to it: such consent was given with a view to ensure and to increase the happiness of the governed, above what they could enjoy in an independent and unconnected state of nature. The consequence is, that the happiness of the society is the *first* law of every government. . . . Then representatives are reminded whose creatures they are; and to whom they are accountable for the use of that power, which is delegated unto them. The first maxims of jurisprudence are ever kept in view—that all power is derived from the people—that their happiness is the end of government.[16]

Carl L. Becker—who touted Jefferson's reliance on Locke for the wording of the Declaration of Independence in his classic book *The Declaration of Independence* (1922)—credited Wilson with "preparing the minds of the colonists for the general theory which Jefferson was later able to take for granted as the common sense of the matter." Becker did not argue that Jefferson copied from Wilson, only that he wrote what others were thinking, and had been, since the late 1760s.[17]

Writing from the opposite end of the spectrum by arguing that Jefferson was more influenced by Scottish writers, Garry Wills also uses this portion of Wilson's writings to establish indirectly Jefferson's reliance on Jean-Jacques Burlamaqui (whom Wilson acknowledged), the primary source, Wills believes, for Thomas Hutcheson's ideas.[18] Thus, Wills argues that as Jefferson read Wilson, he further indebted himself to the Scottish philosophers, not Locke.

It is important to note that both Becker and Wills might have pursued this matter further than they did regarding Wilson's possible influence on Jefferson's "Rough draught" of the Declaration of Independence. Toward the end of the pamphlet, Wilson listed the powers of the king relative to the American colonies:

> He makes war: he concludes peace: he forms alliances: he regulates domestick trade by his prerogative, and directs foreign commerce by his treaties with those nations, with whom it is carried on. He names the officers of government; so that he can check every jarring movement in the administration. He has a negative on the different legislatures throughout his dominions, so that he can prevent any repugnancy in their different laws.[19]

Although he enumerated the king's powers as Jefferson did in the *Summary View*, also published in 1774, Wilson actually placed the primary blame on the Parliament for problems that existed with England and the soon-to-be rebels. Two years later, Jefferson turned the argument around to show how the king was to blame for the colonists' separation from Great Britain. More importantly, in not considering further connections between Jefferson's draft and Wilson's pamphlet, both Becker and Wills were able to concentrate on their primary agendas—demonstrating the influence of Locke and Hutcheson, respectively, on Jefferson. Both Mason and Wilson emphasized that people have the right to pursue happiness, and Wilson made happiness a specific end of government. But only Mason said that it is the right of the people to *pursue* happiness and emphasized in the first and third points of his Declaration of Rights that the people's *safety* is connected with their happiness.[20]

The words of Mason's draft of the Declaration of Rights made such an impression on Jefferson because since early May he had been hard at work, as Maier notes, on a draft of a constitution for Virginia. By the time Mason's draft reached him, Jefferson had most likely completed his first draft of the Virginia constitution, including as a preamble the listing of charges against George III that he later copied almost verbatim into the Declaration of Independence. That his attention was focused on Virginian affairs is also seen in the fact that he changed his original list of charges to conform to the "Resolutions of the Virginia Convention Calling for Independence," which arrived in Philadelphia on May 26 or 27.[21]

Further evidence of his attentiveness to Virginia's affairs may be found in his concerns about not being able to attend Virginia's constitutional convention. As Boyd pointed out in his discussion in the *Papers* regarding Jefferson's draft of the Virginia Constitution, Jefferson would have preferred to be in Virginia instead of in Philadelphia. Because of his intense interest in the convention's deliberations, he wrote to a friend in the convention suggesting that the group recall its delegates to Philadelphia for the purpose of assisting the writing of the state constitution. "In truth," he declared, "[writing Virginia's constitution] is the whole object of the present controversy." Otherwise, Virginia might as well stay under the current association with Great Britain and avoid "the risk and expence of contest." Recognizing the nature of his position, however, Jefferson hastened to add that he spoke in confidence since "a hint to any other [concern than national matters] is too delicate however anxiously interesting the subject [Virginia's constitution] is to our feelings." In a postscript, Jefferson noted that "the other colonies who have instituted government . . . recalled their delegates leaving only one or two to give information to Congress of matters which might relate to their country particularly."[22]

Jefferson's choice of the word "country" in this context is especially pointed. He became so distressed at being stuck in Philadelphia that he wrote to George Gilmer asking that he not be renominated to the Continental Congress so he could participate in the debates of the Virginia Convention. The request threw his friends into something of a panic regarding whether to press his credentials, and Jefferson became distressed when he heard that he had come in "next to the [last]" in the voting. "It is a painful situation to be 300. miles from one's country," he lamented to William Fleming on July 1, 1776, "and thereby open [oneself] to secret assassination without a possibility of self-defence. I am willing to hope nothing of this kind has been done in my case, and yet I cannot be easy. If any doubt has arisen as to me, my country will have my political creed in the form of a 'Declaration &c.' which I was lately directed to draw. This will give decisive proof that my own sentiment concurred with the vote they instructed us to give." On July 8, he sent copies of the Declaration as he framed it, and as the Congress amended it, to Richard Henry Lee with the news that he would leave Philadelphia for Virginia on August 11. If his successor came prior to that date, he said he hoped "to see you and Mr. Wythe in Convention, that the business of Government, which is of everlasting Concern, may receive your aid."[23] Unfortunately for Jefferson, the convention finished its work before he could arrive.

Finally, the Virginian influences on the Declaration of Independence may be seen by focusing more fully on Jefferson's shift of attitudes toward George III. In *Summary View*, Jefferson petitioned the king for changes in Parliamentary and executive actions; in 1776, he blamed him for the separation of the colonies from England. In 1774, Jefferson described George III as "the central link connecting the several parts of the empire" and as "chief officer of the people"—the man most able to reconcile the peoples of England and Virginia. Two years later, Jefferson listed twenty specific charges against George III, each intended to convince "a candid world" that the king intended to establish "an absolute tyranny" over the American states.

Why the shift of emphasis? Defenders of American rights throughout the British colonies were learning that blaming one person establishes motive more convincingly than indicting a group, but more than rhetoric forms the basis of Jefferson's language regarding the king. Throughout most of 1775, Jefferson and other colonial leaders clung to a belief that the Parliament was primarily responsible for America's problems. As co-author with John Dickinson of the "Declaration of the Causes and Necessities of Taking up Arms" (June 1775), Jefferson wrote sections that contained nearly identical phraseology as that employed in *Summary View*, except expressed now within a national context. Americans possessed, Jefferson argued, "the full & perfect powers of legislation" and were associated with Great Britain through "one common king who thus became the link of union between the several parts of the empire."[24]

The first indication in Jefferson's papers of a change in attitude toward the king appears in his correspondence of November 1775, when he learned that Virginia's royal governor ordered attacks on Norfolk and Hampton, Virginia.[25] Immediately, he blamed the king for Dunmore's actions. "It is an immense misfortune to the whole empire," he wrote concerning the attack on Hampton, "to have a king of such a disposition at such a time. We are told and every thing proves it true that he is the bitterest enemy we have." The king might have learned from prior "petitions" (*Summary View* being chief among those "petitions") that independence would follow bloodshed. "That step is now pressed upon us," Jefferson concluded, ". . . under the fostering hand of our king."[26]

Then, some time in January, Jefferson received a copy of the *Virginia Gazette* containing the text of the king's speech in the Parliament on October 26, 1775, in which George III had asserted that the "British nation" had formed the American colonies. This assertion flew directly in the face of Jefferson's argument in *Summary View* that "America was conquered, and her settlements made and firmly established, at the expence of individuals, and not of the British public." "A king who can adopt falshood, and solemnize it from the throne, justifies the revolution of fortune which reduces him to a private station," Jefferson asserted in his "Refutation of the Argument that the Colonies Were Established at the Expense of the British Nation." From January 1776 onward, in Jefferson's eyes George III was no more than "a petty king of Britain."[27]

In addition, as Jay Fliegelman points out, the "Refutation" marks an important departure from Jefferson's argument in *Summary View* where he left open the possibility that the king was "a victim of partisan misinformation" due to the fact that he relied too heavily on his advisors. In the "Refutation" and later the Declaration of Independence, Jefferson emphasized the fact that the king acted without constraint. "His will," Fliegelman writes, "is arbitrary, in the eighteenth-century sense: willful rather than random. . . . By demonizing George, the Declaration stigmatizes individual willfulness at the same time that it articulates an ideology of individual liberty. . . . [The king] is the responsible party, an example of the horrible cost of willful action, of designing."[28]

Perhaps, as so many of Jefferson's biographers have written, the fate of state and nation were so perfectly harmonized that in promoting his country's interests, he also furthered those of the United States. As noted previously, very late in his life Jefferson cultivated this idea, that in drafting the Declaration of Independence he "aim[ed neither] at originality of principle or sentiment, nor yet copied from any particular and previous writing, . . . [but intended it] to be an expression of the American mind, and to give to that expression the proper tone and spirit called for by the occasion."[29] In taking credit for "inventing America," however, there is no reason to think that he wanted to diminish his role in helping to chart the future course of his country. A focus on the Virginia roots of the Declaration of Independence suggests that Jefferson wrote his famous document less as a statement of American nationalism than as evidence that his views coincided with those of his gentry peers at Virginia's constitutional convention. Absent from deliberations on his *Summary View* (Chapter 2) and anxious to contribute to his country's break from the past, Jefferson felt compelled to establish his unity with the group. The best he could do in July 1776 was to provide what became the preamble for the Virginia Constitution and to draft the Declaration of Independence, whose preamble melded his own writings with Virginia's Declaration of Rights.

II

By August 1776, Jefferson was home in Virginia. In October he declined appointment to the mission to France in order to join the Virginia Assembly in Williamsburg, where he reached the pinnacle of his devotion to reforming the lives of his countrymen by trying to get the Assembly to abandon the Virginia Constitution in favor of a better one. "[W]ritten in haste and urgency . . . by persons long in authority and never popularly ratified," in Daniel P. Jordan's words, the new constitution "inevitably retained much of the colonial system and epitomized tradition rather than innovation." As in the colonial period in Burgesses, members of the gentry class in the Assembly exercised a firm control over Virginian society as "an entrenched squirearchy." The gentry controlled not only the Assembly, which elected the governor (who had no veto power and had to rule through a Privy Council), but also the judicial system through county courts. In the counties, "self-perpetuating family oligarchies" controlled the judicial process and selected the justices of the peace.[30]

In addition to empowering entrenched families and providing for a generally conservative political climate to block fundamental change, the constitution included no provision for amendment. Jefferson was one of the first assemblymen to push for a new constitution, popularly ratified by the people, but his views were decidedly in the minority during the Revolutionary period. He also pressed again, as he had in his draft of the constitution, for the abolition of slavery, but without success. He had some limited success in abolishing entail and primogeniture, but Jefferson's suggestions to lower property qualifications for voting and to separate the powers of government attracted little support. Only with the spread of population to the west—the 1820 census revealed that the population of western counties was increasing while it declined or remained stable in the east—did sectional pressures lead eventually to a new constitutional convention.[31]

Two bills in particular—the Statute for Religious Freedom and the "Bill for the More General Diffusion of Knowledge" (Chapter 7)—received the bulk of Jefferson's attention and energy while he served as an assemblyman. Both proceeded from his commitment to ensure that the American Revolution charted a new path for his society.

The appearance of Baptists and other dissenters in Virginia at the time of the Great Awakening forced the gentry to scrutinize their behavior and their culture. Emphasizing equality, the Baptists dressed plainly, sometimes welcomed slaves into some of their back-country meetings, and sought to build a close, supportive, and orderly community. The Baptists did not challenge the gentry's wealth or control of the colony, but they did contribute to a growing sense of crisis among certain of the colony's leaders on the eve of the American Revolution.[32]

Also in the 1740s and 1750s, Scottish merchants opened new stores throughout the Piedmont area and extended credit against future tobacco crops. As a result of this increased supply of money in the community, gentry squires extended themselves even further beyond their means, and many flaunted luxury items in their communities. Conspicuous consumption and increased reliance on the labor of others created concern among many members of the gentry class.[33] Younger sons seemed especially vulnerable to a life of luxury and money-seeking. Traditionally, the gentry groomed their heirs for seats in Burgesses—the linchpin of gentry control in Virginia. If individualism replaced social solidarity, however, and if craving for luxury items negated virtue, gentry control of Virginia might crumble. When the Baptists condemned public drunkenness, physical aggression in dueling and cock fighting, and other forms of "sin" in the colony, many gentry reacted defensively and tried to force Baptist ministers to conform to the system. In 1771, Baptists achieved their largest number of congregations in the pre-war period, and articles in Virginia newspapers attacked them as a "contemptible class of the people." The next year, Baptists threw Burgesses into turmoil by petitioning for "protection from persecution" under the seventeenth-century English Toleration Act.[34]

Attacks on the Baptists and other religious dissenters were anathema to Jefferson and to others who feared that religious intolerance bred anti-libertarian policies. From the early 1770s, the region around Charlottesville was a center of agitation for religious toleration. Article XVI of Mason's Declaration of Rights guaranteed to "all men . . . the free exercise of religion," but following independence Burgesses passed a series of acts further strengthening the authority of the Anglican Church in Virginia.[35] If the gentry closed their minds to change and restricted individual initiative in the area of religion, where would such behavior stop? The depth of Jefferson's fears in this regard is revealed by comparing the Statute for Religious Freedom as he drafted it, the contents as the Assembly passed it in 1786, and sections of *Notes on the State of Virginia* dealing with religion. This investigation also demonstrates how Jefferson's ideas about rights and government, first developed in *Summary View* and expanded in the Declaration of Independence, continued to evolve during his service as an assemblyman and later as governor.

Jefferson began his version of the Statute for Religious Freedom with a ringing assertion of empiricism. "[T]he opinions and belief of men depend not on their own will," he wrote, "but follow involuntarily the evidence proposed to their minds." According to Jefferson, God created people with minds capable of judging the accuracy of all opinions through reason and further extended this freedom by "making [the mind] altogether insusceptible of restraint. . . . [T]he opinions of men are not the object of civil government, nor under its jurisdiction." The Assembly struck each of these ideas from the statute.[36]

In Jefferson's view, freedom of religion flowed naturally out of his statements on legislative authority expressed in *Summary View* and the Declaration of Independence. When people formed societies, they gave to their elected representatives "the sovereign power of legislation" (*Summary View*). But in *Notes*, he limited the power of assemblies to "[c]ivil government . . . compos[ed] of the freest principles of the English constitution, with others derived from natural right and natural reason." In one of the most celebrated passages in *Notes*, Jefferson argued that

> our rulers can have authority over such natural rights only as we have submitted to them. The rights of conscience we never submitted, we could not submit. We are answerable for them to our God. The legitimate powers of government extend to such acts only as are injurious to others. But it does me no injury for my neighbor to say there are twenty gods, or no god. It neither picks my pocket nor breaks my leg. . . . What has been the effect of coercion? To make one half the world fools, and the other half hypocrites. To support roguery and error all over the earth.

Following the Revolution, he posited, Virginians became careless of their liberties and disregarded their rights. If rights and liberties were not secured "while our rulers are honest, and ourselves united," people would "forget themselves, but in the sole faculty of making money, and will never think of uniting to effect a due respect for their rights."[37]

"Freedom of conscience," therefore, constitutes only one aspect of Jefferson's interest in religious freedom. When the gentry limited their natural rights in this area, they endangered liberty in Virginia in all areas. Also, if people were not capable of reform following the momentous separation from Great Britain, when could they be trusted to ensure rights? Seen in this way, by establishing religious freedom in the state Jefferson was committing his peers to preserving liberty throughout Virginian society. Unfortunately, he believed that one legislature could never "restrain the acts of succeeding Assemblies," a point he first developed in *Summary View*. To mitigate the possibility that a subsequent legislature might revoke the statute altogether, Jefferson concluded his version with the declaration "that the rights hereby asserted are of the natural rights of mankind, and . . . if any act shall be hereafter passed to repeal the present or to narrow its operation, such act will be an infringement of natural right."[38] This statement is the closest Jefferson ever came to saying that one legislature could bind another. When the resolution was adopted by the Virginia Assembly in 1786, he may have hoped that the gentry were committing themselves, however belatedly, to his principles.

In fact, it is doubtful that the gentry saw his proposal in this light. As Rhys Isaac persuasively argues, "the traditional Episcopal gentry leaders" bowed to change only because they hoped by separating church and state to diffuse pressures from backcountry areas for more fundamental reforms in the political system. Only as the gentry "received clear indications that a continuing mobilization of religion into politics might shatter their customary dominance at the polls did they grant religious freedom." As with everything else in the society, religious freedom must be seen in relation to social and political power:

> The parish church, where all were symbolically together in their due rank and order for the corporate worship of God, was seen to be threatened by break-away sectarianism. But the violence really came when the Baptist evangelists' campaigns of conversion cut into the little (and not so little) communities at the very base of society—the households, including the large plantations. Wives might be set in defiance of husbands, children divided from parents, and, most menacing of all, slaves set against masters. It seemed imperative to many to stop the mass gatherings for preaching and to enclose the sectaries within the safe bounds of licensed meeting-houses that could be put off-limits to slaves, unless they had their masters' permission.[39]

Charles Irons agrees. Following the American Revolution, Baptist leaders removed discussions of slavery from their churches in order to defuse disagreements and minimize conflicts among members. Irons documents how this decision to move discussions about slavery to the legislature made Baptists less of a threat to the Anglican majority and at the same time produced unity within the ranks of the faithful.[40]

Seen in these terms, Jefferson's limited accomplishment in the area of religious liberty takes on new light. The Statute for Religious Freedom secured, there would be no further fundamental reforms in Virginian society throughout the 1780s, and beyond.

III

When the Assembly first discussed and failed to adopt the Statute for Religious Freedom in the summer of 1779, Jefferson was not able to debate his bill since in June he began the first of two terms as governor of the state. And when the British army attacked first South, then North Carolina and finally Virginia, Jefferson had to confront military problems that had previously plagued only northern states.[41] His inability to deal with these problems nearly cost him his life. In the end, he lost only his reputation.

Chief among his problems were scarcity of soldiers (both militia and regular troops) and supplies—food, clothing, arms, and ammunition. By October 1780, he was receiving letters from commanders in the field that no more men should be sent to the army without the necessary equipment for immediate service.[42] Otherwise, Nathanael Greene warned in December, he would be forced to send them home. "Your troops may literally be said to be naked," Greene wrote. "It will answer no good purpose to send men here in such a condition, for they are nothing but added weight upon the army and altogether incapable of aiding in its operations. . . . No man will think himself bound to fight the battles of a State that leaves him to perish for want of covering; nor can you inspire a soldier with the sentiment of pride whilst his situation renders him more an object of pity than envy. . . . [B]e assured you raise men in vain unless you cloathe, arm, and equip them properly in the field."[43] When Benedict Arnold led a British invasion of the state in January 1781, Friedrich Wilhelm Ludolf Gerhard Augustin, Baron von Steuben reported that the Virginia militia were either without arms or equipped with guns that were mostly unfit for service. "I just beg leave to suggest to your Excellency," Steuben wrote, "that Men without arms can Answer no purpose but the Consumption of Provisions."[44]

Added to these problems were an inability to collect taxes in Virginia's sprawling counties; unwillingness on the part of the Assembly to commandeer horses, wagons, and provisions; and an infuriatingly slow pace in every governmental agency. In addition to functioning as the governor, Jefferson also acted as quartermaster and in July, August, and September as chief of intelligence.[45]

During May and June 1781, he even played host to the Assembly on the run from British troops.

These activities notwithstanding, contemporaries complained that the governor did too little to halt the British advance. In February 1781, for example, George Washington wrote from New York, "It is mortifying to see so inconsiderable a party committing such extensive depredations with impunity: but considering the situation of your state, it is to be wondered you have hitherto suffered as little molestation."[46] In Virginia, Steuben candidly observed that British changes in tactics did not result from "any Efforts of ours." As commanding officer, he ruefully observed that "the shamefull opposition" to the invasion fell "in some measure" on himself. But chief blame rested elsewhere in Steuben's mind. "I cannot but reckon it among my misfortunes," he wrote, "to have been here at this time. My wish is to prevent a Repetition of the Disgrace but . . . I can do nothing without the Assistance of Government."[47]

In early June 1781, Lieutenant Colonel Banastre Tarleton very nearly captured the governor and most of the assemblymen at Monticello, and Jefferson fled south to his property at Poplar Forest. There his term as governor expired, and he decided to leave the office of governor vacant for more than a week rather than continue to serve until a successor could be named. Based upon this decision and the general mayhem resulting from the British invasion of the state, some assemblymen pressed for an official investigation of Jefferson's conduct as governor.[48]

Could he have done more? This question defies easy answers. First, to make government more efficient would have required fundamental constitutional reforms that Jefferson had pursued between 1777 and 1779 as an assemblyman without success. Even in the face of an invasion of the state, government worked at an exasperatingly slow pace. Jefferson's written communications to the Assembly reveal more deference than decisiveness; certainly, his experiences did not lead him in the direction of increasing executive powers. He provided information and waited for a response. He gave advice and then followed the Assembly's lead. He stalled; he obfuscated; he apologized; he excused.[49] When he tried to execute the laws passed by the Assembly, he lacked sufficient enforcement procedures when people failed to follow orders.[50] In short, he accommodated himself to the inefficiencies of the system, having tried and failed as an assemblyman to make it more responsive to change.

Second, Jefferson frequently found himself caught between political and military officials who often worked at cross-purposes to each other. The Virginia Assembly expected more help from the Congress and the other states than it received. After most of Virginia's regular troops surrendered with the rest of the southern army at Charleston (May 1780), fighting the war fell totally on the militia. The Assembly commissioned troops, sent them to the field (expecting to receive credit on Continental ledgers as a result), and relied on the Congress to feed, clothe, and equip the soldiers in the field.[51] Army leaders then discharged the troops because they had no supplies, and each side blamed the other for lack of support. In these controversies, Jefferson sided with the Assembly and not with the army or the Congress.[52]

Third, the slowness of politics and the leisurely rhythms of the Virginia gentry left Jefferson unprepared for the speed and effectiveness of British actions in Virginia. In August 1777, he disparaged the ability of the British to conduct operations in the state at all. "[General William Howe] may destroy the little hamlet of Williamsburgh, steal a few slaves, [but he will] lose half his army among the fens of our lower country, or by the heats of our climate." Following the fall of Charleston, he feared the British would move northward but hoped "the cautious principles of the military art" would delay their progress.[53] In other words, his own beliefs about the region's climate and the nature of warfare compounded his problems of governmental inefficiency and narrowed his options when he had to act quickly. In early 1781, a thousand obstacles forestalled progress and frustrated the state's ability to fight the enemy.

In the final analysis, Jefferson's prejudices may have complicated his already serious situation, but it is difficult to believe others would have fared better in the same circumstances. Indeed, many in Virginia and other states did worse. Julian Boyd concluded that "no governor worked more devotedly than he against odds more completely insuperable. None administered a larger or more vulnerable territory." Boyd also noted that if Jefferson could have delayed his resignation for five months the American victory at the Battle of Yorktown would have vindicated his efforts.[54]

Nonetheless, on June 12, 1781, the Assembly adopted a resolution to conduct "an inquiry . . . into the conduct of the Executive of the State for the last twelve months." The charges of incompetence and dereliction of duty that were leveled at him caused Jefferson in August to turn down an appointment as a peace commissioner in order to deal with the accusations, and allusions to cowardice in the face of the enemy tarnished his final vindication.[55]

IV

Despite the Assembly's questioning of his leadership abilities, on April 11, 1782, his Albemarle neighbors elected Jefferson to the Virginia Assembly. Two days later, François Jean, Marquis de Chastellux, arrived at Monticello and found his host to be in a very bad humor, "his manner grave and even cold." Despite what Chastellux took to be Jefferson's impressive list of accomplishments—"Musician, Draftsman, Surveyor, Astronomer, Natural Philosopher, Jurist and States-man"—the Frenchman recorded that Virginians "mingled with [respect] too many misgivings" on account of his service as "Governor of Virginia, . . . during the invasions of Arnold, Phillips, and Cornwallis." Despite Jefferson's recent appointment as minister to France, the nobleman learned that Jefferson had declined the honor and planned to retire from public service, "because he loves the world only insofar as he can feel that he is useful, and because the temper of his fellow citizens is not as yet prepared either to face the truth or to suffer contradiction."[56]

True to what he told Chastellux, Jefferson on May 6 refused to serve in the Virginia Assembly.[57] Although no formal record exists for this session of the legislature, Edmund Randolph wrote to James Madison on May 16 that the House of Delegates voted not to accept Jefferson's resignation due to his statement based "upon his own principles, delivered on a similar occasion." That same day, the Speaker of the House wrote to Jefferson that

> the Constitution in the Opinion of the Members will not warrant the acceptance of your resignation. . . . I suppose your reasons are weighty, yet I wou'd suggest that good and able Men had better govern than be govern'd. . . . In times of Peace Men of moderate abilities perhaps might conduct the affairs of the State, but at this time when the Republic wants to be organized and requires but your influence to promote this desirable End, I cannot but think the House may insist upon you to give attendance without incurring the Censure of being siezed.[58]

Jefferson did not answer the Speaker's letter directly but rather indirectly in a most remarkable letter to James Monroe that reveals, primarily, the depth of his distress over the accusations that followed his resignation of the governorship.

At the beginning of the letter, Jefferson explained that thirteen years of public service had damaged his "private affairs" and that he had his own family plus the children of "a deceased friend [Dabney Carr] whose memory must be for ever dear to me." Then, at the end of the letter, he confided that following the birth of his daughter on May 18, his wife was "and still continues very dangerously ill." Dumas Malone concluded that the letter's tone of "extreme anxiety" could only be explained in the context of his concern over the health of his wife, who died September 6; perhaps he is correct. Still, if the language of the letter can be taken at face value, Jefferson was angry that the same people who had charged him with incompetence and cowardice as governor were now threatening to force him to serve in their midst. "[T]he affection of my countrymen . . . was the only reward I ever asked or could have felt" from serving for so long, he wrote. Yet, despite the "exculpatory declaration" of the Assembly, "I stood arraigned for treasons of the heart and not mere weakness of the head. And I felt that these injuries . . . had inflicted a wound on my spirit which will only be cured by the all-healing grave." He followed this impassioned statement with a detailed and emotional legal brief designed to prove that the law could never compel a person to serve. To do so, he wrote, "would be slavery and not that liberty which the bill of rights has made inviolable and for the preservation of which our government has been changed . . . [and] would contradict the giver of life who gave for happiness and not for wretchedness, and certainly to such it were better that they had never been born."[59]

The fact that Jefferson in this hour of extreme discomfort paraphrased the Declaration of Independence and called attention to the Virginia Declaration of Rights—both of which established the existence of inalienable rights residing in individuals that government was created to protect—is highly significant. By the time of his wife's death, Jefferson had effectively given up hope that his peers would protect the liberties that the American Revolution promised. Slavery persisted in Virginia, and not only for African Americans; the promise of religious freedom was dead; and the state's Constitution denied rights to all the country's inhabitants living in western regions. Jefferson soon made public the depth of his disappointments in his countrymen's behaviors in *Notes on the State of Virginia*.

Of Manna, Mouse, and Mammoth

Notes on the State of Virginia as Jefferson's Pentateuch

The structure of Thomas Jefferson's *Notes on the State of Virginia* perplexes most Jefferson scholars (not to mention college undergraduates) because it has the appearance of haphazardly gathered data. In Charles A. Miller's words:

> The book is very much mis-titled insofar as "notes" implies a relatively brief or ill-considered compilation of material. Yet it is not a systematic and unified treatise, nor is it written with a sense of literary proportion. It veers wildly, from tables of Indian populations, names of plants, and weather data to hymns to the Natural Bridge and the independent farmer. One of the queries . . . is only seventeen words long. Another . . . is approximately a thousand times that length.[1]

To Dumas Malone, *Notes* appeared to be "an *ad hoc* work, like practically everything else he ever wrote; it was unpretentious and unlabored, and at no time was he much concerned about its literary form." Recent Jefferson scholars respond in a like manner. Andrew Burstein calls it "fact-filled (and argument-prone)"; Joseph J. Ellis, "part travel guide, part scientific treatise and part philosophical meditation."[2]

This chapter argues that during revisions undertaken during the winter of 1783–84, when he revised and expanded his original manuscript "to nearly treble bulk,"[3] Jefferson imbedded keys within *Notes* that help to unravel its complexity. Because he began writing in a bound notebook, when he expanded the book he often cut the pages to change their order or pasted addenda onto them to accomplish the editing job.[4] This process of editing and rearranging not only increased the size of the book but also changed its character.

Notes is best viewed as a book within a book. Its organizational framework is modeled on Denis Diderot's and Jean Le Rond d'Alembert's great *Encyclopédie*, where nature reorders knowledge. Within this larger work is Thomas Jefferson's Pentateuch for Virginia—beginning with genesis (Genesis, in the

Bible) and ending with a reformulation of his country's laws (Deuteronomy, in the Bible)—to try to save Virginians from their self-destructive behaviors. Far from an incoherent mass of tables and charts, *Notes* stands as Jefferson's primary prospectus for reforming the behavior of his countrymen.

I

First, some background on how Jefferson happened to write the book. He began his work in response to a general request in 1780 to the governors of the states from François, marquis de Barbé-Marbois, a member of the French legation to the United States, for information about the states. In November, Jefferson noted to a correspondent that he was "busily employed for Monsr. Marbois without his knowing it."[5] In this letter, Jefferson did not say precisely how he planned to organize his thoughts, but he did mention that he was "exceedingly anxious to get a copy of Le grande Encyclopedie."[6]

Although the precise date that he first received a copy of the *Encyclopédie* cannot be ascertained from his *Papers*, one of his book buyers acknowledged having purchased a copy of it for the State of Virginia at Jefferson's request on April 1, 1781.[7] It is likely that he had it by May and consulted it during his first draft of *Notes*, which he sent to Marbois in December of that year.[8]

The fact that *Notes* bears striking similarities to the *Encyclopédie* has not escaped the notice of all of Jefferson's students. Merrill Peterson describes *Notes* as "in one aspect . . . a glorified guidebook, descriptive, crammed with facts, informative on a broad range of subjects from cascades and caverns to weights and measures, all treated in clear, effortless prose touched with philosophy."[9] According to Douglas L. Wilson, *Notes* was to be merely the beginning of "a project with an even more ambitious scope: an encyclopedic depiction of America . . . , something that attempted to do for the New World what the *Encyclopédie* had done for the Old."[10]

In ordering Marbois's questions, Jefferson, in Peterson's words, "sorted and arranged the whole . . . , the order proceeding from the natural through the civil to the generally social and moral."[11] David Waldstreicher agrees: "[I]nstead of starting with the unresolved problem of government in the new republic, as Marbois had, Jefferson begins with the most striking—and impressive—features of American nature. . . . The story told here is one of progress from the wildness of nature to the calm of human settlement."[12]

Marbois's twenty-two queries, as Jefferson received them, were skewed toward information relative to commercial capabilities (Queries 12, 13, 14, and 19) and mineral wealth (20 and 21) in the American states.[13] The Frenchman's bias is especially evident in the wording of Query 21—"some samples of [the] mines and extraordinary stones. In short a notice of all what can increase the progress

Table 2. A Comparison of Marbois's and Jefferson's Queries

Marbois's Queries	Jefferson's Queries
1. The Charters of your State.	1. Boundaries of Virginia
2. The present Constitution.	2. Rivers
3. An exact description of its limits and boundaries.	3. Sea-Ports
4. The Memoirs published in its name, in the time of its being a Colony and the pamphlets relating to its interior or exterior affairs present or ancient.	4. Mountains
5. The History of the State.	5. Cascades
6. A notice of the Counties Cities etable Townships and how far they are navagible. Cascades Caverns Mountains Productions Trees Plants Fruits and other natural Riches.	6. Productions Mineral, Veg- and Animal
7. The number of its Inhabitants.	7. Climate
8. The different Religions received in that State.	8. Population
9. The Colleges and public establishments. The Roads Buildings &c.	9. Military Force
10. The administration of Justice and a description of the Laws.	10. Marine Force
11. The particular Customs and manners that may happen to be received in that State.	11. Aborigines
12. The present State of Manufactures Commerce interior and exterior Trade.	12. Counties and Towns
13. A notice of the best Sea Ports of the State and how big are the vessels they can receive.	13. Constitution
14. A notice of the commercial productions particular to that State and of those objects which the Inhabitants are obliged to get from Europe and from other parts of the World.	14. Laws
15. The weight measures and the currency of the hard money. Some details relating to the exchange with Europe.	15. Colleges, Buildings, and Roads
16. The public income and expences.	16. Proceedings as to Tories
17. The measures taken with regard of the Estates and Possessions of the Rebels commonly called Tories.	17. Religion
18. The condition of the Regular Troops and the Militia and their pay.	18. Manners
19. The marine and Navigation.	19. Manufactures
20. A notice of the Mines and other subterranean riches.	20. Subjects of Commerce

Table 2. *(continued)*

Marbois's Queries	Jefferson's Queries
21. Some Samples of these Mines and of the extraordinary Stones. In short a notice of all what can increase the progress of human Knowledge.	21. Weights, Measures, and Money
22. A description of the Indians established in the State before the European Settlements and of those who are still remaining. An indication of the Indian monuments discovered in that State.	22. Public Revenue and Expences
	23. Histories, Memorials, and State Papers.

of human knowledge." By linking progress to wealth, Marbois surely caught Jefferson's eye. Jefferson shifted questions concerning mineral wealth to Query 6 ("productions mineral, vegetable and animal")—by far the longest (one-fourth of *Notes*) and most structurally complex of the queries—and placed the subjects of the least amount of interest to him (manufactures; commerce; weights, measures, and money; public revenue and expenses) near the end, Queries 19, 20, 21, and 22, respectively.

Jefferson changed other questions as well. Whereas the French diplomat began his list with requests for information on the state's charter, constitution, treaties, and history, Jefferson demonstrated a preference for nature by first addressing boundaries, rivers, seaports, mountains, cascades, minerals, vegetables, animals, and climate. In order to elevate nature but also to gratify other biases, Jefferson relegated other topics to lesser positions. "Religion" drops from twelfth position on Marbois's list to twentieth on Jefferson's; "history" drops from fifth to twenty-third (a new, last item).

Similarly, in Query 12 (counties and towns), the subject matter is the same, but the definitions are not. Jefferson corrected the Frenchman in his nomenclature, that Virginia's "towns . . . [are] more properly [called] . . . villages or hamlets" because the large number of navigable rivers ("trade [thereby] brought generally to our doors, instead of our being obliged to go in quest of it") made towns unnecessary. On occasion, representatives in the House of Burgesses had passed "*laws* . . . [that] there shall be towns; but *Nature* has said there shall not, and they remain unworthy of enumeration."[14]

In Query 19, "manufactures," Jefferson contended that the people of Virginia generally made their own necessary articles and exchanged their agricultural products "for finer manufactures than they are able to execute themselves." Because of the "immensity of land courting the industry of the husbandman," he deemed it unwise for Virginians to abandon agriculture for manufacturing. Immediately following this statement, Jefferson inserted one of the most-quoted sections from *Notes*: "Those who labor in the earth are the chosen people of God, if ever he had a chosen people, whose breasts he has made his peculiar deposit for substantial and genuine virtue." Exchanging agriculture for manufactures might increase a preference for towns or cities, an undesirable development for Jefferson, who asserted that "mobs of great cities add just as much to the support of pure government, as sores do to the strength of the human body."[15]

In Query 20, "subjects of commerce," Jefferson disparaged Virginia's primary export, tobacco, by saying that its importance was "fast declining" (Chapter 1). Further, he called it "a culture productive of infinite wretchedness" and suggested that "those employed in it are in a continued state of exertion beyond the powers of nature to support." Following this denigration of tobacco, he advocated cultivating wheat because it harmonized with nature by "cloathing the earth with herbage, preserving its fertility," and providing food for animals and mankind. "We find it easier," he wrote, "to make an hundred bushels of wheat than a thousand weight of tobacco, and they are worth more when made." From this description, one would never guess, except from the chart he provided, that the total annual value of tobacco exported exceeded that of wheat nearly threefold.[16]

II

But *Notes* is more than simply a paean to nature. Most of the queries are less a description of what currently existed in Virginia than what might exist or should exist if nature were in control. In the words of Robert Booth Fowler, "Jefferson constructed a nature that embodied his values and employed it as a force against much in his own society—and many other societies—he disliked."[17] Far from *ordering knowledge* based upon observations of nature, as Peterson and Wilson argue, *Notes* is most remarkable for the way in which it *reorders knowledge* based upon Jefferson's emerging political agenda. To appreciate this reordering, it is necessary to look more closely at the structural complexity of the great French *Encyclopédie*.

According to French cultural historian Robert Darnton, Diderot and d'Alembert intended the *Encyclopédie* to be both a compilation of knowledge and a manifesto of *philosophie*—"that is, valid knowledge, the kind derived from the senses and the faculties of the mind as opposed to the kind dispensed by church and state."[18] The "jumble of information [the authors provided] on everything from *A* to *Z*" obscured the fact that the *Encyclopédie* radically reformulated perceptions of the way the world operated by drawing "new lines between the known and the unknown." "Setting up categories and policing them," Darnton reminds us, "is . . . a serious business" because it focuses attention squarely on the relationship between knowledge and power.[19] The *Encyclopédie* dismissed traditional learning as "nothing but prejudice and superstition," and "excluded everything that could not reach reason through the senses . . . [thereby cutting] orthodox religion off the map, . . . and thus [excluding] it from the modern world of learning."[20]

Because the *Encyclopédie*'s notions of knowledge were heretical, they had to be hidden from government and church censors. Looking in the *Encyclopédie*, for example, under "religion," a person would find nothing that would cause a censor to blanch. But beginning to read about a seemingly mundane topic leads the reader into a maze that winds from one spot to another, eventually reaching an anticlerical reference. "Finding [the heretical statements]," according to Darnton, "became a game . . . [; the] Encyclopedists stimulated their readers to seek for meaning between the lines and to listen for double-entendre."[21]

In a similar fashion, Jefferson constructed *Notes* in order to provide a *game* for his book's readers. For example, in Query 1 (letter *A* in Jefferson's encyclopedia) he described Virginia's boundaries as established by royal charters, legal arrangements with neighboring colonies, and the Treaty of Paris. But Jefferson was not content simply to delineate his country's recognized limits. Rather, he moved from description to inference with the calculation that these boundaries established Virginia's area at 121,525 square miles. Thus, he reckoned Virginia's size to be "one third larger than the islands of Great-Britain and Ireland, which are reckoned at 88,357 square miles."[22] In using size to establish importance, Jefferson was repeating the same strategy that Thomas Paine used in *Common Sense*, when he wrote, "Small islands not capable of protecting themselves, are the proper objects for kingdoms to take under their care; but there is something very absurd, in supposing a continent to be perpetually governed by an island."[23]

The game deepens in Query 2 (rivers), which contains Jefferson's first expansion of the original manuscript where he pasted additional information. Jefferson did not limit his discussion of the rivers of Virginia to those in his native state, since he included the Mississippi, the Missouri, the Illinois, the Tennessee, and known tributaries of the Ohio. The listing proceeds seemingly without order or point. Neither the size at the mouth of the river nor its navigability explains its importance to the author. The emphasis, rather, seems to be on completeness—to tell the reader everything that is known about all the rivers that extend outward from Virginia.

The additional material Jefferson added to the original draft finally brings the discussion of rivers to a conclusion. Based upon the calculations of Virginia's size in Query 1, he concluded that "the country watered by the Missisipi and its eastern branches constitutes five-eighths of the United States, two of which five-eighths are occupied by the Ohio and its waters." He then offered the opinion that a competition would develop relative to trade with the Atlantic among three of the rivers—the Mississippi, the Potomac, and the Hudson. Downriver, the Mississippi was unrivaled, "but the navigation through the Gulph of Mexico is so dangerous, and that up the Missisipi so difficult and tedious, that it is thought probable that European merchandize will not return through that channel." Which of the other two would control European trade with the Ohio valley and the west? Calculating that it was only 420 miles from Lake Erie to Alexandria via the Ohio and Potomac River systems with only two portages, whereas the Hudson involved 825 miles and five portages (plus the problem of ice in the winter), Jefferson hoped that the west would be tied to Virginia rather than to New York. Therefore, Virginia's lack of ports (Query 3) would present no problems for the state as it competed for European trade.[24]

In Query 6 Jefferson continued his use of numerical comparisons and his revision of the first version of his book in order to refute theories advanced by the French naturalist Georges Louis Leclerc, Comte de Buffon, that animal species (including human beings) were smaller in the New World because North and South America had a defective climate. Jefferson also addressed in Query 6 the ideas of writer and historian Guillaume Thomas François Raynal, who expanded Buffon's theories to include European immigrants. Integral to these refutations are Jefferson's investigations regarding the mammoth—the largest then-known animal in the New World—and North American Indians.

European naturalists had attributed the skeletons of mammoths to various Old World species, including elephants and hippos. Jefferson, however, asserted that the mammoth was a unique species, separated by nature from the elephant, since the mammoth lived in the north and the elephant in the south. Based upon fossil remains, Jefferson inferred that the mammoth was the largest animal known to man and that it still lived in America.[25]

At first glance, Jefferson appears to take the wrong side of this argument (he was later proved to be correct; mammoths and elephants are of different species). Why not admit that mammoths were extinct elephants, especially since they were larger than elephants, and that they lived only in North America? Instead of comparing mammoths and elephants, Jefferson tested Buffon's theories by comparing the sizes of 26 known quadrupeds common to both Europe and America, concluding that 7 were larger in America, 7 were of equal size with those in Europe, and 12 were undetermined.[26]

These calculations refuted Buffon's theories regarding animals, but Jefferson did not stop here. Rather, he estimated that America contained a total of 100 species of animals, the rest of the world an additional 126, or a ratio of 4 to 5. But this calculation proved to be too high because when one controlled for America's size "the exact proportion would have been but 4 to 8."[27] Why compare land areas? The meaning of this investigation becomes apparent only when following Jefferson's shift from comparing animals to human beings in the New World.

From considerations of sexual prowess to strength and dexterity, from a lack of tenderness toward their children to horrid treatment of their wives, Buffon concluded that American Indians were not fully human. Based on empirical evidence, however, of what he had seen "of man, white, red, and black, and what has been written of him by authors, enlightened themselves, and writing amidst an enlightened people,"[28] Jefferson considered and destroyed each of Buffon's arguments. Even where the noted French naturalist was accurate in his generalizations (that the natives were uncivilized), Jefferson argued that Buffon missed the point. Only a lack of contact with whites had kept Indians below Europeans in civilization. Jefferson's subsequent treatment of Africans, by way of contrast, established the validity of both white and native virtues because in his telling they have no redeeming qualities (more on this point later).

Finally, Jefferson reached the end of his game by arguing that if animals and Indians had thrived in this environment, civilized people would prosper even more. But where was the proof of this assertion? Where, Europeans asked, were the cultured inhabitants of America—the poets, the musicians, the theorists? Americans had produced, Jefferson conceded, only three examples of genius— George Washington, Benjamin Franklin, and David Rittenhouse. But wait; size of population must be considered:

The United States contain three millions of inhabitants; France twenty millions; and the British islands ten. We produce a Washington, a Franklin, a Rittenhouse. France then should have half a dozen in each of these lines, and Great-Britain half that number, equally eminent. It may be that France has: we are but just becoming acquainted with her, and our acquaintance so far gives us high ideas of the genius of her inhabitants. It would be injuring too many of them to name particularly a Voltaire, a Buffon, the constellation of Encyclopedists, the Abbe Raynal himself, &c. &c. We therefore have reason to believe she can produce her full quota of genius. The present war having so long cut off all communication with Great-Britain, we are not able to make a fair estimate of the state of science in that country. The spirit in which she wages war is the only sample before our eyes, and that does not seem the legitimate offspring either of science or of civilization. The sun of her glory is fast descending to the horizon. Her philosophy has crossed the channel, her freedom the Atlantic, and herself seems passing to that awful dissolution, whose issue is not given human foresight to scan.[29]

Jefferson controlled for land area in comparing animal species, therefore, so he could use the size of populations in order to turn Raynal's conclusions on their head: the United States had already produced its quotient of geniuses, first of whom was Washington. Why was Europe, especially Great Britain, lagging behind?

Experience in teaching *Notes* to undergraduates confirms the wisdom of Darnton's statement about the game imbedded within the *Encyclopédie*. Students easily miss the punch line and, therefore, the fun, because they are so easily distracted by the wealth of details. But once they are trained to delve into the passages for subtle meanings, they are rewarded.

This experience is instructive when we consider the primary audience Jefferson envisioned for his book. If one views a general reading public as the audience for *Notes*, the topics of the book take center stage, and the book gives the appearance of a poorly structured, topical treatise. But Jefferson never intended for his book to reach a mass audience. Writing to Madison in May 1785, Jefferson told him that he had received the two hundred copies of *Notes* from the publisher. "[I] do not put them out of my own hands," he warned him, "except two or three copies here, and two which I shall send to America, to yourself and Colo. Monroe." He continued:

> I beg you to peruse it carefully because I ask your advice on it and ask nobody else's. I wish to put it into the hands of the young men at the college [of William and Mary], as well on account of the political as physical parts. But there are sentiments on some subjects which I apprehend might be displeasing to the country perhaps to the assembly or to some who lead it. I do not wish to be exposed to their censure, nor do I know how far their influence, if exerted, might effect a misapplication of law to such a publication were it made. Communicate it then in confidence to those whose judgments and information you would pay respect to.[30]

He expanded on these points in a subsequent letter:

> The strictures on slavery and on the constitution of Virginia . . . are the parts which I do not wish to have made public, at least till I know whether their publication would do most harm or good. It is possible that in my own country these strictures might produce an irritation which would indispose the people towards the two great objects I have in view, that is the emancipation of their slaves, and the settlement of their constitution on a firmer and more permanent basis. If I learn . . . that they will not produce that effect, I have printed and reserved just copies enough to be able to give one to every young man at the College. It is to them I look, to the rising generation, and not to the one now in power for these great reformations.[31]

Only when it was clear that he could not prevent unauthorized publications of the book did he agree to allow British bookseller John Stockdale to republish *Notes* in 1787, with the admonition that the publisher reproduce it "without additions, alterations, preface, or any thing else but what is there."[32] As William Peden and others who admire the book note, Jefferson certainly took pride in *Notes* as its author,[33] but it is also true that he envisioned the book's value more as enlightenment for the young and as amusement for his friends than as a "popular" offering.

III

But there's another remarkable aspect to Jefferson's reconstruction of *Notes* aside from this game that he hoped readers would play. The book is filled with sections that suggest a far deeper meaning. Consider, for example, Query 4 (mountains), where he describes "[t]he passage of the Patowmac [River] through the Blue ridge [Mountains]" as

> perhaps one of the most stupendous scenes in nature. You stand on a very high point of land. On your right comes up the Shenandoah, having ranged along the foot of the mountain an hundred miles to seek a vent. On your left approaches the Patowmac, in quest of a passage also. In the moment of their junction they rush together against the mountain, rend it asunder and pass off to the sea. The first glance of this scene hurries our senses into the opinion, that this earth has been created in time, that the mountains were formed first, that the rivers began to flow afterwards, that in this place particularly they have been dammed up by the Blue ridge of mountains, and have formed an ocean which filled the whole valley; that continuing to rise they have at length broken over at this spot, and have torn the mountain down from its summit to its base. . . . [It is the scene] of a war between rivers and mountains, which must have shaken the earth itself to its center.[34]

It is possible to become so captivated by his description of the two converging rivers as to miss the fact that his description crashed against accepted epistemological premises. Jefferson's "senses" told him that the "earth was created in time" and that "the mountains were formed first, that the rivers began to flow afterwards." What we have here is an affront to biblical accounts of Creation where dry lands appeared *after* the waters had receded.

This section of *Notes* is also one that Jefferson added during his expansion of the manuscript during the winter of 1783–84. What is especially interesting about this revision is that compared to his composition of *Summary View* (Chapter 2) and the Declaration of Independence (Chapter 3), where he borrowed phrasings from George Mason and others without attribution, Jefferson identified the source of these ideas—Charles Thomson. Thomson was secretary of the Second Continental Congress who had sent Marbois's queries to Jefferson, and he offered suggestions for revision to Notes, addenda that Jefferson included in his book as Appendix 1. Although it is unclear which version of Notes Thomson critiqued,[35] it is likely that Jefferson's visit to the site of modern-day Harpers Ferry in October 1783, just prior to his winter of revisions, led Jefferson to rely so heavily on Thomson's observations. If this is so, Jefferson certainly concurred with Thomson's conclusion that the remarkable scene had been created by "some violent convulsion, and that the face of [the country] must have been changed from what it probably was some centuries ago."[36]

The fact that Jefferson identified his source allows us to compare the texts directly. Juxtaposing them reveals that Jefferson did not take all of Thomson's suggestions. In his commentary on Query 4 (mountains), Thomson included other examples in New York and Pennsylvania of similar instances of rivers cutting through mountains. Jefferson chose to omit these references. Neither did Jefferson include Thomson's information "that at York town in Virginia, in the bank of York river, there are different strata of shells and earth, one above another, which seem to point out that the country there has undergone several changes; that the sea has, for a succession of ages, occupied the place where dry land now appears; and that the ground has been suddenly raised at various periods."[37] Jefferson neither confirmed nor negated Thomson's report, but the information may have caused him to make another change in the first version of Notes and further challenge religious authoritarianism.

Early in Query 6, Jefferson took up the anomaly of shells being found not at Yorktown, as Thomson advised, but rather at higher, western elevations. "I have received petrified shells of very different kinds," he writes, "from the sources of the Kentucky, which bear no resemblance to any I have ever seen in the tidewaters. It is said that shells are found in the Andes, in South America, fifteen thousand feet above the level of the ocean." Such evidence had caused many "both of the learned and unlearned" to believe in "a universal deluge." Jefferson argued in Notes, however, that floods of such magnitude were "out of the laws of nature" because there was not enough water on the earth to overrun the height of these mountains. "History renders probable some instances of a partial deluge in the country lying round the Mediterranean sea . . . [and] that sea may thus have been raised as to overflow the low lands adjacent to it, as those of Egypt and Armenia, which, according to a tradition of the Egyptians and Hebrews, were overflowed about 2300 years before the Christian aera. . . . But such deluges as these will not account for the shells found in the higher lands."[38]

In seeking to explain these anomalies aside from the biblical explanation of a flood covering the entire globe, Jefferson explored two additional theories, one offered by Thomson and one not. The first additional interpretation summarizes Thomson's explanation "that, in times anterior to the records either of history or tradition, the bed of the ocean, the principal residence of the shelled tribe, has, by some great convulsion of nature, been heaved to the heights at which we now find shells and other remains of marine animals."[39] Jefferson then questioned the accuracy of this theory by stating that "no fact has taken place, either in our own days, or in the thousands of years recorded in history, which proves the existence of any natural agents, within or without the bowels of the earth, of force sufficient to heave, to the height of 15,000 feet, such masses as the Andes."

The second "solution of this difficulty" that Jefferson investigated was one offered by François Marie Arouet (pen name Voltaire) that pressure in the earth had combined materials in such a way as to produce perfect copies of shells. "But," Jefferson wrote, "[Voltaire] has not established it. He has not even left it on ground so respectable as to have rendered it an object of enquiry to the literati of his own country." In the end, Jefferson dismissed all three theories because each was "equally unsatisfactory." He, therefore, concluded "that this phaenomenon is as yet unsolved. Ignorance is preferable to error; and he is less remote from the truth who believes nothing, than he who believes what is wrong."[40]

Later in Query 6, in his discussion of the origin and size of the mammoth, are additional statements that pose a direct challenge to biblical interpretations of divine intervention in history. As indicated above, Jefferson used the mammoth primarily in order to contradict Buffon's theories regarding inadequacies the French scientist saw in the climate of the New World. But imbedded within this rebuttal is another passage that is easily overlooked:

> The truth is, that a Pigmy and a Patagonian, a Mouse and a Mammoth, derive their dimensions from the same nutritive juices. The difference of increment depends on circumstances unsearchable to beings with our capacities. Every race of animals seems to have received from their Maker certain laws of extension at the time of their formation. Their elaborative organs were formed to produce this, while proper obstacles were opposed to its further progress. Below these limits they cannot fall, nor rise above them. What intermediate station they shall take may depend on soil, on climate, on food, on a careful choice of breeders. But all the manna of heaven would never raise the mouse to the bulk of the mammoth.[41]

The manuscript copy of *Notes* indicates that Jefferson not only added this section to his original version but also in the second account wrote something other than "mouse" that he scratched through, and that he originally used the word "elephant," later changing it to "mammoth." While it is possible that he

4. Views of *Mammuthus columbi* and *Mammuthus jeffersonii*. Although Jefferson believed there was only one species of the mammoth, in fact there were several. The species named for him is actually *Mammut americanum*. Still, he was correct that they were not elephants. These specimens are on display at the University of Nebraska State Museum. Photo courtesy of Nancy Lindsley-Griffin, Department of Geosciences, University of Nebraska.

may have been more interested in developing alliteration than in challenging biblical theories, the passage—read in conjunction with Jefferson's letters concerning the primary audience for the book—provides important keys for understanding how Jefferson tied issues together in *Notes* and for what purposes. As addressed above, in his letter to Chastellux he said he did not write his book for a general audience because he did not want to "indispose the people towards the two great objects I have in view, that is the emancipation of their slaves, and the settlement of their constitution on a firmer and more permanent basis."[42] *Manna, mouse,* and *mammoth* unite these objectives in two important ways.

First, the presence of the mammoth rather than the elephant in North America carried great weight with Jefferson. A creator god, in Jefferson's view, bound nature at the start of time with laws that through observation human beings could discover, if not fully comprehend. As Eugene R. Sheridan writes, Jefferson rejected the basic foundations of Christianity—especially the belief in the divinity of Jesus and the miracles his disciples attributed to him—because they were "contrary to human reason." Jefferson also rejected the view that God would have restricted his knowledge to the Jews (a view that Sheridan believes he may have borrowed from Henry St. John Bolingbroke) but rather revealed himself to everyone through "the natural wonders of the created universe."[43]

In Jefferson's cosmology, at creation God separated elephants and mammoths with "a belt of separation," thereby establishing "the constitution of the one in her extreme of heat, and that of the other in the extreme of cold."[44] Eight queries later, Jefferson used this fact to explain differences that he had observed between blacks and whites:

> The first difference which strikes us is that of colour. Whether the black of the negro resides in the reticular membrane between the skin and the scarf-skin, or in the scarf-skin itself; whether it proceeds from the colour of the blood, the colour of the bile, or from that of some other secretion, the difference is fixed in nature, and is as real as if its seat and cause were better known to us . . . [and] is a powerful obstacle to the emancipation of these people.[45]

Aside from Jefferson's ideas about blacks' color and behavior—ideas that jar the modern reader but were for the most part derived from English cultural biases[46]—it is important to note that these views appear not in Query 6 (nature's "belt of separation") but rather in Query 14 (laws). As noted earlier, Merrill Peterson believes that *Notes* proceeds from natural to civil and moral topics. In the Bible, however, "laws" (Exodus and Deuteronomy) follows "genesis" (Genesis). Not only did Jefferson write a text within a text, but also he provided readers with the necessary clues by which to follow the message to its conclusion.

Second, if Jefferson intended for Query 6 to be read in connection with Query 14, we should devote more attention to his assertion that "all the manna from heaven would never raise a mouse to the bulk of a mammoth." This reference to the Israelites' exodus from Egypt appears in others of Jefferson's writings. In August 1776, he became involved in discussions with Benjamin Franklin and John Adams concerning a seal for the United States. Franklin suggested that the seal contain a drawing of Pharoah in a chariot being overwhelmed by the Red Sea during the Israelites' escape from bondage in Egypt, with "rays from a pillar of fire in the cloud, expressive of the divine presence, and command, reaching to Moses who stands on the shore." Jefferson modified Franklin's design by secularizing it. Jefferson proposed a picture of "the children of Israel in the wilderness, led by a cloud by day and a pillar of fire by night; and on the other side, Hengist and Horsa, the Saxon chiefs from whom we claim the honor of being descended, and whose political principles and form of government we have assumed."[47]

Nearly thirty years later, Jefferson revisited this issue in the second inaugural address when he requested "the favor of that Being in whose hands we are, who led our fathers, as Israel of old, from their native land and planted them in a country flowing with all the necessaries and comforts of life."[48] As Thomas E. Buckley points out, Jefferson frequently acknowledged "dependence on a divine Providence overseeing the American experiment."[49]

More contemporaneous with the writing and rewriting of *Notes*, Jefferson alluded to the Israelites' escape from Egypt in a letter he wrote to David Rittenhouse in July 1778. After asking the budding American scientist (who had received wide acclaim for his creation of a mechanical representation of how the universe operated) if he would be able to make two clocks for him, Jefferson chided Rittenhouse for abandoning his scientific interests for "the civil government of your country."

> I . . . am myself duly impressed with a sense of the arduousness of government, and the obligation those are under who are able to conduct it, yet I am also satisfied there is an order of geniusses above that obligation, and therefore exempted from it. No body can conceive that nature ever intended to throw away a Newton upon the occupations of a crown. . . . I doubt not there are in your country many persons equal to the task of conducting government: but you should consider that the world has but one Ryttenhouse, and that it never had one before.

Then, these words: "Without having ascended mount Sina[i] for inspiration, I can pronounce that the precept, in the decalogue of the vulgar, that they shall not make to themselves 'the likeness of any thing that is in the heavens above' is reversed for you, and that you will fulfill the highest purposes of your creation by employing yourself in the perpetual breach of that inhibition."[50]

While Jefferson was writing this letter to Rittenhouse, he was deeply involved in trying to change the Virginia Constitution (Chapter 3), and it is possible that he saw himself during this struggle as a latter-day Moses, ascending "mount Sina[i]" for "a decalogue of the vulgar." If this is so, we are led again to Query 14 in *Notes* (laws) where Jefferson reprised his failure five years earlier to obtain fundamental changes in his country's constitution. Here, Jefferson listed *ten* of the "most remarkable alterations" he proposed to the Assembly from 1777 through 1779.[51] Because his peers rejected each of these suggested changes, he became, at least in that regard, a failed Moses.

There are further surprises in Query 14 that help to link it with Jefferson's treatment of the mammoth in Query 6. At the end of Query 14 he included a warning: "In every government on earth is some trace of human weakness, some germ of corruption and degeneracy, which cunning will discover, and wickedness insensibly open, cultivate, and improve. Every government degenerates when trusted to the rulers of the people alone. The people themselves are its only safe depositories."[52]

Although the idea that government rests on public involvement is a common theme of Jefferson's which he raised many times in his life,[53] he did not exhaust his development of the topic in *Notes* in Query 14. Instead, he returned to it two more times, in Query 17 (religion) and Query 18 (manners). In Query 17, he worried that Virginians, like the Israelites, had been in declension since their liberation. "From the conclusion of [the American Revolution]," he wrote, Virginians had been "going down hill," and people were forgetting their rights. Instead, they were single-mindedly devoted to "the sole faculty of making money," and had neglected the need to "effect a due respect for their rights. The shackles, therefore, which shall not be knocked off at the conclusion of this war, will remain on us long, will be made heavier and heavier, till our rights shall revive or expire in a convulsion."[54]

Next, in Query 18, he revealed why slavery needed to be abolished: "There must doubtless be an unhappy influence on the manners of our people produced by the existence of slavery among us."[55] Because young people saw the "boisterous passions" between masters and slaves in the form of "unremitting despotism on the one part, and degrading submissions on the other," Jefferson feared that they would emulate their parents' behavior. Also, because the climate of Virginia made people want to avoid working in the fields, they would become lazy—"no man labour[ing] for himself who can make another labour for him." Then, these words:

And can the liberties of a nation be thought secure when we have removed their only firm basis, a conviction in the minds of the people that these liberties are the gift of God? That they are not to be violated but with his wrath? Indeed I tremble for my country when I reflect that God is just: that his justice cannot sleep for ever: that . . . a revolution of the wheel of fortune, an exchange of situation, is among possible events: that it may become probable by supernatural interference! The Almighty has no attribute which can take side with us in such a contest.—But it is impossible to be temperate and to pursue this subject through the various considerations of policy, of morals, of history natural and civil. We must be contented to hope they will force their way into every one's mind. . . . The spirit of the master is abating, that of the slave rising from the dust, his condition mollifying, the way I hope preparing, under the auspices of heaven, for a total emancipation, and that this is disposed, in the order of events, to be with the consent of the masters, rather than by their extirpation.[56]

This passage (added to his manuscript during the winter of 1783–84) supplies the context necessary to understand his entry about the mouse and the mammoth eight queries previous. Manna from heaven did not, indeed *could not* make a mouse into a mammoth because their sizes had been fixed at creation. God *could*, however—indeed, *might*—intervene in history to punish Virginians for practicing slavery.

Jefferson's words are harsh, perhaps intended to scare young people attending the College of William and Mary into making a commitment to abolish slavery, but they are no harsher than one can find in Deuteronomy, Chapter 8, following the Israelites' exodus from Egypt, their years of wandering in the desert, and their inattentiveness to Moses' reading of the Ten Commandments:

> And thou say in thine heart, My power and the might of mine hand hath gotten me this wealth. But thou shalt remember the Lord thy God: for *it is* he that giveth thee power to get wealth, that he may establish his covenant which he sware unto your fathers, as *it is* this day. And it shall be if thou do at all forget the Lord your God, and walk after other gods, and serve them, and worship them, I testify against you this day that ye shall surely perish. As the nations which the Lord destroyeth before thy face, so shall ye perish; because ye would not be obedient unto the voice of the Lord your God.[57]

IV

When Jefferson rewrote *Notes* during the winter of 1783–84, he perhaps recalled how as a member of the Virginia Assembly he had tried repeatedly from 1776 through 1779 to make changes in the Virginia Constitution. In this effort—as with his attempts to end slavery, create a system of public education, and institute religious toleration—Jefferson met largely the hostility of his peers.[58] As a result, he became cautious and jaded. Writing to George Wythe in November 1778, Jefferson noted his concern regarding his attempts to reword a bill "for proportioning crimes and punishments in cases heretofore capital." "I wished," he wrote, "to exhibit a sample of reformation in the barbarous style into which modern statutes have degenerated from their antient simplicity. And I must pray you to be as watchful over what I have not said as what is said."[59] Given the extreme hostility that his attempted reforms had produced among his peers, therefore, it makes sense that he shifted the audience to younger people who were less wedded to the past, but he could not completely contain his anger over past events.

That Thomas Jefferson intended *Notes* to be "the book of Moses" for his country opens its author to new interpretations. Although Jefferson kept a personal copy of *Notes* in which he kept addenda and corrections that might have formed the nucleus of a second edition of the book, he never published a revision.[60] Nor did he ever follow through with his plans to abolish slavery, and he continued to benefit from the labor of his own slaves until his death (Chapter 7). Seen in this light, *Notes* established Jefferson's azimuth in his efforts to reform his society.[61]

Perhaps in his old age, however, Jefferson *did* finish *Notes* when he edited the New Testament as a complement to his Pentateuch.[62] If so, it must be emphasized that in his revised New Testament Jefferson rejected the divinity of Jesus Christ. In Jefferson's reordered Bible, only in *Notes* did he speculate that God might intervene in history—not to create a universal deluge or to alter the size of species or the divisions established among them at creation—but rather to punish the Virginia gentry for holding people in perpetual bondage.

Refreshing the Tree of Liberty
with the Blood of Patriots and Tyrants

Defending Virginia with Extremist Language in the 1780s and 1790s

It is now 125 years since John Fiske termed the mid- to late-1780s "the critical period" in U.S. history and argued that the ratification of the U.S. Constitution rescued the nation from disaster.[1] In the subsequent decade, these controversies melded with concerns over the French Revolution, the resulting wars involving the British and the French, and Alexander Hamilton's financial plans, all of which polarized Americans into political parties.

Thomas Jefferson escaped direct involvement in the turmoil attendant to the drafting and ratification of the Constitution because he was in France. There, he used extremist language in his letters to express the depth of his concerns over the political events that raged in the United States. With regard to the Constitution, Jefferson's initial impressions of the document contradicted the decisions of fellow Virginians George Washington and James Madison, who believed that too much liberty in the hands of the states under the Articles of Confederation threatened national existence. Instead of replacing the Articles of Confederation with a new document, wrote Jefferson to John Adams in November 1788, he would have preferred to add the "three or four" good aspects of the Constitution to the Articles, the Articles being a "good, old, and venerable fabric, which should have been preserved even as a religious relique."[2] In an extended, contemporaneous letter to Adams's son-in-law, William Stephens Smith, Jefferson chose hyperbolic language with which to criticize the delegates meeting at Philadelphia for threatening to abolish the people's right to resist tyranny (Chapters 3 and 4). Rebellion, he cautioned, was always preferable to "lethargy, the forerunner of death to the public liberty":

> What country can preserve it's liberties if their rulers are not warned from time to time that the people preserve the spirit of resistance? Let them take arms. . . . What signify a few lives lost in a century or two? The tree

of liberty must be refreshed from time to time with the blood of patriots and tyrants. It is its natural manure.[3]

How can we explain this and other radical-sounding statements of Jefferson from the period? The best explanation for his radicalism, Jefferson's biographers agree, lies in his residency in Paris. There, as the French moved toward a bloody revolution, Jefferson's language became increasingly inflammatory, perhaps even irrational.[4]

The first part of this chapter explores an alternative explanation, that Jefferson's initial responses to events rested more on deeply felt biases concerning the conduct of politics in Massachusetts compared to his native Virginia than on his views of European politics. A close examination of his commentary on American events from 1784 through 1789 leads to the conclusion that Jefferson formed his opinions about the U.S. Constitution based upon the meaning he assigned to Shays's Rebellion, not the French Revolution.

The second part of the chapter explores how his time in Paris and Shays's Rebellion marked important turning points in Jefferson's life. Whereas in *Notes on the State of Virginia* he took his peers to task for their failures to live up to the possibilities for change that the American Revolution opened (Chapter 4), during "the critical period" of the 1780s he shifted his attention away from attempts to change Virginian society. Instead, he devoted his energies to alerting white Virginians to preserve the liberties—now endangered under the Constitution— they enjoyed. A decade later in the wake of conflicts with Alexander Hamilton over domestic and foreign policy issues, Jefferson again used extreme language in private letters, in his *Anas*, and in the Kentucky Resolutions in order to rouse his countrymen to oppose the unchecked powers of the national government.

I

When Thomas Jefferson left the United States for France to replace Benjamin Franklin as U.S. minister on July 5, 1784, he had developed his most important political ideas and also had participated in many notable events. In spite of these accomplishments, however, Jefferson's life had not gone exactly as he might have planned. His wife's death in September 1782, while innuendoes of cowardice as governor swirled about him, was an especially heavy blow (Chapter 3). Perhaps he felt refreshed after his attack on his countrymen's destructive behaviors during his revision of *Notes* in the winter of 1783–84 (Chapter 4), and the appointment to the mission in France promised a respite from Virginia's political intrigues and memories of his personal tragedies. The especially fast passage (nineteen days) might have seemed portentous of good things to come during his stay.

From the beginning, the American minister drew comparisons between life in Virginia and Europe, and an awakened appreciation for his country dominates his letters, especially those to his younger correspondents. To James Monroe, he advised that a visit to Europe "will make you adore your own country, it's soil, it's climate, it's equality, liberty, laws, people and manners. My god! How little do my countrymen know what precious blessings they are in possession of, and which no other people on earth enjoy."[5] When a young acquaintance traveling in Europe asked his advice on where he might receive the best education, Jefferson admitted that acquiring "the habit of speaking the modern languages" could best be done abroad, but he advised that "every other article can be as well acquired at William and Mary College." Following college, "to prepare . . . for public life," Jefferson suggested that the young man study either law or medicine. For the latter subject, he believed that Europe was preferable, but for law "where can [a student] apply so advantageously as to Mr. [George] Wythe [Jefferson's mentor—Chapter 1]?" Otherwise, all a youth would learn in Europe amounted to "drinking, horse-racing and boxing" in England, and on the Continent "a fondness for European luxury and dissipation," including "a partiality for aristocracy or monarchy." It would be preferable, Jefferson advised the young man, to ask himself: "[W]ho are the men of most learning, of most eloquence, most beloved by their country and most trusted and promoted by them? They are those who have been educated among them, and whose manners, morals and habits are perfectly homogeneous with those of the country."[6]

With respect to France, his initial views were mostly those of a tourist. Language was a problem, finding suitable accommodations and clothing occupied his time, and attending court functions presented numerous difficulties. Once he and his daughter Martha went to Versailles to view the queen at her entrance to the palace, but when the queen's coach arrived, they could not see her. Next, they tried to view a military display and were shunted away by soldiers. "You can calculate," he wrote to John Adams, probably tongue-in-cheek, "the extent of mortification."[7]

While observing life in France and pressing American requests for additional trade opportunities, Jefferson kept informed about American affairs as best he could through trusted correspondents and American newspapers. On December 11, 1786, courtesy of Smith in London, he first learned of Shays's Rebellion and disorders in other New England states. In an accompanying letter, Smith informed Jefferson "of the expectation of a General Indian War and that Congress are raising troops on that ostensible Ground and for that ostensible reason." To Smith, the plan seemed flawed and suggested an ulterior motive; the Confederation Congress might intervene directly in Massachusetts' internal affairs. "How they mean to employ 2 Companies of Dragoons of 120 Rank and File in this service I am not yet informed," he wrote.[8]

Jefferson did not respond to Smith until December 20, the same day that he received a lengthy letter from Secretary of Foreign Affairs John Jay that portrayed the rebellion in Massachusetts in the worst possible light. "A Spirit of Licentiousness," wrote Jay, "[produced by a] Reluctance to Taxes, and Impatience of Government, a Rage for Property, and little Regard to the Means of acquiring it, together with a Desire of Equality in all Things, seem to actuate the Mass of those who are uneasy in their Circumstances."

The problem with the rebellion, according to Jay, lay in the effect it would have on "the Minds of the rational and well intentioned." Because they would worry about their "Peace and Security, they will too naturally turn towards Systems in direct Opposition to those which oppress and disquiet them. If Faction should long bear down Law and Government, Tyranny may raise its Head, or the more sober part of the People may even think of a King."[9]

Jay's response to Shays's Rebellion must have greatly alarmed Jefferson because he mentioned it several times. In answer to Smith's letter, he said that he "first viewed the Eastern disturbances as of little consequence" until he received a letter (Jay's) that "represented them as serious." In like manner, Jefferson admitted to John Adams that "Mr. Jay's letter on the subject had really affected me" until he received one from Adams advising him not to be "allarmed at the late turbulence in New England." Adams attributed the rebellion to a tax, "rather heavier than the People could bear," laid by the Massachusetts Assembly. Based on this letter, Jefferson assured members of the Adams family that he had no further concerns about the rebellion.[10]

After he overcame the initial shock of Jay's letter, Jefferson organized his thoughts on Shays's Rebellion around two primary foci. First, he placed this most recent event within his strongly held attitudes relative to politics and society in New England in general and Massachusetts in particular. Cryptic but consistent comments in correspondence reveal Jefferson's basic attitude toward life in Massachusetts. In his first letters to the Adamses in London and to Ezra Stiles, the president of Yale, Jefferson chose similar words to dismiss the implications of the rebellion. To John Adams he said, "I can never fear that things will go far wrong where common sense has fair play." To Abigail Adams, "Let common sense and common honesty have fair play and they will soon set things to rights." To Smith, "I hope . . . that the good sense of the people will be found the best army." Finally, to Stiles, "Let common sense and common honesty have fair play and they will soon set things to rights."[11]

For Jefferson, Massachusetts' problems were lodged not in the people but rather in the state's form of government. Writing to Adams in 1813, Jefferson distinguished between "a natural aristocracy . . . the grounds of which are virtue and talents" and an artificial aristocracy "founded on wealth and birth, without either virtue or talents" (Chapter 1). It was this latter group, Jefferson believed, that had dominated politics in Massachusetts since colonial days. By way of contrast, "in Virginia, we have nothing of this." From the earliest times, Jefferson believed, the electorate in Virginia had learned to discriminate between natural and pseudoaristocrats.

Another area where Virginian society was superior to that of Massachusetts related to the power of the clergy in the two states. In Massachusetts, Jefferson believed, a "strict alliance of church and state" prior to the American Revolution allowed ministers to attain a higher status than they deserved. In Virginia, however, fixed salaries for clergymen discouraged rivalries and accumulation of riches and thereby prevented their "acquiring influence over the people."[12] He viewed Virginia, therefore, as a land of tranquillity where men of virtue and talent rose to the top of society unaided by privilege, especially following his own efforts to abolish entail and primogeniture and to disestablish the Anglican Church (Chapters 3 and 4). In Massachusetts, however, the people had no recourse to liberty except through rebellion because of the tight control that ministers exercised over political affairs in the state.

In explaining how he believed that government had gone wrong in Massachusetts, Jefferson turned primarily to newspapers and tried not to rely on information he received from those like the Adamses whom he believed were infected by superstitions and heresies perpetrated by religious leaders in the state. From the newspapers, Jefferson concluded that the rebels were closing the courts because they did not have money to pay their foreign debts and state taxes. Prior to the American Revolution, he reasoned, New Englanders had exported their whale oil and fish to England and the Mediterranean, the former closed in the 1780s by duties, the latter, by pirates. Then, the Massachusetts Assembly "in their zeal for paying their public debt had laid a tax too heavy to be paid in the circumstances of their state." He emphasized that the rebels had refrained from injury to persons or property and did not remain a day in any one place.[13]

For his friends in European countries like C. W. F. Dumas at The Hague, or those who shared republican sympathies in France, like the Marquis de Lafayette, Jefferson placed the rebellion in the best possible light to quell possible alarms on their part. To American correspondents, however, he voiced different concerns. First, Jefferson was aware that many states in the nation had suspended the collection of debts during the American Revolution as a form of debtor relief. Indeed, unlike Massachusetts, most southern states, including Virginia, did not reopen their courts until the 1790s. Throughout the period of Shays's Rebellion, Jefferson received letters from correspondents in Virginia and South Carolina ruing the day the courts would eventually reopen and creditors would dun debtors to repay loans, as was already happening in New England.[14]

Second, Jefferson correctly concluded from his newspapers that the citizens of Massachusetts were caught in a "chain of debt" stretching from London to Boston to Worcester and Springfield. Part of the problem involved a British rush after the war to dump surplus manufactured goods in the former colonies. Jefferson laid most of the economic dislocation, however, at the feet of overly zealous New England merchants who, anticipating demand for British goods to be high after the war, bought large amounts of goods on credit. Unfortunately, a depressed economy led to few purchases and a subsequent flow of specie to England to pay creditors.[15]

Jefferson did not fully understand the complexities of this situation, but he offered good advice to a friend in Boston in the summer of 1785 to beware of merchants in that area "who undertake to trade without capital; who therefore do not go to market where commodities are to be had cheapest, but where they are to be had on the longest credit. The consumers pay for it in the end, and the debt contracted, and bankruptcies occasioned by such commercial adventurers, bring burthen and disgrace to our country."[16]

The theme of luxury and Americans' aping European tastes was a favorite of Jefferson's, and nowhere did he find more cause for alarm than in Boston. In this connection, he might have recalled the problems Virginians faced when asked to sign agreements not to import British products in the 1770s (Chapter 2) and might have extended some sympathy to Bostonians. Instead, his criticisms centered on societal flaws. In the aftermath of the rebellion, he wrote to Abigail Adams that "the disturbances in Massachusets are not yet at an end. [A correspondent] . . . gives me a terrible account of the luxury of our ladies in the article of dress. He sais that they begin to be sensible of the excess of it themselves and think a reformation necessary. That proposed is the adoption of a national dress. I fear however they have not resolution enough for this."[17]

Anticipations of British involvement in the events surrounding Shays's Rebellion went far beyond credit problems and clothing fads, however, whether in Virginia or Massachusetts. Jefferson convinced himself that Americans who wanted a stronger central government—and perhaps a restitution of the English king—planned to use Shays's Rebellion as their justification for constitutional change. In an extended letter in mid-January to Edward Carrington, the Virginian he hoped to use in place of James Monroe as his mouthpiece and informant in the Confederation Congress, Jefferson compared the nature of government in America and in Europe. Those societies with minimal government, Jefferson argued, based their rights on public opinion, whereas all European governments "under pretense of governing . . . [divide] their nations into two classes, wolves and sheep. I do not exaggerate. This is a true picture of Europe."[18]

One week later, he received a second letter from Jay deploring the fact that the Massachusetts government had treated the insurgents lightly, blaming Great

Britain for inciting Indians to warfare, and hoping that the British would not inflame the differences between eastern and western territories that surfaced in discussions over the Jay-Gardoqui Treaty. On January 30, Jefferson repeated and embellished upon much of his letter to Carrington in one to Madison, but his mind was on Jay. "I hold it," Jefferson wrote in one of his most quoted passages, "that a little rebellion now and then is a good thing, and as necessary in the political world as storms in the physical." Governments should see that even the minor evil of volatility in the people produces much good—interest in and commitment to liberty. "Honest republican governors," therefore, should be "so mild in their punishment of rebellions, as not to discourage them too much." Then, immediately following, this sentence: "If these transactions give me no uneasiness, I feel very differently at another piece of intelligence, to wit, the possibility that the navigation of the Missisipi may be abandoned to Spain."[19] Jay had misplaced his concerns, Jefferson thought. A rebellion in Massachusetts should not be allowed to create such an alarm, even when linked (erroneously, he believed) with British intrigue; and Jay should not exonerate his inept negotiations with such a lame excuse either.

Three days later, Jefferson received a letter from Abigail Adams containing language similar to Jay's, characterizing Shays and his followers as "Ignorant, wrestless desperadoes without conscience or principals, [who] have led a deluded multitude to follow their standard under pretence of grievances which have no existence but in their imaginations." Taken one way, Jefferson's response to Abigail—"I like a little rebellion now and then. It is like a storm in the Atmosphere"—seems harsh and punitive. Rather, he may have been reacting to the second half of Abigail's letter wherein she expressed the belief that in spite of "much trouble and uneasiness" the rebellion would provoke "an investigation of the causes which have produced these commotions":

> Luxery and extravagance both in furniture and dress had pervaded all orders of our Countrymen and women, and was hastning fast to sap their independance by involving every class of citizens in distress, and accumulating debts upon them which they were unable to discharge. Vanity was becoming a more powerfull principal than patriotism. The lower order of the community were prest for taxes, and tho possest of landed property they were unable to answer the demand, whilst those who possest money were fearfull of lending, least the mad cry of the mob should force the Legislature upon a measure very different from the touch of Midas.

In spite of his penchant for repeating pithy statements in private correspondence, I doubt that Jefferson would have reprised the "little rebellion" statement in his letter to Abigail unless he expected her to agree with him.[20] The extreme similarity in their views on part of the underlying causes of the rebellion must have led him to believe he could repeat to her the sentence he had used in Madison's letter. When she reacted differently from his expectations (by writing less often and avoiding politics even when she did), Jefferson dropped the topic altogether.

But with his other correspondents, he turned to another, deeper problem inherent in Shays's Rebellion. In Jay's and Adams's first letters to Jefferson about the revolt, both men wrote that they expected the rebellion, in Adams's words, to "terminate in additional Strength to government."[21] In contrast to their views, Jefferson fretted that the revolt in Massachusetts would lead to the formation of a stronger central government in the United States.

As citizens of the most populous and wealthy state in the union, Virginians were confident that their state could handle affairs without outside interference. Indeed, the chief reason for Virginians' active involvement in revolutionary events after 1774—as Jefferson himself had expressed so clearly in *Summary View* (Chapter 2)—had been the fear that England would overturn Burgesses' control of Virginia's affairs. As governor, Jefferson had felt the need for a more concerted action on the part of the states to meet the wartime needs of the nation (Chapter 3), and as minister to France he came to believe that a stronger union of the states would improve the conduct of foreign policy. But these attitudes never influenced his views of domestic affairs. If Jay and the Confederation Congress were able to raise an army to suppress an internal convulsion in Massachusetts under the guise of preparing for an Indian war, what would prevent disturbances in other states from provoking a similar response, or worse, of creating a more powerful central government over the states?

By mid-June, Jefferson had heard from Madison, Franklin, and other valued correspondents that Shays's Rebellion had ended peaceably, with pardons for the participants and the election of a new governor.[22] Thus, he was able to write the last chapter of this part of the story in a letter to David Hartley, an American residing in England. The causes of the rebellion, Jefferson opined, were internal to Massachusetts and revolved around an inability to pay debts. "I believe you may be assured," Jefferson wrote confidently, "that an idea or desire of returning to any thing like their antient government never entered into their heads." Then, some quantitative evidence: one insurrection in thirteen states in eleven years meant that any single state could expect only one rebellion every 143 years! Far from providing an example of weakness in American governments, Shays's Rebellion proved how inherently stable the American republic was.[23]

Not all of his countrymen agreed with this optimistic view of the rebellion. The actions of the Massachusetts debtors alarmed James Madison, George Washington, and other Virginians who gathered in Philadelphia in the summer of 1787 to discuss problems under the Articles of Confederation. Reports Jefferson received from Madison indicating that the convention might propose a new constitution revived Jefferson's concerns that the members of the convention might overreact to the events in Massachusetts.

In mid-July he received a letter from Madison containing a list of the delegates in Philadelphia and a lengthy discussion of the impression John Adams's *Defence of the Constitutions of the United States of America* was having on those men. Madison feared that the book would further incline the representatives from the eastern states toward "the British Constitution" and prove to be "a powerful engine in forming the public opinion."[24] By August, Jefferson entertained the prospect that some Americans would prefer monarchical to republican government. He also considered lobbying the representatives to make "one nation in every case concerning foreign affairs, and separate ones in whatever is merely domestic." States should be made to execute national laws (especially payments on the national debt), he felt, but this pressure should be light and "peaceable."[25]

Some time in early November, Jefferson saw the Constitution for the first time, courtesy of John Adams. Again, his first reactions provide important clues to his attitudes. Writing to Adams, Jefferson immediately railed against the powers of the executive officer. Characterizing the president as "a bad edition of a Polish king" because he could be reelected every four years for life, Jefferson prophesied that the office would at every election be "worthy of intrigue, of force, and even of foreign interference. It would be of great consequence to France and England to have America governed by a Galloman or an Anglo-man."[26]

He repeated the same ideas to Smith, but as before he wrote with more emphasis. First, he blamed the British for "impudent and persevering lying" regarding the instability of government under the Articles of Confederation:

> The British ministry have so long hired their gazetteers to repeat and model into every form lies about our being in anarchy, that the world has at length believed them, the English nation has believed them, the ministers themselves have come to believe them, and what is more wonderful, we have believed them ourselves. Yet where does this anarchy exist? Where did it ever exist, except in the single instance of Massachusets?

Then follow a repeat of his calculations about the number of revolutions per state per year and the statement (quoted at the beginning of this chapter) about blood being the "natural manure" of the tree of liberty. "Our Convention," he wrote, "has been too much impressed by the insurrection in Massachusets; and in the spur of the moment they are setting up a kite to keep the hen yard in order."[27]

Jefferson's worst fears had now materialized; rebellion in Massachusetts threatened liberty in his country because panicked national leaders might use this incident to increase the powers of the national government over the states. Drew McCoy and Lance Banning remind us that Madison's nationalism had strict limits and developed in response to fears that Virginia's prominent role in the nation was declining in the waning years of the Articles of Confederation,[28] but Jefferson's location in Paris caused him to worry that Madison had lost his local bearings. Therefore, he used excessive language in his letters to his friend to warn him, Washington, Carrington, and the other Virginia delegates to the Constitutional Convention not to allow Massachusetts' problems to undermine liberty in Virginia.

Shays's Rebellion could occur, Jefferson reasoned, only in a state like Massachusetts where clergy and aristocratic families stifled freedom. Although he had earlier been critical of his countrymen for their reluctance to improve Virginian society by switching from tobacco to grains, for refusing to institute a system of public education, for clinging to a state-sponsored religion, and for failure to abolish slavery (Chapters 3 and 4), his reform impulses dissolved when confronted with the specter of an overly powerful central government that threatened to destroy local control. Far away from his home, Jefferson used this "little rebellion" to caution his countrymen not to trade their liberties for the illusive dream of "a more perfect union."

II

When Jefferson returned home in November 1789, he hoped to settle the debts of his father-in-law and return to Paris. While on his way to Monticello, however, he received an invitation from newly elected President George Washington to join his cabinet as secretary of state. Following a personal visit and letters of encouragement from Madison, Jefferson agreed to accept the post.

By the time he arrived in New York City in late March 1790, the collaborative spirit that had led Madison and Hamilton to cooperate in drafting *The Federalist* had disappeared, and Madison had already taken a leading role in opposing Hamilton's emerging financial and diplomatic plans. Viewing Hamilton as a sectionalist intent on shifting the nation's wealth from south to north and from west to east, Madison also believed that the secretary of the treasury had designed plans that would move power "from the body of the people to a few rich men whose fortunes would expand dramatically as a result of federal largesse."[29] In addition, whereas Hamilton saw trade with Great Britain and protection of the British navy as integral to his plans for financing the national debt, Madison sought to break American dependence on the British by having the Congress place discriminatory tariffs on the trade of nations without commercial treaties with the United States.[30]

Another issue dominated Madison's concerns about Hamilton's and other northerners' emerging plans for the new national government—the permanent location for the nation's capital. Representatives from New York, Pennsylvania, and New England sought to keep the capital at New York and then move it permanently to the Susquehanna River in Pennsylvania, but Madison favored a location more favorable to western and, especially, southern farmers. In the words of Lance Banning, "Madison had every reason to believe that the allegiance of the westerners [especially Kentuckians] was hanging by a thread and that the location of the seat of government could be decisive for the future of the Union."[31]

Reacting to these emerging differences between Hamilton and Madison, Jefferson eventually brokered a deal between the two men that more than anything else came to define the parameters within which the political warfare in the nation operated for the next three decades. The details are familiar. In return for passage of Hamilton's financial plans (including payment of the national debt at face value, assumption of state debts, and payment to states, like Virginia, that would have received less than others, like Massachusetts), the capital of the United States would be moved from New York to Philadelphia until it would be established permanently on the Potomac River.

Complete historical understanding of the complexities involved in the "Capital Compromise" remains elusive. Recent scholars emphasize that the fragility of the Union likely turned the tide and put the pieces together. Most directly, Melvin Yazawa writes, "Against the backdrop of the ideologically charged and seemingly fragile national political situation of the 1780s, 'men of sound heads and honest views' apprehensively engaged 'in mutual sacrifices of opinion' to preserve the union, promote a sense of national identity, and perpetuate the 'glorious prospect' of the revolution." In addition, Yazawa makes the excellent point that Jefferson gave "separate and variant versions" of the political deal (especially regarding the specific role he played) at the time and in the 1818 version that he wrote into his *Anas*.[32]

Yazawa may be correct when he emphasizes that the Capital Compromise involved more than a political deal "among wily, self-serving participants," but two lasting results of Jefferson's involvement in the arrangement deserve emphasis. First, as Norman Risjord delineates, working out the details of the agreement allowed Jefferson to cement the sectional arrangement between Pennsylvania and Virginia that Madison had cultivated for at least a year prior to the final settlement. According to Risjord, the negotiations over the funding of the debt and the location of the capital "reaffirm[ed] the Pennsylvania-Virginia alliance." By the time of Jefferson's election as president, Pennsylvania had become "the keystone of the Democratic arch," and its politicians firmly backed Jefferson and his program (Chapter 6).[33]

Secondly, although Madison dissented from the final resolution of Hamilton's Report in the House, it is clear that he agreed with the compromise because he helped to switch the key votes behind the scenes that allowed the measure to pass.[34] From that point forward, he and Jefferson joined in "a great collaboration" to protect their country's preeminent position in the new republic as the most populous and largest state.[35] Working frequently in tandem, they opposed in sequence Hamilton's national bank, his tax on whiskey, and his manufacturing plan. As Jefferson later recorded in his *Anas* concerning these matters, "nothing rescued us from their liberticide effect but the unyielding opposition of those firm spirits who sternly maintained their post in defiance of terror until their fellow citizens could be aroused to their own danger, and rally and rescue the standard of . . . 'federal union, and republican government.'"[36]

Jefferson's devotion to "federal union, and republican government" resulted from a long, evolutionary development. His interest in federalism—shared political authority between central and local governments—began during the colonial period and provided a primary impetus for *Summary View* (Chapter 2). Similarly, he argued in the Declaration of Independence that republicanism (people's control of government, including a right of revolution [Chapter 3]) provided the justification for the existence of the United States. In his first inaugural address in 1801 (Chapter 6), he linked the two ideas when he said, "We have called by different names brethren of the same principle. We are all republicans, we are all federalists. . . . Let us, then, with courage and confidence pursue our own federal and republican principles, our attachment to union and representative government." It was in the 1790s during his battles with Alexander Hamilton over domestic and foreign policy issues that Jefferson finally worked out the logic of these principles.

It is unclear from his *Papers* exactly when he became convinced that Hamilton and others in the administration were undermining the Constitution by making the national government supreme in all matters and by ruling the nation as a minority faction bent on restoring monarchical rule. The editors of Jefferson's *Papers* dated the rift to the closing months of 1790, and they ended Volume 18 of the *Papers* with an appendix entitled "The First Conflict in the Cabinet," where they argued that Hamilton fought for the privileged few and Jefferson for the many.[37] An alternative beginning point appears in a February 1791 letter to his old collaborator George Mason (Chapters 2 and 3), where Jefferson referred to the existence "among us [of] a sect" who believed that the Constitution was a "kind of Halfway-house, [to] the English Constitution." The only way to counter these tendencies, he surmised, was to increase "the numbers in the lower house, so as to get a more agricultural representation, which may put that interest above that of the stock-jobbers."[38]

The letter to fellow countryman Mason is important because in it Jefferson linked Hamilton's emerging agenda with issues of federalism and republicanism. In calling Hamilton and others in the government a "sect," Jefferson differentiated them from those who may have had legitimate differences on specific issues but who agreed that the primary purpose of the Constitution was to limit the powers of government to secure maximum liberty for individual actions. In late April 1791, Jefferson wrote that he welcomed the publication of Thomas Paine's *Rights of Man* because it would stand "against the political heresies which have sprung up among us."[39] Although publication of his letter as preface to Paine's pamphlet caused Jefferson considerable embarrassment and opened him to personal attacks in newspapers, he never retracted his charge. In defending his actions to Washington in early May, Jefferson wrote that "Anglomen" feared "that this popular and republican pamphlet . . . is likely at a single stroke to wipe out all the unconstitutional doctrines. . . . I certainly never made a secret of my being anti-monarchical, and anti-aristocratical."[40] Jefferson blamed John Adams for newspaper articles written against him signed with the name "Publicola," but his wrath fell primarily on Hamilton for accusations that Jefferson's views on Paine's pamphlet "marks my opposition to the government. Thus endeavoring to turn on the government itself those censures I meant for the enemies of the government, to wit those who want to change it into a monarchy."[41]

Jefferson's comments on the constitutionality of Hamilton's National Bank, written in mid-February 1791, help to clarify further the meanings he assigned to the terms "sect" and "political heresies." Although what became the Tenth Amendment to the Constitution was not ratified until December 1791, in Jefferson's reckoning it formed "the foundation of the Constitution" since it reserved to the states and to the people powers not delegated to the national government. "To take a single step beyond the boundaries thus specially drawn around the powers of Congress," he wrote, "is to take possession of a boundless feild of power, no longer susceptible of any definition." If the Congress voted to create a bank, the body would exceed its enumerated powers and thereby destroy the federal division of powers on which the Constitution rested. Therefore, the only remedy in Jefferson's mind lay in the presidential veto power. "It is chiefly for cases where [the legislature] are misled by error, ambition, or interest," Jefferson concluded, "that the constitution has placed a check in the negative of the President."[42]

In July, he extended his thinking on federalism in a letter to James Sullivan, that the Constitution had "partitioned . . . sovereignty . . . between the general and particular governments . . . , the constitution having foreseen it's incompetency to all the objects of government and therefore confined it to those *spe-*

cially described." Unless state governments exercised their authority over those unassigned matters, the national government might "[fly] to monarchy for that semblance of tranquility which it is the nature of slavery to hold forth." Happily, Jefferson concluded, "a due poise and partition of powers between the general [national] and particular [state] governments" would extend "the benign blessings of republicanism over still greater tracts of country than we possess."[43]

When Hamilton defended his plans for creating a national bank in newspapers, Jefferson changed his nomenclature, but not his sentiments, toward the treasury secretary and the Federalists. Writing to Madison, Jefferson said that Hamilton was now "daring to call the republican party *a faction*," and this term began to replace "sect" in Jefferson's vocabulary when he referred to Federalists.[44] Richard Hofstadter in his classic book on the evolution of the two-party system in the United States captured Jefferson's thinking perfectly. A *faction* was "the instrument with which some small and narrow special interest could impose its will upon the whole of society, and hence . . . become the agent of tyranny."[45]

In describing his opponents beginning in late December 1794, Jefferson consistently used the words *faction* and *party* in order to discredit the Federalists and contrast them from the Republicans. That month, Jefferson wrote that the "faction of Monocrats" were denouncing "the democratic societies . . . whose avowed object is the nourishment of the republican principles of our constitution." In other words, whereas Republicans were simply voicing popular anxiety over policies that benefited the few at the expense of the many, Federalists were determined to subvert the Constitution. In the wake of Jay's Treaty, Jefferson accused the factious Federalists of entering "into conspiracy with the enemies of their country" to destroy the nation. Writing to Philip Mazzei in late April 1796, Jefferson confided that "an Anglican, monarchical and aristocratical party has sprung up, whose avowed object is to draw over us the substance as they have already done the forms of the British government. . . . It would give you a fever were I to name to you the apostates who have gone over to these heresies, men who were Samsons in the field and Solomons in the council, but who have had their heads shorn by the harlot England."[46]

This thinly veiled attack on Washington in Jefferson's letter to Mazzei (a version of which was later published in Federalist newspapers) proved to be the final breaking point between the two Virginians. Beginning in late August 1791, Jefferson had made notes on his conversations with Washington, Hamilton, and others in the administration so that he could document Hamilton's machinations and Washington's acquiescence in these matters. Following a meeting with the president in late February 1792, Jefferson recorded that Washington had expressed fears that "he really felt himself growing old, his bodily health less

firm, his memory, always bad, becoming . . . worse, and perhaps the other faculties of his mind shewing a decay to others of which he was insensible himself."
Six months later, following a similar meeting, Jefferson wrote that the president
"was sensible . . . of a decay in his hearing[, and p]erhaps his other faculties
might fall off and he not be sensible of it."[47]

Washington was also hypersensitive, Jefferson believed, to perceived personal attacks contained in Republican newspapers. In response to Jefferson's accusations that Hamilton and others were pushing the nation toward monarchy,
Washington stated that he feared that the nation might degenerate into anarchy
rather than a monarchy and disparaged articles that he was seeing in Philip Freneau's *National Gazette* attacking the government's policies. "He was evidently
sore and warm," Jefferson recorded. When Washington suggested that Jefferson
fire Freneau from his position in the State Department, Jefferson wrote, "I will
not do it. [Freneau's] paper has saved our constitution which was galloping fast
into monarchy, and has been checked by no one means so powerfully as by that
paper. . . . [T]he President, not sensible of the designs of the party, has not with
his usual good sense . . . looked on the efforts and effects of this free press and
seen that tho some bad things had passed thro' it to the public, yet the good had
preponderated immensely."[48]

As for Washington's views, Jefferson blamed Hamilton and Secretary of War
Henry Knox for playing on the old man's irrational fears that the emerging
Republican party was an *"antifederal and discontented faction . . . [that] would
by their corresponding societies in all the states draw the mass of the people,
by dint of misinformation, into their vortex and overset the government. . . . I
opposed it totally, told the President plainly in their presence, that the intention
was to dismount him from being the head of the nation, and make him the head
of a party."*[49]

III

It is within this context of antiparty ideology and Jefferson's evolving ideas
about federalism and republicanism that the Kentucky Resolutions are best understood. In his final use of extremist language prior to his election as president,
Jefferson sought to defend the rights of his country against an all-powerful national government. Again, for early American historians the backdrop of the
famous document approaches common knowledge. When the Congress passed
the Alien and Sedition Acts during the height of the war scare with France in
1798, Jefferson and Madison provided legislation—the Kentucky and Virginia
Resolutions, respectively—that became the rallying point for Democratic-
Republicans throughout the nation.[50]

Less well understood is the fact that Virginian events shaped Jefferson's interest in the matter. As Adrienne Koch pointed out several decades ago, a little-known incident in the spring of 1797 involving a federal grand jury's indictment of Samuel Jordan Cabell, Republican representative from Albemarle County to the U.S. Congress, set the stage for Jefferson's document. In the words of the grand jury presentment, Cabell had "endeavor[ed] at a time of real public danger to disseminate unfounded calumnies against the happy government of the United States . . . and to increase or produce a foreign influence ruinous to the peace, happiness and independence of these United States."[51]

Jefferson immediately viewed Cabell's indictment as an attack on federalism. Writing to James Monroe in early September 1787, Jefferson argued that Virginia's courts "(and among them the General Court as a court of impeachment) are originally competent to the cognisance of all infractions of the rights of one citizen by another citizen: and they retain all their judiciary cognisances not expressly alienated by the federal constitution." Because the Constitution had not shifted responsibility from the states to the nation, state authority "is therefore not alienated, but remains under the protection of the courts."[52]

In debating how best to counter the usurpation by the national courts of this local responsibility, Jefferson initially thought that the Congress might provide redress. "But I knew that to send the petition to the H. of Represent. in Congress," he continued in his letter to Monroe, "would make bad worse. The system of the General Government is to seize all doubtful ground." Therefore, the only possible remedy for the judiciary's unconstitutional actions lay with the Virginia Assembly, which alone "could maintain the authority of our own government over it. . . . We must join in the scramble or get nothing. . . . It is of immense consequence that the States retain as complete authority as possible over their own citizens."[53]

In October, Jefferson enclosed a draft "Petition on the Election of Jurors" that he prepared for the legislature in a letter to Madison. It reprised language he had used earlier in *Notes* (Chapter 4): "the people themselves are the safest deposit of power, and that none . . . should be trusted to others which they can competently exercise themselves . . . [and] that in the establishment of the trial by jury . . . a great inconsistence has been overlooked in this and some other of the states." It remained for the Virginia Assembly, therefore, to "preserve the trial by jury, in its pure and original spirit, as the true tribunal of the people, for a mitigation in the execution of hard laws when the power of preventing their passage is lost, and may afford some protection to persecuted man, whether alien or citizen, which the aspect of the times warns we may want."[54] Jefferson's document eventually led to a resolution from the House of Delegates that branded the actions of the grand jury as "an usurpation of power . . . and a subjection of a natural right of speaking and writing freely." In Koch's words, Jefferson's attempts to secure popular selection of jurors rather than their appointment by national courts would ensure "a proper percentage of Republican jurors, proportioned to their popular strength in Virginia," thereby overturning the ability of Federalist-dominated courts to pack juries.[55]

When Jefferson worked through the Virginia legislature to blunt the effect of Federalist schemes to silence dissent in the state, he set the stage for the most controversial portion of his Kentucky Resolutions, that a state might declare acts of Congress unconstitutional. According to Jefferson, with the ratification of the Constitution, the states did not grant unlimited power to the "general government" but rather reserved to themselves a "residuary mass of right to their own self-government." Neither had the states created the national government as "the exclusive or final judge of the extent of the powers delegated to itself." Therefore, Jefferson wrote into the 8th provision of the Kentucky Resolutions that "every state has a natural right in cases not within the compact . . . to nullify of their own authority all assumptions of power by others within their limits." In Jefferson's view, each state with "it's co-states" were equal parties with the national government under the Constitution, the document that specified the division of powers each type of government exercised. Hence, the Kentucky Resolutions asked the "co-states . . . [to] concur in declaring these acts void and of no force."[56]

Integral to this argument is the idea of federalism that Jefferson had developed during his disputes with Hamilton over the national bank earlier in the decade; the Tenth Amendment reserved powers not specified in the Constitution to the United States either to the states or to the people. Madison, who responded based upon fears of unrestrained state legislatures which might assume absolute powers, disagreed. "Have you ever considered thoroughly," he wrote to Jefferson on December 29, 1798, "the distinction between the power of the *State* and that of the *Legislature*, on questions relating to the federal pact. On the supposition that the former is clearly the ultimate Judge of infractions, it does not follow that the latter is the legitimate organ especially as a Convention was the organ by which the compact was made."[57] In other words, Madison objected not to the basis of Jefferson's understanding of federalism but only to Jefferson's means of implementing the policy—through the states' legislatures.

Jefferson took no small measure of delight in pointing out to Madison in a letter in late January 1799 that various petitions from the New York, New Jersey, and Pennsylvania legislatures against the Alien and Sedition Acts confirmed the validity of his views and of his strategy. "I am in hopes," he wrote, "Virginia will stand so countenanced by those States as to repress the wishes of the government to coerce her, which they might venture on if they supposed she would be left alone."[58]

The final chapter in this episode occurred in August 1799 when Jefferson's fears escalated under the belief that the national government would declare that

English common law had been established in the nation at the time of independence and, therefore, directed the way the nation's courts should function. Writing to Edmund Randolph, Jefferson asserted that prior to the American Revolution "the nation of Virginia had, by the organs they then thought proper to constitute, established a system of laws," including English common law, but nothing of the sort had been done nationally. Virginians had changed the way they made laws in their constitution, but "the nation was not dissolved, was not annihilated; its will, therefore, remained in full vigor." But before the American Revolution, "there existed no such nation as the United States. . . . So that the common law did not become, *ipso facto*, law on the new association; it could only become so by a positive adoption, and so far only as they were authorized to adopt." Were it so, U.S. courts would have "jurisdiction co-extensive with that law, that is to say, general over all cases and persons" and the state courts "may be shut up, as there then will be nothing to hinder citizens of the same State suing each other in the federal courts in every case."[59]

IV

It is not surprising that so many historians argue that the Kentucky Resolutions gave language and purpose to the states' rights position that John C. Calhoun and others later espoused—that a state by itself had the right to nullify acts of the national government. Take, for example, the words of Joseph Ellis, that Jefferson's "line of thought led logically to the compact theory of the Constitution eventually embraced by the Confederacy in 1861."[60]

The extreme language that Jefferson used in the late 1790s, however, must be viewed within the context of his earlier views of Shays's Rebellion and his conflicts with Alexander Hamilton over domestic and foreign policy issues. Writing to John Taylor in early June 1798, Jefferson conceded that "we are completely under the saddle of Massachusetts and Connecticut, and that they ride us very hard, cruelly insulting our feelings, as well as exhausting our strength and subsistence." Some might use the current situation to propose secession, he continued. "But if on a temporary superiority of the one party, the other is to resort to a scission of the Union no federal government can ever exist." Besides, he reasoned, if Virginia and Pennsylvania or Virginia and North Carolina were to secede, the temporary arrangement would not ensure permanent unity, and these states might eventually separate from each other. "A little patience," he counseled, "and we shall see the reign of witches pass over, their spells dissolved, and the people recovering their true sight, restoring their government to its true principles . . . and then we shall have an opportunity of winning back the *principles* we have lost. For this is a game where principles are the stake."[61]

In 1787, Jefferson deliberately downplayed the radicalism of the French Revolution and elevated the dangers he saw on the part of American leaders' reactions to Shays's Rebellion in order to warn his countrymen that a too-powerful national government threatened liberty in the states. As the nation's first secretary of state under the Constitution, he collaborated with his friend and the nation's preeminent congressman James Madison to oppose Alexander Hamilton's domestic and foreign policy programs. In the process, Jefferson and Madison emerged as national political leaders, but the extremist language of the Kentucky Resolutions helps to clarify the fact that Jefferson continued to frame his proposals primarily on what seemed to him to be best for Virginia. By the time of his presidency, this commitment meant increasing his countrymen's attachment to "federal and republican principles."

6

"Pursu[ing] Federal and Republican Principles"

The Unfulfilled Revolution of Jefferson's Presidency

When Thomas Jefferson walked the short distance from his boardinghouse to the Capitol on March 4, 1801, he carried in his hand a blueprint for a Second American Revolution. As he wrote much later to a friend, his presidency presented the opportunity for "as real a revolution in the principles of our government as that of 1776 was in its form."[1]

The word "principle" occurs with the greatest frequency in the inaugural address—eight times—and is commonly modified by an adjective meant to heighten its importance, as in the "*sacred principle*, that though the will of the majority is in all cases to prevail, that will, to be rightful must be reasonable"; or "absolute acquiescence in the decisions of the majority—the *vital principle* of republics, from which there is no appeal but to force"; or the "*essential principles* of our government . . . which ought to shape its administration" (*emphases added*). Jefferson's most famous use of the word comes early in the speech when he said "every difference of opinion is not a difference of principle. We have called by different names brethren of the same principle. We are all republicans—we are all federalists. . . . Let us . . . with courage and confidence pursue our own federal and republican principles, our attachment to our union and representative government."[2]

With these statements, Jefferson melded his experiences as secretary of state and vice-president with ideas formed earlier in his life that he recorded in *Summary View* (Chapter 2) and *Notes on the State of Virginia* (Chapter 4). When the voters removed the Federalists from power in the election of 1800, Jefferson must have felt that his country's perspectives on national affairs had been vindicated. The doubts that he had earlier entertained with regard to life in Virginia and his criticisms of his countrymen's failures to accomplish fundamental reforms melted away. Nothing stood in the way of Virginia—and, now, the nation—in their mutual paths to peace and progress. Drew McCoy caught the essence of this feeling perfectly when in the frontispiece of *The Elusive Republic* he quoted from F. Scott Fitzgerald's *The Great Gatsby*: "He had come a long way to this blue lawn, and his dream must have seemed so close that he could hardly fail to grasp it."

This chapter investigates how during two foreign policy episodes—the Louisiana Purchase in 1803 and the British attack on the U.S.S. *Chesapeake* that occurred in the middle of Aaron Burr's trial for treason in 1807—Jefferson turned his back on many of the principles that he outlined in his inaugural address. In acquiring Louisiana from France, he relied on Alexander Hamilton's doctrine of implied powers to justify taking the territory by treaty and incorporating it into the United States. Then he used Hamilton's financial system to finance the purchase.

Second, at Monticello during the summer of 1807, he determined that a war with Great Britain was necessary in order to salvage the nation's honor and establish future security from British attacks. When he returned to Washington in the fall of 1807, Jefferson could not achieve the war that he felt the country required to defend its honor against the British, but his reversals from the principles he enunciated in 1801 set the stage for James Madison's final revocation of these principles during the War of 1812.

Finally, the chapter integrates Jefferson's domestic life into national affairs by examining the context of Sally Hemings's conception of her fourth son and final child, Eston, in August 1807. At the height of his retreat as president from the provincial principles he outlined in his first inaugural address, local values continued to inform his behavior in his personal life.

I

Federalism—sharing of government's powers between national and local authority—and republicanism—popular election of the people's representatives at the national and local levels—formed the basis of Jefferson's (and Madison's) criticisms of Alexander Hamilton's domestic and foreign policy agendas in the 1790s (Chapter 5). In Jefferson's view, Hamilton's Federalist party was a minority faction dedicated to reestablishing a monarchy in the United States. Jefferson envisioned this occurrence under several scenarios. The doctrine of implied powers might abolish federalism by negating the Tenth Amendment; or the executive branch of government would destroy the constitutional balance of powers the Constitution had instituted by subordinating the legislative and judicial branches to the presidency; or Hamilton could initiate a military coup in order to bring back George III.

In 1799, Jefferson anticipated much of what he said in March 1801, in a letter he wrote to Elbridge Gerry of Massachusetts. As Roger Brown notes, Gerry along with Virginians Richard Henry Lee and George Mason had been "[t]he most active limited amendment Antifederalists"—those who favored a Constitution but not without a bill of rights—and initially opposed ratifying the document. Unlike Lee and Mason, Gerry accommodated himself to government under the Constitution and found Republican party domestic and foreign policy initiatives attractive in the 1790s. As one of John Adams's special envoys to France, he was also well-positioned politically to disrupt New England Federalist unanimity in the election of 1800. In the letter to Gerry, Jefferson outlined what he termed "my principles," which, he added, were also "unquestionably the principles of the great body of our fellow-citizens."[3] Integral to these "principles" were both federalism and republicanism.

First, he told Gerry, he sought to "preserv[e] to the States the powers not yielded by them to the Union, and to the legislature of the Union its constitutional share in the division of powers."[4] This view stemmed directly from Jefferson's disagreement with Hamilton's plan for funding the national debt and for creating a national bank. Responding to President George Washington's request for his opinion on the bank's constitutionality, Jefferson asserted that the Tenth Amendment had clarified the fact that the Constitution limited the powers of the national government in many areas. "To take a single step beyond the boundaries thus specially drawn around the powers of Congress," he wrote, "is to take possession of a boundless feild of power, no longer susceptible of any definition. The incorporation of a bank, and other powers assumed by this bill have not, in my opinion, been delegated to the U.S. by the Constitution. . . . It was intended to lace them up straitly within the enumerated powers." Therefore, Jefferson urged the president to use his veto power as the only "shield provided by the constitution to protect against . . . cases where [members of Congress] are misled by error, ambition, or interest."[5]

Simultaneously, Jefferson wrote to Virginian confidant George Mason, informing him that the only corrective to Hamilton's schemes was to "augment . . . the numbers of the lower house, so as to get a more agricultural representation, which may put that interest above that of the stock-jobbers."[6] By the following year, Jefferson was convinced that congressmen were no longer independent members of the national government but rather were the minions of the secretary of treasury. In two biting letters to Washington, Jefferson renewed and deepened his charges that Hamilton's financial system of permanent debts and a centralized bank were destroying republican government. In May, he wrote that "the ultimate object of all this [financial system] is to prepare the way for a change, for the present republican form of government, to that of a monarchy, of which the English Constitution is to be the model. That it was contemplated in the [Constitutional] Convention, is no secret. . . . To effect it then was impracticable; but they are still eager after their object, and are predisposing every thing for it's ultimate attainment."[7] In September, Jefferson charged that Hamilton's financial system "flowed from principles adverse to liberty calculated to undermine and demolish the republic, by creating an influence of his department over the members of the legislature . . . for the purpose of subverting step by step the principles of the constitution, which he has so often declared to be a thing of nothing which must be changed."[8]

Second, Jefferson wrote to Gerry, "I am for a government rigorously frugal and simple, applying all the possible savings of the public revenue to the discharge of the national debt; and not for the multiplication of officers and salaries merely to make partisans, and for increasing, by every device, the public debt, on the principle of its being a public blessing."[9] This view also appeared earlier in his September 1792 letter to Washington, where Jefferson said that he "was duped . . . by the Secretary of the Treasury and made a tool for forwarding his schemes, not then sufficiently understood by me." Whereas Jefferson initially thought that Hamilton devised his Report on Public Credit (1791) to establish the nation's financial stability by paying off the war debt left from the American Revolution, Jefferson convinced himself that Hamilton was intent on creating a permanent debt by which he could "corrupt & manage the legislature." A permanent debt would also create the need for a host of federal positions—hundreds of "clerks of his department, [a] thousand excisemen, custom-house officers, loan officers &c. &c. appointed by him, or at his nod . . . spread over the Union."[10] Four months later, Jefferson wrote to William Short that "[t]here are in the U.S. some characters . . . high in office . . . fondly looking to England as the staff of their hope. These I named to you on a former occasion. . . . The little party above mentioned have espoused [the Constitution] only as a stepping stone to monarchy."[11] While Jefferson and Madison portrayed Hamilton as dedicated to establishing an artificial aristocracy of wealth and power leading to monarchy, they projected themselves as drawing support from the people of the nation and called themselves Democratic-Republicans.

Third, he informed Gerry, "I am for relying, for internal defence, on our militia solely, till actual invasion, and for such a naval force only as may protect our coasts and harbors from such depredations as we have experienced." Neither did he favor a standing army, "nor . . . a navy, which, by its own expenses and the eternal wars in which it will implicate us, will grind us with public burthens, and sink us under them."[12]

In *Notes*, Jefferson wrote that the nation's attachment to commerce would likely involve the nation in wars, but even if wars resulted from defending American trade, the nation need not engage in an expensive war at sea or despair of asserting American rights. Echoing sentiments expressed by Thomas Paine in *Common Sense* (1776) that Americans could use their agricultural products to win friends in Europe, Jefferson wrote that "Circumstances exist, which render even the stronger [European nations] weak as to us. Providence has placed their richest and most defenceless possessions at our door; has obliged their precious commerce to pass as it were in review before us." A small navy, well within the power of Virginia alone to build and outfit, would be sufficient to the task. Besides, "the value of our lands and slaves, taken conjunctly," he calculated, "doubles in about twenty years."[13]

His service as secretary of state and vice-president confirmed to him the wisdom of his views and of the necessity to implement them at the national level. Indeed, the great problem Jefferson and Madison found with Hamilton's foreign policy was that it was based on a premise of American weakness rather than strength. European problems presented Americans with unique opportunities. France should be used as a makeweight in the scale of international relations to break the British monopoly of American trade and credit.[14]

Fourth, he affirmed to Gerry, "I am for free commerce with all nations; political connection with none; and little or no diplomatic establishment." There would no longer be a preference for England over France as with Jay's Treaty (1794) during Washington's administration or the Quasi-War with France (1797–1800) under Adams's term as president. To implement these beliefs, Jefferson ratified the Convention of Mortefontaine (1800) that Adams's emissaries had negotiated, which ended the Treaty of Alliance with France that had been signed during the American Revolution.[15]

As Lawrence S. Kaplan argues so persuasively, most of Jefferson's "isolationism" stemmed from his beliefs that European countries operated under governmental systems different from, and antithetical to, that of the United States—or, as Jefferson explained it in his inaugural address, "nations who feel power and forget right, advancing rapidly to destinies beyond the reach of mortal eye."[16] Because Americans lived by different principles, which Jefferson carefully delineated in 1801, he suggested that it would be foolish to focus attention on foreign nations rather than on themselves. Although Jefferson questioned George Washington's adoption of Hamilton's financial plans and attachment to British foreign policy, Jefferson agreed with Washington's Farewell Address and supported his "Great rule of conduct": "Europe has a set of primary interests, which to us have none, or a very remote relation. . . . Under an efficient government, the period is not far off, when we may defy material injury from external annoyance;—. . . when we may choose peace or war, as our interest guided by justice shall counsel."[17]

Finally, Jefferson promised to Gerry that he would preserve "freedom of religion . . . against all manoeuvres to bring about a legal ascendancy of one sect over another."[18] Religion appears in Jefferson's inaugural address five times. He first broached the subject in the negative context of differing political opinions: "Having banished from our land that religious intolerance under which mankind so long bled and suffered, we have yet gained little if we countenance a political intolerance as despotic, as wicked, and capable of as bitter and bloody persecutions." Later, in a similar context, he promised "equal and exact justice to all men, of whatever state or persuasion, religious or political." Two positive contexts of religion reinforce such statements. Toward the middle of his address, Jefferson expressed his belief that God intended for religion to help people, not to hurt them, because in America people were "enlightened by a benign religion, professed, indeed, and practiced in various forms, yet all of them including honesty, truth, temperance, gratitude, and the love of man; acknowledging and adoring an overruling Providence which by its dispensations proves that it delights in the happiness of man here and his greater happiness hereafter." At the very end of the speech, he developed this theme further: "May that Infinite Power which rules the destinies of the universe, lead our councils to what is best, and give them a favorable issue for your peace and prosperity."[19]

Jefferson may have chosen these conciliatory words to counter warnings from Congregational ministers who during the election of 1800 used their pulpits to warn their congregants against what they perceived as atheism. If these concerns predominated, Jefferson likely would have argued (as John Kennedy did in 1961) that government was God's agent on earth for leading people toward happiness and prosperity. Instead, Jefferson's words suggest that his feelings flowed from sentiments he had expressed as a Virginia assemblyman during the American Revolution.

Integral to Jefferson's view of good government was his belief that people's opinions—especially their religious beliefs—should be removed from government's control. In his "Bill for Establishing Religious Freedom" (1777), Jefferson argued "the opinions of men are not the objects of civil government nor under its jurisdiction."[20] Later, in *Notes* (1787), he wrote: "The legitimate powers of government extend to such acts only as are injurious to others. But it does me no injury for my neighbor to say there are twenty gods, or no god."[21] As president, he reaffirmed in 1802 his belief that "religion is a matter which lies solely between man and his God, . . . that the legislative powers of government reach actions only, and not opinions . . . thus building a wall of separation between Church and State." In the words of Eugene Sheridan, "[U]ltimately, what most concerned [Jefferson] was how men acted in society, not what they believed in religion."[22]

In only one area did Jefferson expand his "principles" from those contained in his letter to Gerry to the enumeration in his inaugural address. Perhaps because Gerry was from Massachusetts, a state devoted to commerce, as were all the New England states, Jefferson did not indicate that he planned to dedicate his administration to the "encouragement of agriculture, and of commerce as its handmaid." As Drew McCoy delineates so masterfully, Jefferson believed that when a country moved from agriculture to manufacturing, the result was misery and stagnation. By expanding across space and by providing markets for the surpluses produced by farmers—described in *Notes* as the nation's "most virtuous and independant citizens"[23]—Jefferson hoped to forestall movement through time from agriculture to commerce to industry.[24]

The theme of hardworking, independent, virtuous citizens was a favorite of Jefferson's, and he seldom missed an opportunity to repeat it. In *Summary View* (Chapter 2), Jefferson reminded the king that "America was conquered, and her settlements made and firmly established, at the expence of individuals, and not of the British public. Their own blood was spilt in acquiring lands for their settlement, their own fortunes expended in making that settlement effectual. For themselves they fought, for themselves they conquered, and for themselves alone they have a right to hold."[25] Twenty years later, in *Notes*, he praised farmers as "the chosen people of God, if ever he had a chosen people, whose breasts he has made his peculiar deposit for substantial and genuine virtue. . . . Corruption of morals in the mass of cultivators is a phaenomenon of which no age or nation has furnished an example."[26]

Only war, Jefferson had concluded by 1801, could prevent the United States from becoming a wealthy, secure nation, and if the powers of the national government were restricted to conducting a foreign policy freed from the need for armies and navies, Virginia (and the other states) would be free to concentrate on local matters. Were this to occur, the people—most of whom were farmers—would live their lives free of external controls beyond those to which they gave their consent. "Young as we are and with such a country before us to fill with people and with happiness," Jefferson said, "we should point in that direction the whole generative force of nature, wasting none of it in efforts of mutual destruction."

II

For a time, things went well, and the principles that Jefferson outlined in the inaugural address provided an effective guide to his actions. Forty-three-year-old Swiss-born Pennsylvanian Albert Gallatin assumed the task as secretary of treasury to eradicate the national debt while cutting the taxes that the Federalist-controlled Congress had imposed during the 1790s. As a three-term congressman, Gallatin had been instrumental in creating and using the House of Representatives' Ways and Means Committee to rein in Hamilton's programs.

As treasury secretary, Gallatin retained much of the structure of the office and left many of Hamilton's appointees in their posts, but he moved swiftly to reverse the first treasury secretary's program.[27] In his first report to Congress, Gallatin recommended appropriating over $7 million annually to debt retirement, a figure that represented approximately three-quarters of the nation's revenues. Initially, Gallatin calculated that it would take sixteen years to retire the debt at that rate of payment, but an unexpectedly brisk sale of public lands and windfall customs duties from expanded European trade later encouraged him to believe by 1803 that the debt might be paid off substantially earlier than his first estimates suggested.[28]

Behind the scenes, however, Jefferson instituted changes into government operations that began to deviate from the principles he outlined in his inaugural address, especially as he broadened the office of the executive from national leader to include the title of "party leader." Political scientist Robert M. Johnstone concludes that Jefferson's presidency was a "pioneering effort in erecting a working model of presidential leadership characterized by persuasion and the cultivation of influence."[29] Most importantly, Jefferson used his political party to enlarge the power of the executive office over political behavior. As a partisan leader, Jefferson acted pragmatically by shrewdly calculating his decisions based on what was possible, and used his personal influence on others to promote harmony and conciliation in government. Put succinctly, the Republican party made the Congress effective, and Jefferson dominated the actions of the Republican party.[30]

Historian Noble E. Cunningham makes similar points from a slightly different perspective. Jefferson's election brought few institutional changes into government, Cunningham argues, but rather inaugurated a fundamental change in the management of government. As the first effective party leader who became president, Jefferson exerted a stronger leadership role in the cabinet and the Congress than had either of his predecessors. More than Washington or Adams did, Jefferson oversaw governmental operations through frequent conversations with office heads and by directing the activities of the cabinet. His dinners, to which he invited mainly Republican congressmen and cabinet officers, were far from informal social gatherings; they were integral to Jefferson's process of government by which system, organization, and consultation prepared the way for effective legislation. Partisanship smoothed the way for every major action of the administration. "The functioning of government under Jefferson," Cunningham concludes, "rested on a party foundation. Republicans in Congress and throughout the country looked to the President as the national leader of the party, and the strength of his leadership depended heavily on the fact that the President and a majority of Congress belonged to the same party."[31]

Since the Republican party arose, in Jefferson's view, in order to wrest government from the hands of a minority faction intent on establishing monarchy and returned government into the hands of the people, it can be argued that the expansion of presidential powers as party leader do not deviate in important ways from the "federal and republican principles" he had emphasized in 1801. If that is the case, the first major deviation from the inaugural address came in 1803 with the Louisiana Purchase. On the surface, the addition of 830,000 square miles of land would appear to be lodged firmly in Jefferson's inaugural promise of stimulating agriculture by expanding dramatically the land available for farming. In fact, the acquisition of the Louisiana territory does not flow smoothly out of the inaugural address because it reversed Jefferson's emphasis on strict constitutional interpretation and frugality in government and also because it placed the first major stresses on party cohesion by not adhering strictly to these principles.

As early as March 1801, Jefferson heard rumors that New Orleans had changed hands from Spain to France. In October 1802, he learned that the French canceled the right of trade on the Mississippi River, thereby creating a foreign policy crisis for the United States. To U.S. Minister to France Robert Livingston, Jefferson wrote that the transfer of New Orleans from Spain to France "fixes the sentence which is to restrain her [France] forever within her low water mark." Reversing his (and Secretary of State James Madison's) principles that the United States should use France to break a dependence on Great Britain, Jefferson hyperbolized to Livingston, "From that moment we must marry ourselves to the British fleet and nation."[32]

Contemporaneous with this strong letter, Jefferson dispatched James Monroe to Paris to offer Napoleon Bonaparte as much as $10 million for New Orleans and Spanish possessions east of the Mississippi River (Florida, he hoped). Before Monroe could arrive, however, Napoleon told his finance minister to meet with Livingston and to work out the details of the transfer of New Orleans and everything France owned *west* of the Mississippi. When Monroe learned of this change in direction, he overcame doubts about violating his instructions and agreed that the United States would pay $15 million for the territory.

Why did Napoleon decide to sell property that he had only three years previously worked so hard to obtain? Traditional wisdom has it that Jefferson used the problems France was having in financing the wars of Europe in order to benefit from Napoleon's distress. Far more than the president realized at the time, however, the land purchase hinged less on American negotiations with Napoleon than the success of a slave rebellion in the French colony of Saint Domingue.

From the date of the secret treaty with Spain, the Treaty of San Ildefonso

(1800), Napoleon planned for Louisiana to be the base of a new French empire in North America, providing agricultural products for French possessions in the West Indies, the crown jewel of which was the colony of Saint Domingue. Containing more than three thousand sugar, cotton, indigo, tobacco, and cocoa plantations (one of them belonging to Napoleon's wife, Josephine), Saint Domingue had been in rebellion since 1791 due to a slave revolt led by Toussaint-Louverture. In December 1801, Napoleon's brother-in-law General Charles Victor Leclerc landed there with 20,000 French troops, but the slave armies and tropical diseases quickly decimated the French army. Leclerc managed to capture Louverture and send him to France where he subsequently died in jail, but the war continued without his leadership. When Leclerc himself succumbed to yellow fever in November 1802, French losses stood at more than 21,000 troops and 2 million francs without an end in sight.

In the words of Robert Paquette, "The strain of providing for Leclerq's expedition and the subsequent drain of resources to Saint Domingue disrupted operations in Louisiana that crucially depended on money, coordination, and timing." With the renewal of war with Great Britain looming, Napoleon decided to sell Louisiana to the United States rather than risk the possibility of British conquest and to "try to salvage what he could in Saint Domingue." Therefore, in Paquette's view, the sale of Louisiana hinged more on European than American considerations. Alexander Hamilton offered a similar analysis: "To the deadly climate of St. Domingo, and to the courage and obstinate resistance made by its black inhabitants are we indebted for the obstacles which delayed the colonization of Louisiana, till the auspicious moment, when a rupture between England and France gave a new turn to the projects of the latter, and destroyed at once all her schemes as to this favourite object of her ambition."[33]

As complicated as these issues were, in the end the acquisition of Louisiana required overcoming more domestic than foreign complications. Many Federalists opposed adding so vast a territory to the United States because they felt that its distance from the other states would make it difficult to govern. The need for money to pay for the purchase caused Gallatin to rely on Hamilton's establishment of the national credit to borrow from a London banking house the $15 million necessary for the purchase. As a result of the loan, the national debt soared to the highest point it would reach prior to the Civil War. The irony of the situation was certainly not lost on Hamilton, who gloated that "Republicans—the traditional opponents of government expenditures—were able to speak of a debt of $15 million as 'a triffling sum.'"[34]

In addition, opponents questioned the constitutionality of the purchase. Nowhere in the Constitution does it allow territory to be added by treaty without the consent of the inhabitants. Jefferson's answer to these charges is especially interesting in the light of his emphasis on "principles" of strict construction of the Constitution in his inaugural address. Writing to Kentucky senator John Breckinridge in August 1803, Jefferson acknowledged that "the executive . . . have done an act beyond the Constitution" and contemplated asking the Congress for ex post facto legislation or even an amendment to the Constitution to cover all the ambiguities. In the end, however, he opted for speed and convenience and asked the members of the House and the Senate to

> see their duty to their country in ratifying and paying for [the acquisition], so as to secure a good which would otherwise probably be never again in their power. . . . The Legislature in casting behind them metaphysical subtleties, and risking themselves like faithful servants, must ratify and pay for it, and throw themselves on their country for doing for them unauthorized, what we know they would have done for themselves had they been in a situation to do it. . . . I pretend no right to bind you [Congressmen should say to their constituents]: you may disavow me, and I must get out of the scrape as I can: I thought it my duty to risk myself for you. But we shall not be disavowed by the nation, and their act of indemnity will confirm and not weaken the Constitution, by more strongly marking out its lines.[35]

Ironically, after Jefferson's death John Marshall's Supreme Court—the branch of government that Jefferson constantly railed against as being the only one out of the power of the majority to control—validated the purchase in *American Insurance Company v. Canter* (1828) when it ruled that the Constitution confers on the national government "the power of acquiring territory, either by conquest or by treaty."

It is not surprising, therefore, that Jefferson took a full measure of satisfaction from the elections of 1804 as confirming his beliefs that the nation approved not only of the Louisiana Purchase but also of the other actions of his first administration. He lost only 14 of 176 electoral votes in the presidential election, and Federalist strength in the House and the Senate shrank to only about 20 percent of each body.[36] At the end of his second inaugural address, delivered in March 1805, the president alluded to the fact that "the union of sentiment now manifested so generally" would bring "harmony and happiness" to the nation and said that he anticipated that "our doubting brethren will at length see, that the mass of their fellow citizens, with whom they cannot yet resolve to act, as to principles and measures, think as they think, and desire what they desire."[37]

At the beginning of the address, he harkened back to the first inaugural ("I declared the principles on which I believed it my duty to administer the affairs of our Commonwealth") and affirmed, "My conscience tells me that I have on every occasion acted up to that declaration according to its obvious import and to the understanding of every candid mind." Still, he may have felt some lingering pangs of conscience concerning controversies surrounding Louisiana because early in the message he twice referred to the acquisition. In discussing the administration's reduction of taxes, he alluded to it indirectly when he wrote that taxes on foreign trade "enable us to support the current expenses of the government, to fulfil contracts with foreign nations, to extinguish the native right of soil within our limits, *to extend those limits*, and to apply . . . a surplus to our public debts" (*emphasis added*). Shortly thereafter, he referred to the acquisition directly: "I know that the acquisition of Louisiana has been disapproved by some, from a candid apprehension that the enlargement of our territory would endanger its union." The answer to this dissent comes next, couched in three rhetorical questions: "But who can limit the extent to which the federative principle may operate effectively? . . . [I]s it not better that the opposite bank of the Mississippi should be settled by our own brethren and children, than by strangers of another family? With which shall we be most likely to live in harmony and friendly intercourse?" Finally, he rephrased James Madison's argument in *Federalist* #10 that a large republic would prevent the formation of a large majority faction by saying that "[t]he larger our association, the less will it be shaken by local passions."

III

A second retreat from the principles Jefferson enunciated in his first inaugural address centers on that portion that promised "peace, honest friendship & commerce with all nations, entangling alliances with none." In 1803, the lull in the wars between Great Britain and France that had been so lucrative for American shipping ended, and the difficulties the United States had experienced under Washington's and Adams's administrations in steering a neutral path between the two great European powers returned with a vengeance. Those wars entered a far more difficult stage in 1805 when the British defeated a combined French and Spanish fleet at the Battle of Trafalgar and became ruler of the oceans. In that same year, Napoleon defeated a combined Austrian, Prussian, and Russian army at the Battle of Austerlitz and became master of the land. Increasingly, the United States became trapped between the British "shark" and the French "tiger." But because the British navy controlled the seas, Americans continued to feel the power of the former mother country more than their former ally. In the summer of 1807, while the president was home at Monticello, an event graphically demonstrated this fact when the H.M.S. *Leopard* attacked the U.S.S. *Chesapeake* just outside Norfolk harbor.

At the time of the attack on the *Chesapeake*, Jefferson was already preoccupied with another event that was taking up far more of his time than he would have wanted—Aaron Burr's trial for treason. The broad outlines of the Burr trial and Jefferson's direct involvement with it are easily summarized. In his December 1806 message to Congress, Jefferson asserted that Burr had led an expedition against Spanish provinces in the West and, thereby, involved his nation in an act of war. A grand jury in Frankfort, Kentucky, failed in December to indict Burr for committing acts of treason, as did one in Mississippi in February 1807. When Burr fled to West Florida, he was captured and taken to Richmond, Virginia, for trial because of the president's belief that a successful case could be made there that he had plotted treason in Ohio Territory, which was in Virginia's jurisdiction. At Richmond, however, Jefferson found himself at odds both personally and politically with both Burr and Chief Justice John Marshall, in whose district the trial now rested.

In a notable understatement, Merrill Peterson writes that Jefferson involved himself in the trial more actively "than constitutional duty alone seemed to require." More directly, Roger Kennedy concludes, "When Burr entered the southwest of his mind, Jefferson became unjeffersonian." A system of riders between Washington and Richmond kept him informed concerning the prosecution of the trial. He directed George Hay, the chief government prosecutor, to pardon any conspirator who would testify against Burr and authorized him to undertake "any expense necessary" to prosecute the trial. Undoubtedly aware of Jefferson's direct oversight of the case, Burr tried to have the president brought to Richmond to testify. Although Jefferson successfully avoided appearing at the trial, he conceded that he might have been compelled to testify, and he failed utterly to establish a case for treason under Marshall's strict interpretation of the Constitution. Consequently, Burr was set free on August 31.[38]

On June 25, during the time when he was under subpoena to appear in Richmond, Jefferson heard for the first time of the *Leopard*'s attack on the *Chesapeake*.[39] Although these two events occurred sequentially, most of Jefferson's biographers fail to pursue the fact that he viewed them as causally related. Jefferson believed that the British had carefully synchronized the two events to embarrass the administration or to provide the impetus for rallying pro-British Federalists to overthrow the government. Writing to his son-in-law (Virginia congressman John W. Eppes) on July 12, 1807, Jefferson said that the attack on "the *Chesapeake* seems to have come in as an interlude during the suspension of Burr's trial."[40]

As Peter Onuf points out, in his first inaugural address Jefferson had distinguished between Federalist leaders and followers, holding out the possibility that the former still adhered to "federal and republican principles." But as

president, Jefferson believed that punitive British foreign policies had embold-
ened many New England Federalists to propose sectionalist policies (including,
eventually, secession) in order "to destroy the union and forge an alliance with
their secret British sponsors. . . . [H]aving lost their national base of support,
the unreconstructed 'monarchists' exploited sectional grievances in order to
prepare the way for disunion and foreign alliances."[41]

Further, in Onuf's words, "[f]or Jefferson, Burr was a sort of honorary Federalist . . . who shared and acted on their notorious contempt for the 'federal and
republican principles.'" Adulatory correspondence from others reinforced the
president's beliefs. Republicans from Chenango County, New York, for example,
referred to "[f]oreign enemies and *domestic Traitors*: like Burr," and the Maryland legislature feared "the demon of conspiracy[,] the offspring of desperate
and abandoned men who backed by foreign aid expect to benefit and aggran-
dize themselves from the destruction of the Constitution which has exalted us
to our now elevated station."[42] Thus, the Burr trial offered Jefferson the opportunity to strike directly at both his internal and external enemies.

In early September, while at Monticello, he made the link between the British and Burr explicit. "[Burr] is preserved," he wrote to George Hay, "to become
the rallying point of all the disaffected and the worthless of the United States,
and to be the pivot on which all the intrigues and the conspiracies which foreign governments may wish to disturb us with, are to turn." To Thomas Paine:
"That war with us had been predetermined may be fairly inferred . . . being so
timed as to find us in the midst of Burr's rebellion as they expected." Finally, to
James Wilkinson: "The scenes which have been acted at Richmond are such as
have never before been exhibited. . . . They are equivalent to a proclamation of
impunity to every traitorous combination which may be formed to destroy the
Union; and . . . a centre for all the intrigues and machinations which foreign
governments may nourish to disturb us."[43]

As Burton Spivak notes, beginning in late June, a new tone appeared in
Jefferson's letters. His mood was "angry, . . . insistent, and strangely ebullient";
his "emotions . . . awakened in Jefferson an uncharacteristic fondness for strong
executive power."[44] As late as March 25, 1807, the president had suffered from
migraine headaches, the severity of which, in his words, left him "but an hour
and a half each morning capable of any business at all."[45] By the summer, however, the attack on the *Chesapeake* cleared his mind and charted his course. At
last the enemies of the nation would be known. War would unite the nation
in the same way as the shots fired at Lexington had in 1775. All ambiguities
were wiped away by the "extraordinary occurrence and the state of things that
brings on."[46]

On July 16, the president wrote to Virginia governor William H. Cabell
that "everyday is restoring to us our best means for carrying [war] on." Dur-

ing two weeks of cabinet meetings beginning in late July, Jefferson developed a strategy to invade Canada using militia units eligible for service in any state and laid plans for financing the war effort.[47] Beginning in August (perhaps to avoid problems he had encountered as Virginia's governor during the American Revolution [Chapter 3]), he undertook an almost daily correspondence with Cabell. Jefferson was careful to pledge the national government's support to cover Virginia's expenses in preparing for a possible British invasion while endeavoring simultaneously to conserve valuable supplies.[48] And when Cabell expressed hesitation to go beyond the letter of the law, as Jefferson had done while governor, the president demonstrated that he was willing to utilize executive powers to their fullest, as he had during his agonizings over the constitutionality of the Louisiana Purchase. "It is our consolation and encouragement that we are serving a just public," Jefferson wrote at the end of a long letter full of legal disputations, "who will be indulgent to any error committed honestly, and relating merely to the means of carrying into effect what they have manifestly willed to be a law."[49]

Confident that the British had timed their attack on the *Chesapeake* to correspond with the Burr trial, Jefferson decided to ask the Congress in the fall for war with Great Britain. On August 20, he wrote to Secretary of State Madison that "on the meeting of Congress, we should lay before them everything that has passed to that day, and place them on the same ground of information we are on ourselves. They will then have time to bring their minds to the same state of things with ours, and when the answer arrives, we shall all view it from the same position."[50] Eight days later, he wrote to the secretary of war, Henry Dearborn, that Indians in the Northwest should be apprized "that a misunderstanding having arisen between the United States and the English, war may possibly ensue."[51] On September 3, he informed Secretary of the Navy Robert Smith:

> I do not see the probability of receiving from Gr. Britain reparation for the wrong committed on the Chesapeake, and future security for our seamen, in the same favorable light with Mr. Gallatin & yourself. . . . [T]he present ministry, perhaps no ministry which can now be formed, will not in my opinion, give us the necessary assurance respecting our flag. . . . [I]n that case, it must bring on a war soon, and if so, it can never be in a better time for us. I look to this therefore as most probably now to take place.[52]

In early October, he wrote to Thomas Paine, "We shall never again have so favorable a juncture of circumstances," and confided to Attorney General Caesar Rodney, "[e]verything we see and hear leads in my opinion to war." Smith wrote to Jefferson on October 19 that his message to Congress would "present to them a ground upon which to found . . . war measures."[53]

Unhappily for Jefferson, the unanimity of purpose that he expected failed to materialize. As Spivak points out, in planning for war Jefferson had to keep his plans secret in order to keep the British from discovering them. Also, delaying the war declaration from the summer to the fall would allow American seamen and uninsured American commerce to return home. In addition, the president had to mask his objectives or risk losing the financial support of key investors.[54] Secrecy had the negative effect, however, of confusing congressmen and others of his supporters and leading them to believe that the administration was not doing anything to address the attack on the *Chesapeake*. By mid-August, Jefferson was also encountering problems with Smith, who worried about the effect of war on the nation's small navy and private shipping, and with Gallatin, who did not see how the government would cover its expenses during a war. By late summer, Secretary of War Henry Dearborn joined Smith and Gallatin when plans to create the militia force necessary for offensive purposes failed to materialize. Paraphrasing Spivak, both manpower and money proved to be elusive during the *Chesapeake* summer.[55]

When Gallatin saw Jefferson's draft of his October message to Congress, he characterized it as "a manifesto issued against the British government on the eve of a war" and openly opposed the president's plans. By November, when Jefferson realized that key Republican congressmen also had shown little enthusiasm for war, he backed away from the plans that he had spent the summer developing. On November 1, he reported to Cabell, "Here we are pacifically inclined, if anything comes which will permit us to follow our inclinations."[56]

In contrast to the first term, when consensus and compromise produced solutions, Jefferson found that the Congress found it difficult to agree on anything. Roll call analysis of voting in the Tenth Congress reveals that various blocs developed among Republican members, and confusion existed in all sections of the nation except for the South and the West. In addition, factional disputes in Pennsylvania, New York, and Maryland (perhaps in anticipation of the next presidential election) further divided the majority party into warring groups.[57]

Not only did the president retreat from his war stance but also he refused to provide the Congress with alternatives short of war. Rather, he reconciled himself to the Congress's "snail-paced gait for the advance of new ideas" and left Madison and Gallatin to work with the body. Thus the embargo that cleared the seas of American ships trading with Great Britain and France was likely more Madison's or Gallatin's idea than Jefferson's.[58]

Some measure of Jefferson's disappointment with the Congress's actions may be seen in his increased activism as president to enforce the new law. As Spivak and Drew McCoy argue, Jefferson's faith in man's moral capacity of self-government in a local setting gave way to a stronger view of the powers of the national government.[59] Jefferson thereby transformed the embargo from a defensive strategy to buy time to work out a more effective policy for dealing with the two belligerents into a policy of economic coercion, development of the home market, and isolation from Europe. When New Englanders violated the embargo by smuggling goods from Canada, Jefferson advocated that Secretary Gallatin take all measures necessary to arrest and punish the criminals. Resistance to the national authority, he urged, had to be met with force. But when the embargo failed to produce the desired result, Jefferson did not follow through with his threat to punish those who violated it.[60]

The subsequent war with England became "Mr. Madison's War" because Jefferson did not push the issue in 1809 when, again left to their own direction, Republican members of the Congress joined with Federalists to repeal the embargo without substituting war.[61] The War of 1812, which was the logical extension of Jefferson's policies in the summer of 1807, greatly increased the powers of the national government at the expense of the states, and at the end of the war Madison embraced most of Hamilton's economic program of the 1790s, including asking the Congress to charter a Second National Bank. This "Second War for American Independence" united the country and paved the way for a period of national expansion by using Republican means to achieve Federalist ends. Writing to Benjamin Austin in 1816, Jefferson said, "[E]xperience has taught me that manufactures are now as necessary to our independence as to our comfort; . . . in so complicated a science as political economy, no one axiom can be laid down as wise and expedient for all times and circumstances."[62] Thus did the Republican party abandon the "federal and republican principles" that Jefferson outlined in his first inaugural address.[63]

IV

Not only do scholars downplay Jefferson's belief that the British timed the attack on the *Chesapeake* to occur during Burr's trial but also they do not fully appreciate the fact that another, more personal, event directly involving the president occurred during August 1807—the conception of Eston Hemings. This occurrence offers a new platform from which to investigate Jefferson's retreat as president from the principles of his first inaugural address by focusing on his relationship with his Albemarle neighbors.

As discussed above, Jefferson used portions of his second inaugural address to note, and rebut, allegations that his acquisition of Louisiana had exceeded his presidential powers under the Constitution. Toward the end of the address, Jefferson observed that other controversies had also prevented there being perfect unanimity during his first term. "During this course of administration, and in order to disturb it," he wrote, "the artillery of the press has been levelled against us, charged with whatsoever its licentiousness could devise or dare." State laws might have been employed to counter the charges, he said, "but public duties more urgent press on the time of public servants, and the offenders have therefore been left to find their punishment in the public indignation." Shortly thereafter, he repeated the phrase "falsehood and defamation" and said that voters had answered the charges through the elections of 1804. "[B]y suffrage, they pronounced their verdict, honorable to those who had served them. . . . [T]he public judgment will correct false reasonings and opinions, on a full hearing of all parties. . . . If there be still improprieties which this rule would not restrain, its supplement must be sought in the censorship of public opinion."

In railing against "false and defamatory publications," the president perhaps referred to Federalist newspapers which frequently reprinted Jefferson's first inaugural address in order to subject it and its author to scathing criticism. The (Hartford) *Connecticut Courant*, for example, criticized the president in October and November 1801 for not living up to his promise to conciliate differences between Republicans and Federalists. "On your inauguration your flatterers announced the commencement of a new era which was to be a kind of political millennium; a period when the satan of discord and anti-republican principles was to be bound for a thousand years and cast into the bottomless pit; and the citizens of the United States, regenerated and exalted, should lose the imperfections of their nature, and live and reign in the enjoyment of uninterrupted blessedness, surrounded with the glories of their political savior." In spite of such promises, the president had removed Federalists from their positions and appointed Republicans.[64] Federalist newspapers responded with continued attacks on the president during the second term, especially in the wake of the Embargo of 1807.

It is also possible, however, that in this portion of the address Jefferson alluded to other charges that appeared not in New England Federalist newspapers but rather in the *Richmond Recorder* of September 1, 1802. There, disaffected Republican office-seeker James Thomson Callender reported that Jefferson "for many years has kept, as his concubine, one of his own slaves. Her name is SALLY [Hemings]."[65]

Although most of Jefferson's biographers disparage the accuracy of Callender's accusations, the validity of his charges received new credence when the November 1998 issue of *Nature* broke the news that DNA evidence establishes that a male Jefferson fathered Eston Hemings, one of Sally Hemings's five known children.[66] In the intervening years, a consensus position has emerged based on the DNA evidence; a newspaper interview in 1873 with Madison Hemings, Eston's older brother, just before his death; and a test of when Jefferson visited Monticello compared to the known conceptions of Hemings's children. In Annette Gordon-Reed's words, "[T]he third president of the United States, Thomas Jefferson, . . . fathered a family of children with Sally Hemings."[67]

The fact that Eston was conceived sometime in late August 1807 highlights the fact that despite the nationalistic impulses, including the movement toward war that he was orchestrating, Thomas Jefferson remained fixed in time and place. As Paul Rahe writes, "Despite the distaste that he expressed for the propensity of slaveholders and their relatives to abuse their power, Jefferson either engaged in such abuse himself or tolerated it on the part of one or more members of his family."[68]

Joshua Rothman raises similar issues in his suggestion that many of Callender's allegations in 1802 must have come from Jefferson's Albemarle neighbors. "That Callender got so much of the story right," Rothman writes, "is a remarkable testimony to the extent and transmission of social knowledge about private interracial sexual affairs in Virginia communities."[69] Rothman argues that white Virginians likely shared rumors and gossip with Callender because interracial sex was ubiquitous in both its variety and its notoriety. The most interesting part of Rothman's investigation is his conclusion that Callender's only error was to publicize the liaison, thereby "violat[ing] an unwritten cultural code by bringing the story out of the realm of gossip." Jefferson, by way of contrast, acted honorably by never publicly acknowledging the existence of the affair.[70] Only when interracial couples involved such public matters as personal finance, for example, as in the case of David Isaacs (a Jewish merchant in Charlottesville) and Nancy West (a free woman of color and a baker) did Virginians react negatively and expose the relationship to public scrutiny.[71]

Catherine Clinton's earlier research into southern mores supports Rothman's conclusions. According to Clinton, when Jefferson's father-in-law John Wayles became a widower, "he followed common practice among Colonial planters" by "[t]aking a woman of color as a bed mate." Betty Hemings (who was Wayles's wife's personal maid) saw five of her children by Wayles included in Martha Wayles's dowry to Jefferson, and one of them—Sally—followed "the prescribed southern custom" of becoming Martha's servant prior to her untimely death. "And as in the same instance," Clinton continues, "a home servant, more frequently mulatto than not, was the likeliest surrogate wife for a planter after the death of her mistress. Thus, if Sally Hemings had indeed become Thomas Jefferson's paramour and a mother of his children, they would have been well within a characteristic, virtually dynastic pattern of black and white sexual relations in the slave South."[72]

Instead of following Clinton's lead, Rothman instead folds his research into that of Bertram Wyatt-Brown concerning the cultural constraints under which a master might have sexual relations with a slave. According to Wyatt-Brown, a slave partner had to be sexually attractive to others, the slave owner had to be a man not given to other problems, and the man could neither acknowledge the liaison nor its offspring.[73]

In the end, Clinton's and Wyatt-Brown's investigations lead to the same point. As Rothman concludes, "Jefferson acted with sufficient discretion" that most of his neighbors did not object to his actions. "If there ever was such a thing in white eyes as the ethical amalgamator," Rothman concludes, "Thomas Jefferson was the prototype."[74]

The research of one of Jefferson's earliest biographers, Henry S. Randall, supports this line of investigation. Although Randall never specifically named the master of Monticello as the father of Sally Hemings's children, a close reading of his book and of Randall's personal correspondence suggests that Randall knew that he was.

In his 1858 biography, Randall disparaged Callender's character and impugned his motives but stopped short of negating his conclusions. Describing Callender as possessing "much coarse, vigorous ability," Randall lamented that "his course was steadily downward, owing to habits of inebriety and of consorting with vicious and degraded men" and concluded that Callender "[sank] into the impotence of a common blackguard . . . catering to the appetite for scandal in those who are beneath attack." Easily missed in this litany is Randall's admission that "[e]very enemy" of Jefferson's in Virginia "emptied into this ready conduit [i.e., Callender] all the old gossip, exploded calumnies and base suspicions which can be picked up among low neighbors and unscrupulous enemies in regard to any prominent man; and they swelled the putrid stream of such new and monstrous fabrications as they chose."[75]

While he was writing his *Life of Jefferson*, Randall corresponded with Virginia historian Hugh B. Grigsby, and their letters help to clarify why Randall chose the words he did. "By the by," Randall wrote to Grigsby in 1856, "[Callender] was helped by some of Mr. Jefferson's *neighbors*; . . . these are old stories, & I have not thought it advisable to rake them up one by one, & then attempt to prove *negitious*—that they were not true. . . . Still, I have written the whole biography with an eye steadily on those charges,—& taken the course which I thought would most effectually &, at the same time, most dignifiedly, refute them." In addition to portraying his subject in the best possible light (more on this in the Conclusion), Randall was conscious that his book was "considered 'authorized'" by Jefferson's family because Thomas Jefferson Randolph had allowed Randall to take many of his grandfather's papers to New York, and Randall corresponded frequently with other members of the family while he was writing his book.[76]

A subsequent biographer of Jefferson, James Parton, did not find this record completely satisfactory, because in the course of writing his 1874 biography Parton wrote to Randall concerning the paternity of Hemings's children. In response, Randall told Parton about a trip that he made to Monticello in 1868 with Thomas Jefferson Randolph when, according to Randall, the grandson tried to dispel allegations that his grandfather had a sexual relationship with Hemings. Randall recalled that while "walking about mouldering Monticello one day with [Randolph], he showed me a smoke blackened and sooty room in one of the collonades, and informed me it was Sally [Hemings's] room."[77] Identifying that room as Hemings's emphasized the distance between her chambers and his grandfather's. In addition, Randall reported that Randolph, especially, would have known if private encounters had occurred between the two persons because his room was so close to his grandfather's that "[he] slept within sound of his [grandfather's] breathing at night."[78]

In fact, the layout of Monticello casts considerable doubt on Randolph's story or Randall's telling of it. As genealogist Helen F. M. Leary explains, an 1802–3 reconstruction of the house added two hidden entrances from the dependencies below to the top floor. Slaves used a hidden stairway to move from below to ground level, and that stairway ended in a hallway outside Jefferson's study. Further, the reconstruction added porticles (louver-sided verandas) that hid the exterior entrance to Jefferson's study. "The porticles may not have been built specifically to facilitate Sally's nocturnal visits," Leary concludes, "but they certainly would have concealed them."[79]

Similarly, staff historians at Monticello confirm that in 1807, Sally Hemings was likely living in one of the south dependencies, between the main house and the "honeymoon cottage" where Jefferson had lived with his bride following their marriage in 1770, with easy access to the hidden stairway and, therefore, Jefferson's rooms. Finally, Jack McLaughlin's research casts doubt on Randolph's and Randall's reporting of sleeping arrangements at the mansion because no other bedrooms were close to the master's.[80]

An additional aspect of the letter Randall wrote to Parton deserves attention. Following Randall's inclusion of Randolph's denial of a relationship between his grandfather and Sally Hemings, Randall wrote cryptically to Parton regarding additional conversations that he had with two other nonfamily members who knew Jefferson well—his personal physician Dr. Robley Dunglison and University of Virginia professor George Tucker (more on Tucker in the Conclusion). Following Jefferson's death, both of these men moved to Philadelphia and met with Randall while he was writing his *Life*. "The secrets of an old Virginia Manor house were like the secrets of an Old Norman Castle," Randall wrote to Parton. "Mr. [Dunglison] and Professor Tucker had lived near Mr. Jefferson in the University, and were often at Monticello. They saw what others saw. But Dr. D told me that neither he nor Prof T. ever heard the subject named in Virginia. An awe and veneration was felt for Mr. Jefferson among his neighbors which in their view rendered it shameful to ever talk about his name in such a connexion."[81]

In conclusion, although we cannot say with complete certainty that Thomas

Jefferson fathered Eston, the timing of the conception is significant. In August and September 1807, Jefferson reached the height of his war preparations with Great Britain—a war that eventually reversed the principles he enunciated in his inaugural address—and his personal behavior at Monticello reveals how inextricably bound he was to the slaveholding culture of his time and place.

If, as seems most plausible, Callendar based his 1802 revelation of Jefferson's relations with Sally Hemings on inside information he received from Jefferson's neighbors, then in 1807 Jefferson's family and friends covered whatever they knew of the relations between Sally Hemings and Jefferson. Family-approved biographer Randall did likewise.

Earlier in his life, Jefferson grew angry at the refusal of his peers to adopt his ideas for changing Virginian society (Chapter 3 and Chapter 4). During the *Chesapeake* summer and throughout his retirement beginning in 1809, he must have felt the reverse and taken no small comfort in their silence. In the process, he demonstrated how firmly planted he remained in the habits of the Virginia gentry.

"[My] Country and It's Unfortunate Condition"

Continuing and Reversing Commitment to Change in Later Years

The final months of his presidency appear to have taken their toll on Jefferson's usually optimistic disposition. In March 1809, he wrote similar letters to several correspondents in which he expressed how anxious he was to leave Washington, D.C. For example, to Pierre Samuel du Pont de Nemours, he confided: "Within a few days I retire to my family, my books and farms. . . . Never did a prisoner, released from his chains, feel such relief as I shall on shaking off the shackles of power." To John Armstrong, "Within two or three days I retire from scenes of difficulty, anxiety, and of contending passions, to the elysium of domestic affections, and the irresponsible direction of my own affairs."[1]

On April 3, he responded to the well-wishes of his neighbors on his return to Monticello with these words:

> I gladly lay down the distressing burden of power. . . . [M]y happiness . . . will be complete, if my endeavors to fulfil my duties in the several public stations to which I have been called, have obtained for me the approbation of my country. The part which I have acted on the theatre of public life, has been before them; and to their sentence I submit it; but the testimony of my native country of the individuals who have known me in private life, to my conduct in its various duties and relations, is the more grateful, as proceeding from eye witnesses and observers, from triers of the vicinage. Of you, then, my neighbors, I may ask, in the face of the world, "whose ox have I taken, or whom have I defrauded? Whom have I oppressed, or of whose hand have I received a bribe to blind mine eyes therewith?" On your verdict I rest with conscious security.[2]

Viewed in one way, in asking his countrymen to approve of his actions "in the several public stations to which I have been called," Jefferson perhaps hoped that his service to the nation would finally clear whatever lingering doubts remained of the accomplishments of his terms as governor (Chapter 3). More notable, however, are his reference to his Albemarle County neighbors and friends as the "triers of the vicinage" and his quotation from 1 Samuel 12:1–4, the story of Samuel addressing his people when he raised Saul to govern them.

Because his close friend James Madison had succeeded him as president, Jefferson's allusions to Samuel's anointing of Saul may be apropos. Still, Jefferson's anger is unmistakable, harkening back not only to the trials of his governorship but also to his use of biblical themes in *Notes* to shake the complacency of his countrymen (Chapter 4) and perhaps whatever his friends and neighbors told James Callender about his relationship with Sally Hemings (Chapter 6).

In the years immediately following his retirement, however, his anger cooled. He immersed himself in the agricultural rhythms and the gentry lifestyle of Virginia. As he did while he was home in the 1770s and the 1790s, he charted the progress of the produce in his garden, recorded the temperature on his mountaintop three times a day, and extended the entries in his farm book (Chapter 1).

Then, in 1814, Jefferson plunged into a final major project, the creation of the University of Virginia. This chapter focuses on how Jefferson's plans for the university developed and examines his extreme disappointment that his peers stopped well short of what he envisioned for the school. Just as his plans for creating a system of state-funded education in the 1770s had fallen on barren ground, in the 1820s Jefferson once again felt the full measure of his countrymen's reluctance to change.

While he was overseeing the construction of what became the University of Virginia, Jefferson was also directing the completion of a house seventy-five miles south of Charlottesville on lands in Bedford County that he had gained from his father-in-law's estate. Poplar Forest, as he called it, served not only as his retreat from his routine at Monticello but also as a planned legacy to his grandchildren. The last part of the chapter addresses how his actions at Poplar Forest signaled the full measure of his personal retreat from fundamental change. At the end of his life, we confront a gentry squire deeply entwined in the major inconsistencies of his life and culture regarding slavery.

I

Given the depth of the opposition he received as an assemblyman in the late 1770s to his plans for educational reform in Virginia, why did Jefferson reopen the old wound in the last dozen years of his life? This question is not easily answered, not only because of the Virginia Assembly's reluctance to fund public education but also because of Jefferson's changing commitment to the issue.

Instead of adopting Jefferson's plan for public education, private schools sprang up in Virginia in the years following the American Revolution with various curricula designed by their founders. Then, "academies" arose for those who finished primary education, funded by tuition charged to the students' parents. In 1803, the Virginia Assembly chartered a grammar school for Albemarle County, but nothing came of the venture. Then, in February 1810, Federalist legislator Charles Fenton Mercer introduced legislation in the Virginia Assembly to establish a state literary fund that would have provided education for the state's poor children. By 1816, the reserves in the fund exceeded $1 million.[3]

Because Mercer was a Federalist, there were numerous partisan reasons for Jefferson to object to the creation of the literary fund, but he had philosophical differences with Mercer as well. On October 28, 1813, Jefferson wrote to John Adams (the same letter that appears in Chapters 1 and 5), and outlined his plans for educational reform in Virginia that the legislature had rejected in the 1770s. He proposed dividing "every county into wards of 5. or 6. miles square, like your townships"; and then creating "in each ward a free school for reading, writing and common arithmetic." Each ward would select annually a student to "receive at the public expence a higher degree of education at a district school." Similarly, the district schools would "select a certain number of the most promising subjects to be compleated at an University, where all the useful sciences should be taught."[4] Then follows a recapitulation of Jefferson's ideas in Query 14 of *Notes*, where he proposed that the state educate "youths of genius from among the classes of the poor," so that society would benefit from "those talents which nature has sown so liberally among the poor as the rich, but which perish without use, if not sought for and cultivated."[5]

This outline for educational reform contains two key elements designed to foment revolutionary change among his countrymen. In the first instance, university education would be simply the capstone of a comprehensive system of public-sponsored education. Writing in *Notes*, Jefferson says

> of all the views of this law none is more important, none more legitimate, than that of rendering the people the safe, as they are the ultimate, guardians of their own liberty. . . . Every government degenerates when trusted to the rulers of the people alone. The people themselves therefore are its only safe depositories. And to render them safe their minds must be improved to a certain degree. This indeed is not all that is necessary, though it be essentially necessary. An amendment of our constitution must here come in aid of the public education. The influence over government must be shared among all the people.

History, Jefferson proposed, would form the basis of this three-year curriculum in order to "qualify [people] as judges of the actions and designs of men; it will enable them to know ambition under every disguise it may assume; and know-ing it, to defeat its views."[6]

The key element here is the fact that, as noted in Chapter 4, Jefferson believed that assemblymen chosen from the gentry class were failing as public stewards because they were not involving the people sufficiently as protectors of their rights. Government had to sponsor public education, in other words, so that the people would question the government's actions. "[I]s the spirit of the people an infallible, a permanent reliance?" asks Jefferson rhetorically in Query 17 (Re-ligion) of *Notes*. "From the conclusion of [the American Revolution] we shall be going down hill. . . . [The people] will never think of uniting to effect a due respect for their rights. The shackles, therefore, which shall not be knocked off at the conclusion of this war, will remain on us long, will be made heavier and heavier, till our rights shall revive or expire in a convulsion."[7]

Jefferson's second reason for promoting elementary education extended the first. In his letter to Adams, Jefferson confides that his

> proposition [for educational reform] had for a further object to impart to these wards those portions of self-government for which they are best qualified, by confiding to them the care of their poor, their roads, police, elections, the nomination of jurors, administration of justice in small cases, elementary exercises of militia, in short, to have made them little republics of a country or state. A general call of ward-meetings by their Wardens on the same day thro' the state would at any time produce the genuine sense of the people on any required point, and would enable the state to act in mass, as your people have so often done, and with so much effect, by their town meetings.[8]

"[T]ime and reflection," he wrote in 1816 to Governor Wilson Cary Nicholas, strengthened this dedication to reforming society by dividing counties into wards and creating an elementary school in each ward. "My partiality for that division is not founded in views of education solely, but infinitely more as the means of a better administration of government, and the eternal preservation of its republican principles."[9]

Jefferson urged the Virginia Assembly to create the wards based upon militia units. These locally based companies would vote whether to raise and maintain these schools, which would have no higher authority over them than "the par-ents within each ward." By entrusting this governance to citizens at the lowest, local level, Jefferson returned to ideas he had formed much earlier in his life. In *Summary View* and *Notes*, he argued that government closest to the people should direct their affairs. In the midst of his struggle to create the Univer-sity of Virginia, this language resurfaced. "[T]he way to have good and safe government," he confided to Joseph Cabell, involved "distributing to every one exactly the functions he is competent to. . . . It is by dividing and subdividing these republics from the great national one down through all its subordinations, until it ends in the administration of every man's farm by himself, by placing under every one what his own eye may superintend, that all will be done for the best."[10]

Reforming education, in other words, marked only the first phase of a system that Jefferson designed to produce fundamental changes in government at all levels. If wards, counties, states, and the national government each stood "on the basis of law," their cumulative effect would check and balance government at all levels. The people would learn that they needed to exercise government "not merely at an election one day in the year," Jefferson argued, "but every day. . . . Begin [wards] only for a single purpose; they will soon show for what others they are the best instruments."[11]

Whereas Mercer's literary fund shared some aspects of Jefferson's educational plans (especially educating a few worthy, poor males at public expense), Jefferson's goals for using educational reform to change the behavior of his countrymen year-round were more far-reaching. By 1814, therefore, Jefferson and Mercer were working at cross-purposes to each other, as indicated by Jefferson's actions at a March 25, 1814, meeting of interested citizens in Charlottesville. The meeting had been called to revive plans for an academy for the town. In the words of one of the University of Virginia's historians, "Mr. Jefferson appeared on the street . . . just at this opportune time, and was invited to take part in the conference." Jefferson thereupon advised the group to abandon "their small scheme for a large one—a college where the sciences could be taught in 'a high degree'—and the first step, he told them, was to reorganize their board" to link the plans for a grammar school with Jefferson's for building a college.[12]

II

This change of emphasis—from creating a system of lower schools that would culminate in a college education for a few gifted students to what became a single-minded focus on creating a college located in Charlottesville first—deserves extended attention. A reorganization of the board followed, Peter Carr was elected president, and Jefferson became a trustee. The reorganized board met on April 5, followed by four additional meetings, but they concluded without issue. On August 19, "adjournment was taken to the third Friday in November." Evidently, the board never met again. On September 7, 1814, Jefferson wrote to Carr and advised him to drop the plans. On January 5, 1815, he wrote to Joseph C. Cabell, asking him to introduce a bill in the next Assembly to transfer the money raised for the grammar school to a new project to build a university instead.

The 1st or Elementary grade of education is not developed in this plan; an authority only being asked to it's Visitors for putting into motion a former proposition for that object. For an explanation of this therefore, I am obliged to add to these papers a letter I wrote some time since to Mr. Adams, in which I had occasion to give some account of what had been proposed here for culling from every condition of our people the natural aristocracy of talents & virtue and of preparing it by education, at the public expence, for the care of the public concerns.[13]

Reference to his October 1813 letter to Adams in his January 1815 letter to Cabell suggests the possibility that this letter to his old friend and rival provided the primary stimulus for Jefferson's devotion to educational reform. There are, however, other explanations for the timing of his push.

The most interesting aspect of this intense activism beginning in the fall of 1814 concerns the fact that his devotion to founding the University of Virginia contrasts so sharply with his passivity and resignation in most other areas that also would have benefited from his attention. It is as if he had displaced his frustration with the Virginia gentry's other failings into hopes for this one reform. Indeed, he had. "This corporeal globe, and everything upon it," he wrote to Samuel Kercheval in 1816, "belong to its present corporeal inhabitants, during their generation." In 1819, he confided to Spencer Roane that he wished to "withdraw from all contests of opinion, and resign everything cheerfully to the generation now in place." In 1824, he spoke even more directly to his situation by writing, "I willingly acquiesce in the institutions of my country, perfect or imperfect; and think it is a duty to leave their modifications to those who are to live under them, and are to participate of the good or evil they may produce. The present generation has the same right of self-government which the past one has exercised for itself."[14]

His withdrawal was even more pronounced with respect to efforts to abolish slavery—another reform that he had pushed on his peers in the Assembly following the Declaration of Independence. In May 1815, he wrote to David Barrow that slavery in the South could not be ended for many years. Because slavery was so "deeply seated" and "incorporated with the whole system [of society]," abolition would require "time, patience, and perseverence in the curative process." Drawing on a theme begun in *Notes* (Chapter 4) but now with the opposite conclusion, Jefferson hinted that the system might be beyond the power of people to change. "We are not in a world ungoverned by the laws and power of a superior agent. Our efforts are in his hand, and directed by it; and he will give them their effect in his own time."[15]

Even when he answered appeals from members of the Virginia gentry, Jefferson refused to become involved in attempts to end slavery in his state. In August

1814, Jefferson wrote one of the most remarkable letters of his life to Edward Coles, the person who was largely responsible for rekindling Jefferson's friendship with Adams. Like Jefferson, Coles was born near Charlottesville but was forty-three years younger. Also like Jefferson, Coles had attended the College of William and Mary where, as a student, he determined to free his slaves at some point in his life. In 1814, he was moving to act upon his earlier resolve and wrote to Jefferson to enlist the elder man's aid in the task of promoting legislation for that purpose.

Jefferson demurred. "I have outlived the generation with which mutual labors & perils begat mutual confidence and influence," he wrote. "It shall have all my prayers, & these are the only weapons of an old man." More than this, he advised Coles to "reconcile yourself to your country and its unfortunate condition; that you will not lessen its stock of sound disposition by withdrawing your portion from the mass. . . . And you will be supported [in this decision] by the religious precept, 'be not weary in well-doing.'"[16]

Coles did not follow his elder's advice. In 1820, he broke the chains of his past, left Virginia with his family and property, and moved to Illinois, where he freed his ten slaves. In 1822, he was elected governor of the state on an antislavery ticket and successfully defeated efforts to permit slaveholding there. In 1833, he moved to Philadelphia, where he joined with antislavery friends to work to end slavery in the nation.[17]

By pointing up reforms that he and his society had failed to accomplish, the letter from Coles must have caused his mentor considerable pain. Like Coles, Jefferson might have left his country and its slaveholding society rather than endure its evils. Instead—and likely prodded by Coles's letter more than the one from Adams—Jefferson used the final years of his life to push for his educational reforms. As noted above, the board of advisors for the Albemarle Academy adjourned on August 19 and was scheduled to meet in November, but in September Jefferson wrote to Carr and suggested canceling that meeting. It was during this intervening period that Coles's letter arrived.

Although directed to Coles, the scriptural reference "grow not weary in well-doing" should be seen as primarily self-reflective, and recapturing the commitment to reform he had begun following the American Revolution. If this is the case, the context for the quotation—2 Thessalonians 3—requires scrutiny, beginning with verse 6:

> . . . withdraw yourselves from every brother that walketh disorderly.
> . . . For yourselves know how ye ought to follow us: for we behaved not
> ourselves disorderly among you; neither did we eat any man's bread for
> naught; but wrought with labor and travail night and day. . . . For we hear
> that there are some which walk among you disorderly, working not at all,

but are busybodies. Now them that are such we command and exhort by our Lord Jesus Christ, that with quietness they eat their own bread. But ye, brethren, be not weary in well doing. And if any man obey not our word by this epistle, note that man, and have no company with him, that he may be ashamed.

Of special note in this passage—and reminiscent of Jefferson's address to the citizens of Albemarle County in April 1809—is the anger contained therein. Thessalonica, according to biblical scholars, had become filled with idlers who toiled not for themselves but rather "worked" zealously over other people's affairs. The apostle pointedly chided these busybodies to shut up and get to work; the message to the faithful ones was similar. According to the authors of the *Interpreter's Bible*, the text shifts back and forth between those who are being censured for their disorderly and meddlesome lives and those who are being commended for their fidelity. The latter should "not become weary in their right living. They are surrounded by those who annoy them and make it difficult for them to persevere. However, they are enjoined to continue steadfast and faithful in their daily lives." Although it would be difficult for them, Paul advised the apostles to persevere in their work, having as little as possible to do with the others.[18]

Founding the University of Virginia, in other words, would force the gentry to accept responsibility for their earlier shortcomings and at the same time exonerate Jefferson from his earlier failed efforts. Similarly, the creation of the university would address other problems with which his society wrestled in addition to the training of its youth in science and politics.

In Jefferson's mind, creating the college was necessary by the 1810s because the College of William and Mary was declining in stature rapidly, chiefly in its training of new lawyers. In erecting a curriculum devoted to "useful sciences," Jefferson hoped further to influence the new generation of Virginia's leaders by turning their reading and instruction from William Blackstone and David Hume to John Locke, Sir Edward Coke, and American texts, mixed with natural philosophy and history, mathematics, anatomy and medicine, moral philosophy, and ancient and modern languages. "I fear nothing for our liberty from the assaults of force," he wrote in 1814, "but I have seen and felt much, and fear more from English books, English prejudices, English manners, and the apes, the dupes, and designs among our professional crafts. When I look around me for security against these seductions, I find it in the wide spread of our agricultural citizens, in their unsophisticated minds, their independence and their power, if called on, to crush the Humists of our cities, and to maintain the principles which severed us from England."[19] "You remember," he wrote to Madison a few months prior to his death, "that our lawyers were then all whigs. . . . Nearly all the young brood of lawyers now are all [tories]. They suppose themselves, indeed, to be whigs, because they no longer knew what whiggism or republicanism means. It is in our seminary [the University of Virginia] that that vestal flame is to be kept alive; it is thence to spread anew over our own and the sister States."[20]

Two points deserve attention. First, as David N. Mayer explains, Jefferson devoted himself to implementing English Whigs' views of history and government, which Mayer identifies as "profound distrust of concentrated political power and, with it, an especially intense devotion to the ideal of limited government." Jefferson's ire fell especially on David Hume because of Hume's "apology" for the actions of the arbitrary Stuart kings who ignored ancient ideas concerning rights. Instead, Jefferson valued the Saxons and their defense of political rights against monarchical pretensions.[21]

Second, Jefferson's use of the term "seminary" in connection with the founding of the university is striking, especially in the light of his insistence that the students' studies center on "useful sciences." Jefferson intended for the students at the university to learn to form conclusions about the world, as he had, based on observation and not from the opinions or beliefs of others. University training would break the students' prior education that generally involved primarily studying the Bible. Therefore, in October 1822, Jefferson found it especially troublesome that some people pressed the rectors of the university to include the teaching of religion in the curriculum. On October 7, the rectors discussed this subject and decided that denominations would be encouraged to form buildings for instruction near the university but not on its grounds. "Such an arrangement," Jefferson recorded in his notes of the meeting and amplifying on the point made in his 1813 letter to Adams, "would . . . leave inviolate the constitutional freedom of religion, the most inalienable and sacred of human rights, over which the people and authorities of this state, individually and publicly, have ever manifested the most watchful jealousy."[22]

As he had in the Revolutionary period, Jefferson believed that republican government, education, and religious freedom saved society from slavish devotion to centralized government and state-sponsored churches. As law students and the others at the university studied "science" and banished "emperors, kings, princes, and nobles as [well as] popes, cardinals, archbishops, and priests," they would lead their country as earlier generations had. "[W]ithin twelve or fifteen years from this time," he confidently wrote in 1825, "a majority of the rulers of our State will have been educated here. They shall carry hence the correct principles of our day, and you may count assuredly that they will exhibit their country in a degree of sound respectability it has never known, either in our days, or those of our forefathers."[23]

III

Jefferson's plans, altered after 1814 to focus on creating the University of Virginia at Charlottesville, placed him in direct opposition to Charles Fenton Mercer's plans for the literary fund. On February 8, 1817, Mercer introduced a bill to create a primary school in each township where all free, white children would be educated at state expense, and forty-eight academies for boys and three for girls. Mercer also proposed that any surplus money in the literary fund that might exist after these schools had been created would be distributed among four colleges located throughout the state as well as a central university. Mercer's bill passed the House and went to the Senate to a committee chaired by Jefferson's friend and associate in planning for the creation of the University of Virginia, Joseph C. Cabell.

According to Mercer's biographer, Douglas Egerton, educational funding at this point became deeply entwined with regional tensions and political partisanship. Cabell was able to secure opposition to Mercer's plans from delegates from eastern counties where children were already educated privately and, therefore, would not benefit from the new system. Cabell also believed that Mercer's educational plans sought to boost Federalist strength in western Virginia and were linked to another scheme to create three new state banks to help western investors. In Egerton's words, "The Federalists, routinely excoriated as the party of reactionaries, elitists, and monarchists, were now championing an issue that allied them with the middle and lower classes, who certainly desired free schools." Fearful that industrialization "would make class divisions more severe," Mercer, according to Egerton, sought to create a middle class that would ameliorate divisions in Virginia's social classes. Cameron Addis agrees that Jefferson's collaborations with Cabell marked a complete change of direction in his thinking. "Forced to choose between primary and higher education," Addis writes, "Jefferson acted politically to defeat primary school measures in the late 1810s. . . . He never admitted it, but he now viewed the different levels of schooling in conflict, rather than in conjunction with one another."[24]

By February 1820, Cabell had devised a plan to favor higher education at the expense of everything else. "It is contemplated," he wrote to Jefferson, "to amend [the literary fund], so as to provide that the appropriation for the University shall not interfere with any further appropriation that may be necessary for the education of the poor." When the income from the fund reached $60,000, Cabell proposed that $15,000 be committed to the university, leaving the remainder for the poor. But he was thinking ahead also. "If this bill passes," he continued, "perhaps, our policy will be to invest all our funds in buildings, and get them as far advanced by August as possible . . . [because] Virginians could never be pleased with anything on a small scale." By the end of 1820, Jefferson estimated the cost of buildings for the university in excess of $160,000, and

Cabell was able to secure legislation to borrow that amount incrementally from the literary fund. Further loans for building the Rotunda and other buildings followed.[25]

Although Jefferson and Cabell were able to raise the money necessary to build the University of Virginia, Jefferson still chafed at the fact that the Assembly refused to grant direct funding to the university. In 1818, he confided to Albert Gallatin that his plans for the university were encountering "ignorance, malice, egoism, fanaticism, religious, political and local perversities."[26] Acknowledging that his system would be expensive to operate, Jefferson still believed that the costs were minor, even for the gentry who would bear much of the expenses of the reforms. He complained that many "wealthy members of the counties" viewed his proposals as "a plan to educate the poor at the expense of the rich." In fact, nothing could have been farther from the truth, he wrote to Cabell in 1818:

> When [a wealthy individual's] descendants become poor, . . . their children will be educated by the then rich, and the little advance he now makes to poverty, while rich himself, will be repaid by the then rich, to his descendants when become poor, and thus give them a chance of rising again. . . . It [the educational system] is a provision for his family looking to distant times, and far in duration beyond that he has now in hand for them. Let every man count backwards in his own family, and see how many generations he can go, before he comes to the ancestor who made the fortune he now holds. Most will be stopped at the first generation, many at the 2d, few will reach the third, and not one in the state will go beyond the 5th.[27]

Perhaps it was because Jefferson saw his own estate slipping away—an estate built largely on the efforts of his father in securing fertile lands for his son—that he pushed so hard for his reforms. And because he saw things so clearly, his disappointment must have been all the greater. Six months prior to his death, he confided to Cabell that he felt like he "was discharging the odious function of a physician pouring medicine down the throat of a patient, insensible of needing it."[28] Instead of heeding his advice, his peers insisted on clinging to their old ways, determined (in Drew McCoy's words) "to protect their privileged position."[29]

IV

Despite the considerable attention Jefferson paid to creating the University of Virginia, he also found time during his retirement from the presidency to oversee the final construction and furnishing of a private retreat in Bedford

County that he named Poplar Forest. In 1781, on the run from British troops who nearly captured him and the other state officials at Charlottesville, Jefferson hid out at the overseer's house on this plantation and used the time to begin composing *Notes* (Chapter 4).[30] On September 29, 1805, he noted in his *Memorandum Book* that he would pay Hugh Chisholm, one of his most trusted workers, twenty dollars per month to begin construction of a house for him on the property.[31] Constructed in the shape of an octagon, Poplar Forest emerged slowly over the ensuing years.

By the time of Coles's letter in the summer of 1814, the house and its service wing were largely complete. In the summer of 1816, a visitor remarked on the polished oak floors, the lofty ceilings in the four octagonally shaped and one square-shaped room in the center of the octagon, and large mirrors that covered the walls in the room facing south, where Jefferson most commonly entertained his guests.[32] But he also encountered numerous problems that demanded his attention. Although Chisholm was a competent bricklayer and carpenter, many of the other workers on the building—including Jefferson's slaves on the plantation—were not. The octagon shape of the house required that special bricks be made for its corners, and many of them turned out to be unusable (they ended up in the basement, forming the floor and walls of the wine cellar).[33]

Because Bedford was a working plantation, house construction and attention to the master and his family when they were there meant that slaves had to spend time away from the fields. Also, despite attempts to create a garden near the house, inattention and irregular visits meant that Jefferson had to buy most of the food he consumed when he spent time there, including purchasing provisions from his slaves.[34] In 1819, a devastating hailstorm (with stones the size of partridge eggs, according to some accounts) left extensive damage to the roof and skylights in addition to the triple-hung sash windows throughout the house.[35]

Jefferson had multiple reasons for building Poplar Forest. First, as architectural historian Fiske Kimball notes, in designing the house Jefferson was able to continue to indulge his interest in architecture while creating a personal villa, or "country retreat" in the wilderness. Viewed from this perspective, Poplar Forest was his last construction of himself as a member of the Virginia gentry:

> The designs for Poplar Forest . . . were further experiments along the general lines of Monticello, always with an octagonal projecting salon in the center of one facade. They show a progressive increase in size, with a doubling of the rooms along lateral passages, similar to the development of Monticello itself. Here, however, Jefferson was not hampered by exist-

ing walls and was able to carry through a logical system in the grouping of the bed alcoves along the passages, and in other matters. The most elaborate of the series has an octagonal room on each side, with a complete theoretic symmetry on both axes.[36]

Also, as Kimball and others note, the construction of Poplar Forest gave Jefferson the opportunity to experiment with landscape architecture. The broad, sunken lawn at the rear of the house and the east and west artificial mounds provided a practical dumping spot for the dirt from the lawn and hid two "necessaries" from view. Around these privies, Jefferson planted mulberry trees to screen them from the nearby circular road; on top of them he "planted 5. Calcanthuses" and "4. Monticello aspens at the N. foot of the W. Mound & 3. do. At the N. foot of the E. Mound."[37]

A second reason for constructing the house relates to Jefferson's inveterate consumerism. Recent archaeological excavations at Poplar Forest reveal that although Jefferson was by this time hopelessly unable to control his spending, he continued to indulge his love of fine things. Despite his growing financial insolvency, he filled his new house with furniture, ceramics, and crystal that he ordered from different groups of English merchants than he had used for furnishing Monticello.[38] Writing years after her last trip to Poplar Forest with her grandfather, Ellen Randolph Coolidge recalled that "[i]t was furnished in the simplest manner, but had a very tasty air; there was nothing common or second-rate about any part of the establishment, though there was no appearance of expense." Also, he installed embellishments adapted from designs that were being prepared for the pavilions at the University of Virginia in the dining room and anterooms of Poplar Forest.[39]

Finally, as the quote from Ellen indicates, the house also provided Jefferson with an opportunity to spend time with his grandchildren, most typically away from their parents. He took Thomas Jefferson Randolph (age 19 at the time of his first visit) with him to the house in late 1811. His sisters Ellen (age 10) and Cornelia (age 17) went in 1816; Virginia (age 16), in 1818; and Mary (age 16), in 1820. Brother James (age 13) visited the retreat in 1819. Undoubtedly, part of the reason for having the children accompany their grandfather was to assist him while he was there, much in the same way that Martha helped by moving into Monticello with her family after Jefferson's retirement as president in March 1809. In 1856, Ellen recalled that "[h]is young grand-daughters were there to enliven [Poplar Forest] for him, to make his tea, preside over his dinner table, accompany him in his walks, in his occasional drives, and be with him at the time he most enjoyed society, from tea till bed time."[40]

To make life in the house as comfortable for his grandchildren as possible, Jefferson had to redesign the interior to separate their living quarters from the activities of the slaves, who cooked the food and brought it to table. In the process, he revealed much about himself and his attitudes toward his slaves.

The important research of University of Virginia architectural historian Camille Wells documents how Virginia planters changed the layout of their houses during the early national period due to changed attitudes toward slavery. Whereas in most eighteenth-century Virginia houses slaves and masters "used the same on-axis doorways and passages" and "slaves might be *anywhere* in their owners' houses," domiciles built after the turn of the century separated the functions of the two groups by side entrances and back service stairs in order that slaves might pass unseen in and out of the house. An interesting case in point concerns William Randolph's plantation at Tuckahoe where Jefferson spent his earliest years. During the 1700s, slaves mixed with the family and guests in their comings and goings, but after 1800 the house was modified by adding a doorway into a gable end of the house and thereby provided a separate service route into the dining room. More frequently, according to Wells, slave masters built closets, vestibules, and pantries "where slaves could wait until called," added architectural baffles to block the view between one section of their household and another; installed louvered panels to hide from view work being done in service passages and in the yard; and added "back stairs, multiple passages, side doorways, [and] solid partitions" to their dwellings. Whereas the fronts of nineteenth-century Virginia houses "had proper facades with orderly arrangements of doors and windows," the backs of the houses became a tangle of "wings, ells, stairs, and open or enclosed galleries, the principal purpose of which was to bear the traffic of slaves going about their household chores."[41]

As noted in Chapter 6, Jefferson built Monticello in conformity to the newer, not the older style. House slaves came and went without much direct contact with the house's inhabitants, especially after the slave dependencies were added under the pavilion after 1805. Jefferson's architectural designs at Poplar Forest, however, initially reversed this layout and were far closer to the configuration of earlier rather than later houses. Slaves who accompanied him and his family there lived on the ground floor of the main house, and whenever Jefferson visited the house, slaves came into intimate contact with the family, especially his granddaughters. Also, because Jefferson's original plans for the house did not include any ways to enter the house except either from the front or rear of the house, slaves brought food into the dining room at the center of the house by entering through the front door.[42]

In 1808, however, Jefferson added stairways to the eastern and western sides of the house, and in 1814 had a row of service rooms ("offices," he called them) constructed that contained a kitchen and smokehouse, among other dependencies. His granddaughters occupied the bedroom adjacent to the eastern stair-

5. The East Stairwell at Poplar Forest. Jefferson redesigned his original configuration of Poplar Forest first by adding stairwells on the east and west sides of the structure and then by creating an entrance into the east stairwell from a series of outbuildings (including the kitchen). The reconfiguration caused the bed in the room to be enclosed and added an area for food preparation and storage. Courtesy of Thomas Jefferson's Poplar Forest.

way, which meant that slaves had to pass through the girls' room to bring food into and out of the house.

In 1817, he reconfigured access to the upper floor by adding an entryway from the terrace above the outbuildings to the eastern stairway and likely created a pantry out of their bedroom area where food could be prepared and other supplies stored.[43] In other words, once his granddaughters began to accompany him to the house, he substantially redesigned the house so they would not have to interact directly with the slaves who served them.[44]

It is in this context that it is important to note that the admonition "be not weary in well-doing" that Jefferson used in his 1814 letter to Coles occurs not once in the Bible but twice. In Galatians 6, the phrase also appears, and it is in a radically different context—less angry and more hopeful—than in 2 Thessalonians: "Be not deceived; God is not mocked: for whatsoever a man soweth, that shall he also reap. For he that soweth to his flesh shall of the flesh reap corruption; but he that soweth to the Spirit shall of the Spirit reap life everlasting. And let us not be weary in well doing: for in due season we shall reap, if we faint not." "Sowing and reaping" were never very far from what Jefferson held most dear, and biblical scholars comment that both are social as well as individual activities. Self-centered people aim only at maximizing life for themselves, rather than for others, and measure their wealth in terms of immediate rewards. Altruists (men of "virtue," Jefferson might have said) who do not grow weary working for others also gain their reward at the end of a life devoted to giving. According to the *Interpreter's Bible*, "[M]en of faith have every reason to engage in the 'agriculture of the Spirit.' The first half of the verse is the sower's imperative: keep on doing good; the second clause is the sower's reward: life at harvesttime."[45]

In giving his time to his granddaughters and in trying to save the estate for younger daughter Maria's only surviving son, Francis Eppes, Jefferson may have felt he was sowing for the future of his family as he had for his countrymen's sons at the University of Virginia. If so, plans for his family did not work out perfectly either. A year prior to his death, Ellen married a man from Boston and moved there to live. As for Francis, although he inherited Poplar Forest, the value of his inheritance had been greatly reduced by the sale of lands to try to pay off his grandfather's debts, and a hoped-for sale of lottery tickets to pay off the balance of the encumbrances did not materialize. Writing to cousin Virginia's husband in November 1826, Francis decried the fact that

> liberality and generosity, and patriotism of the old Dominion, is on the wane. . . . Yankee notions, and Yankee practices, have wrought a thorough change in the public mind. . . . You may depend, that the settling of this hard-hearted, copper souled race of tin pedlars amongst us, has had a great effect in poisoning the public minds; and that added to the continued emigration of the old settlers from the state, and the more equal distribution of property, has smothered the flame which once burnt in our bosoms.

Two years later, he wrote with even more emotion, reminiscent of his grandfather's ire at the behavior of his cohort: "I see no ties which should bind any descendants of our grandfather to this state. The people are cold to his memory, the soil is exhausted, the staple [tobacco] reduced almost to the prime cost of the materials. . . . What inducement is there to remain!"[46] In May 1829, Francis took his own advice and moved his family to Florida.[47]

V

Sometime near the end of his long life, Thomas Jefferson designed his burial marker and composed his epitaph:

> on the grave a plain die or cube of 3 f. without any mouldings, surmounted by an obelisk of 6 f. height, each of a single stone: on the faces of the obelisk the following inscription, & not a word more

'Here was buried
Thomas Jefferson
Author of the
Declaration of Independance
of the Statute of Virginia
for
religious freedom
& Father of the
University of Virginia'

> because by these, as testimonials that I have lived, I wish most to be remembered.[48]

The three items on Jefferson's epitaph indicate that he was fortunate to have lived until 1826. In founding the University of Virginia, he was able to finish his life with a sense of personal fulfillment. Posterity would see in the contents of the epitaph that he had devoted his life to the right of people to separate themselves from the past. Surely, whatever anger Virginians might feel toward their ancestors' inability to live up to the full measure of the possibilities that freedom from Great Britain promised would fall on his peers rather than on himself.

In his devotion to Poplar Forest, however, Jefferson demonstrated that he was not as far removed from the behavior of his countrymen as he might have wished. Until the end of his life, he continued to live well at the expense of others. At Poplar Forest, he toiled for his white family but not for his slave family. Ellen moved to Boston, Francis to Florida, but those who did the actual sowing and reaping at Poplar Forest and at Monticello—except for the children named Hemings (not Jefferson), who received their freedom but little else—continued to live in bondage after his death, only working for different masters.

Thomas Jefferson accomplished many things in his life, but other promises that he might have achieved, especially working after his retirement as president to abolish slavery, remained unfulfilled. By the end of his life, he had long since reconciled himself to his "country and it's unfortunate condition."

Conclusion

"Whether My Country Is the Better for My Having Lived at All?"
Changing the Meaning of Jefferson's Life

Around the time he was elected as the third president of the United States, Thomas Jefferson ruminated about his contributions to his country, Virginia. "I have sometimes asked myself," he wrote, "whether my country is the better for my having lived at all? I do not know that it is." He listed many projects that he had advanced, including improved navigation of the Rivanna River, the Declaration of Independence, the act abolishing entails and extending inheritance to all children, and legislation ending the importation of slaves. He wrote that he was the primary "instrument" for several on his list, but he was not willing to take total credit for them. Many, he said, "would have been done by others" and added, "some of them, perhaps, a little better." He acknowledged, for example, that the statute for religious freedom passed "by the efforts of Mr. Madison"; concerning a bill he drafted "apportioning crimes and punishments" that passed the Assembly in 1796, Jefferson wrote that the author had to change "the diction of mine" to get it passed. As for legislation he offered "for the more general diffusion of knowledge," he could not say if it would "ever be carried into complete effect."[1]

Aside from two paragraphs in which he discussed securing agricultural products for South Carolina and Georgia, Jefferson devoted the entire memorandum to his contributions to Virginia. As "Note G" in the first edition of his papers (1829), however, it appears in the context of his contributions to the nation, not his country. Thomas Jefferson Randolph made the decision to switch the meaning, and this shift from a local to a national context has shaped most of the commentaries on Jefferson's life ever since. In exploring Randolph's decision, we encounter not only a devoted grandson intent on trying to salvage his grandfather's estate but also a defining moment when emphasis veered from Jefferson's concerns about his contributions to his country to considerations about his legacy for his nation.

I

As early as 1813, Randolph began taking increased responsibility over his grand-father's financial affairs. He was named Jefferson's sole executor following his death and vowed to pay off the debts of the estate, first by selling personal prop-erty, including the slaves. This decision, Randolph later wrote, "was a sad scene. I had known all of them from childhood and had strong attachments to many of them." Shortly thereafter, Monticello itself had to be sold, and Randolph then decided to publish selections of Jefferson's papers as a way of raising money.[2] Several family members objected to Randolph's plan, as did others. Edward Ev-erett suggested that a well-chosen edition published at a future date might raise $100,000, and James Madison also advised a later publication on a subscrip-tion basis. "Probably all of this was excellent advice," according to Randolph's biographer, "but the editor, with his pressing financial obligations, did not feel that he could wait." Initially, an Albany publishing house suggested trying for forty thousand subscriptions, but the offer never materialized; neither did one from another publisher in Boston. In October 1828, Randolph arranged with F. Carr and Company in Charlottesville to print the book, with the proviso that he would personally offer it for sale. The first volume appeared the following spring as *Memoir, Correspondence, and Miscellanies, from the Papers of Thomas Jefferson*.[3]

In the preface to Volume 1, Randolph wrote that as executor of his grandfa-ther's estate and "Legatee of his Manuscript Papers" he believed "that an exten-sive publication from them would be particularly acceptable to the American people." The "memoir," subsequently published as Jefferson's *Autobiography*, would inform Americans about the debates in the Second Continental Con-gress "on the great question of Independence" and "though in compressed form, present the substance of what passed on that memorable occasion." Following the "memoir," readers would find "[n]otes of conversations whilst Secretary of State, with President Washington, and others high in office; and memo-randa of cabinet Councils, committed on paper on the spot, and filed; the whole, with the explanatory and miscellaneous additions, showing the views and tendencies of parties, from the year 1789 to 1800" (later published as the *Anas*). Finally, Randolph stated that Jefferson's correspondence with various other dignitaries of the early Republic would demonstrate Jefferson's "genius, the learning, the philosophic inspiration, the generous devotion to virtue, and the love of country."[4]

Randolph began Jefferson's correspondence in Volume 1 on page 147 with a letter of May 7, 1775, to William Small in which the former student detailed to his mentor problems the colonies faced, specifically the situation as it existed in Boston. Five letters followed this one concerning the causes of separation with England, twenty-eight to George Washington (from June 23, 1779, through May 28, 1781), six to General Horatio Gates, and ten to the president of the Second Continental Congress, ending in 1781. Letters to fifty-three correspondents (most commonly to John Adams [sixteen] and John Jay [seven] from 1784 and 1785) concluded the first volume. Volume 2 consisted of letters devoted to national matters from 1789 to 1803. Volume 3 covered the period from August 1803 through 1826 (including six letters to George Hay during the Burr trial; the July 20 and August 20, 1807, letters to William Duane and Hay regarding the attack on the *Chesapeake*, and the January 9, 1816, letter to Benjamin Austin concerning manufactures [Chapter 6]); but not the letter of August 25, 1814, to Edward Coles [Chapter 7]). Finally, Randolph devoted Volume 4 exclusively to personal correspondence written between 1786 and 1789, including the famous "head and heart" letter to Maria Cosway.

The decision to focus on national rather than local matters was deliberate on Randolph's part. He said he chose the letters "almost exclusively with a view to promote their sale."[5] Not everyone agreed, however, with Randolph's selections. Jefferson's former physician, Robley Dunglison (Chapter 6), questioned the inclusion of particular items, especially those that contained unflattering references to the Marquis de Lafayette. In addition, James Madison warned the editor of his "apprehensions concerning the consequence that might result . . . if proper care were not exercised in the selection" of the political materials in it. Madison was prescient. In 1832, General Henry Lee's son (by the same name) published a series of his father's letters in an effort to counter an unfavorable impression that the memoir gave concerning his father.[6]

As a partial answer to these criticisms, George Tucker (professor of moral philosophy at the University of Virginia [Chapter 6]) published a two-volume biography of Jefferson in 1837.[7] Tucker dedicated the project to Madison and said that he wrote the book because "the publication . . . of some of [Jefferson's] papers and correspondence" had excited the mistaken impression "that the letters actually published were especially selected by him." Tucker acknowledged that Jefferson had arranged the contents of his recollections (known later as the *Anas*) so that it might "no doubt . . . be one day published, in defence of himself and his party, at the discretion of his executor." However, according to Tucker, Jefferson intended for his papers "to be carefully preserved as memorials of his thoughts and feelings, and of the times in which he lived, but not to be used in a manner which might provoke attacks on his memory."[8]

In attempting to undo the mischief that Randolph had unwittingly perpetrated with his four-volume publication, Tucker nevertheless followed Randolph's emphasis on national rather than local affairs. In fact, Tucker noted on page 2 of his book that because the "life of Mr. Jefferson is so intimately connected with the history of his country," it was necessary to include for readers "a brief notice of the polity and institutions of Virginia." In language that he may have borrowed from Jefferson's writings in *Notes*, Tucker indicated that an early demand for tobacco and "the very high price it then bore" caused planters to ignore "other useful processes of husbandry; and thus the management of his dairy and orchard, and the useful operations of manuring, irrigation, and cultivating artificial grasses, are either conducted in a slovenly way or neglected altogether. . . . But the most serious consequences of the tobacco cultivation is to be found in the increase of slaves; for though it did not occasion their first introduction, it greatly encouraged their importation afterwards." In addition, Tucker lamented the fact that because the tobacco planters settled along Virginia's rivers that were "skirted on either side by rich alluvial lands," they had no use for towns ("as the bees which form no hive collect no honey, the commerce which was thus dispersed accumulated no wealth"). He then criticized his ancestors (but not Jefferson) for "love of show, haughtiness, sensuality—and [. . . for] seeking relief from the vacuity of idleness, not merely in the allowable pleasures of the chase and the turf, but in the debasing ones of cock-fighting, gaming, and drinking."[9]

Having indicated that Jefferson quickly distanced himself from this degraded local perspective, Tucker continued Randolph's emphasis on Jefferson's national contributions. In discussions relating to Jefferson's debates and quarrels with Alexander Hamilton, Tucker emphasized Jefferson's accusations that Hamilton and his friends were monarchists seeking to enlarge the powers of the national government at the expense of the states. Jefferson, however, sought "to give to [the Constitution] a more strict and literal interpretation. Most of the southern members belonged to this party . . . ; and Mr. Madison . . . had united them . . . in endeavouring to keep the new government to the letter of its charter."[10]

It is in this partisan context that Tucker addressed the "calumnies of a mercenary writer, James T. Callender."

> The private life of Mr. Jefferson, present and past, was the subject of the closest scrutiny, and wherever he was believed to be vulnerable, no matter for what cause, or upon what evidence, he was unhesitatingly assailed in the grossest and most offensive way. Such too are the debasing effects of party malignity, that there were not wanting those of the federal party who were panderers to this writer's vindictive calumnies, and communicated every piece of scandal or gossip, no matter how unfit for the public eye, how unsupported by evidence, or improbable in itself, which was thought at all likely to lower the chief magistrate in the eyes of the nation. The paper which was the vehicle of these slanders, and which previously circulated scarcely out of Richmond, now found its way to the remotest parts of the Union. It remains to be added that while this wretched libel-

ler, who had now become an habitual sot, was disseminating his slanders and ribaldry with untiring virulence, he was one morning found drowned in James River, where he had been bathing, it was supposed, in a state of intoxication.[11]

Subsequent biographer Henry Randall used only slightly different words in 1858 (Chapter 6).

So too with the Burr trial: "Party spirit . . . further heightened the interest, and sought in this affair new ground of assailing or lauding the administration. It thus became a favourite object with the federal party to obtain Burr's acquittal, and even to maintain his innocence, for the sake of thwarting the measures of the executive, and of proving the President vindictive and tyrannical." In order to squelch the Federalists' "unprincipled determination . . . to screen a state criminal," Jefferson "kept up a regular correspondence with the United States attorney, Mr. Hay, concerning the prosecution and gave his counsel freely throughout its whole progress." Concerning the foreign policy problems that the nation faced in the wake of the British attack on the *Chesapeake*, Tucker intimated that Jefferson could easily have secured from the Congress a declaration of war with Great Britain but opted instead for peace.[12]

Not surprisingly, Tucker devoted many pages in his biography to the creation of the University of Virginia, where he was a professor, concluding that Jefferson's interest in the subject arose in 1814 from the prospect of erecting "an academy in Albemarle." Tucker dated Jefferson's intention to create the university to the January 1815 letter to Joseph C. Cabell (Chapter 7), which Tucker described as "the first germ of that grand system of public schools, which was afterwards adopted by the legislature, but has as yet been but partially executed." Then followed other admiring words for Jefferson's abilities as "the most far-sighted of his countrymen." More than Hamilton or Adams or Jay, Jefferson was credited by Tucker for moving the nation away from British ideas and institutions because Jefferson "saw that principles must change, because time was washing away the foundations on which they rested." His refusal to accept "the accidents of history" as the basis for human actions led "many of his countrymen" to refer to him negatively as a "visionary," but Tucker lauded him primarily for having "the sagacity to see farther than their obtuser vision could reach."[13]

These positive traits notwithstanding, Tucker's conclusion was not overly effusive regarding Jefferson's abilities as a thinker and writer. "Of the peculiar character of his mind," Tucker opined, "it may be said that it was, perhaps, yet more distinguished for justness than quickness; for comprehension than invention; and though not wanting in originality, . . . he has left no memorial that is worthy of his genius; for the public papers drawn by him are admired rather for the patriotic spirit which dictated them than for the intellectual power they exhibit. They presented no occasion for novelty of thought, or argument, or diction. His purpose was only to make a judicious and felicitous use of that which every body knew and would assent to; and this object he has eminently fulfilled."[14]

It may seem surprising that Tucker was so understated in his assessment of Jefferson's intellectual and literary abilities. Still, the author may simply have been paraphrasing Jefferson's language in two letters he wrote near the time of his death, one to Henry Lee (Chapter 3) and one to Roger C. Weightman (Introduction). In the former letter, Jefferson recalled that "the object of the Declaration of Independence . . . [was] not to find out new principles, or new arguments, never before thought of, . . . but to place before mankind the common sense of the subject, in terms so plain and firm as to command their assent." In the latter, Jefferson expressed the hope that the Declaration "will be . . . the signal of arousing men to burst the chains . . . and to assume the blessings and security of self-government."[15] As Jefferson's first major biographer, Tucker gave his subject the last word.

II

A rebuttal to Tucker's biography was not long in coming, and it originated in an unusual source. Joseph Glover Baldwin was born in Virginia in January 1815 but chose to leave the state in 1836 (seven years after Francis Eppes's exit), living first in Mississippi, and then in Alabama, where he spent eighteen years before moving in 1854 to California. Baldwin will be familiar to some readers because of a popular account of his experiences in the Deep South, *The Flush Times of Alabama and Mississippi: A Series of Sketches*.

According to Baldwin in *Flush Times*, Virginians who left the state retained "a passion" for their native land. "It is part of the Virginia character. . . . It makes no odds where he goes, he carries Virginia with him. . . . He may breathe in Alabama, but he lives in Virginia." Baldwin asserted that these émigrés preferred to live in the past rather than the present, recalling especially life in Williamsburg "when the old burg was the seat of fashion, taste, refinement, hospitality, wealth, wit, and all social graces; when genius threw its spell over the public assemblages and illumined the halls of justice, and when beauty brightened the social hour with her unmatched and matchless brilliancy." In addition, Baldwin recounted that a Virginian held "a reverence of great men, that is to say, of great Virginians. This reverence is not Unitarian. He is a Polytheist. He believes in a multitude of Virginia Gods . . . the like of whom cannot be found in the new country he has exiled himself to." And when their discussions inevitably turned to the Revolutionary generation, Baldwin said he never heard

a discussion in which old John Adams and Thomas Jefferson did not figure – as if an interminable dispute had been going on for so many generations between those disputatious personages; as if the quarrel had begun
before time, but was not to end with it. But the strangest part of it to me
was, that the dispute seemed to be going on without poor Adams having
any defence or champion; and never waxed hotter than when both parties
agreed in denouncing the man of Braintree as the worst of public sinners
and the vilest of political heretics.[16]

Like Francis Eppes (Chapter 7), Baldwin blamed much of the decline of Virginia on northerners who believed in paper money ("Rags") rather than the
wealth accumulated from working the land. Referring to the 1850s as an Age of
Brass (rather than Eppes's copper or tin), Baldwin accused northerners of buying
up the lands of Virginia in order to speculate in them. "With the change of times
and the imagination of wealth easily acquired came a change in the thoughts
and habits of the people. 'Old times were changed – old manners gone.'"[17]

Although Baldwin also had negative things to say about his fellow countrymen, much of it reminiscent, ironically, of George Tucker's rants concerning
an ostentatious hospitality, his portrayal of his native land in *Flush Times* is
not overly negative. But Baldwin wrote another book that is less well-known in
which he countered not only Tucker's arguments concerning Jefferson's political contributions to the nation but also questioned Jefferson's consistency as a
politician.

In *Party Leaders,—Sketches of Thomas Jefferson, Alexander Hamilton, Andrew Jackson, Henry Clay, and John Randolph of Roanoke* . . . , which appeared
in 1855, Baldwin praised the Federalists (especially Washington and Adams)
and condemned "the almost ferocious opposition with which every measure
proposed was assailed, on grounds and pretexts, too, for the most part unrea-
sonable and untenable, sometimes even puerile and factious." In this context,
Jefferson (whom Baldwin refers to as "one of the most adroit politicians who
ever lived") received the bulk of Baldwin's criticism for creating opposition to
the Federalist program.[18]

Baldwin's book is important not only because of its early date but also because
he struck a medium between Hamilton (who pushed too hard for consolidation
in the national government) and Jefferson (who defended states' rights)—"we
think both erred," Baldwin concluded. For our purposes, there are two aspects
of Baldwin's account that deserve attention. First, he criticized Randolph for
publishing Jefferson's papers. "We think it a misfortune to Jefferson's memory,"
Baldwin noted, "that his correspondence, at least in its present shape, has been
published. . . . It is certain, that, since the publication of his correspondence,
Jefferson has stood less favorably before his countrymen, at least a large portion

of them, than previously." Baldwin was especially critical of what became the
Anas: "It is unfortunate that those loose memoranda ever saw the light. Some of
these notes are little better than gossip; some of them worse; and none of them
are of any great value as illustrative of the history, or of the personages of the
time." In addition, Baldwin also faulted Jefferson's tendency to propose "many
true principles" but to fail to carry them out. Indeed, Baldwin hyperbolized that
Jefferson "gave out more contradictory ideas than any other American states-
man has published."[19]

The author then compiled a list stretching to thirty pages of other inconsistencies in Jefferson's words and actions that is reminiscent of Jefferson's charges
against George III in the Declaration of Independence. He was initially against
the Constitution, then favored partial ratification and finally accepted the document as drafted. He approved of Hamilton's plans to assume state debts in the
Report on Public Credit and then said he was tricked into supporting the plan.
"His whole administration was, as we have shown, in direct opposition to the
principle of super-strict construction, upon which he organized opposition to
the Federal party." "He announced the doctrine of Nullification in his Kentucky
Resolutions" but wouldn't hear of New England states seceding or blocking the
Embargo. He shifted positions on the subject of a navy so often that he didn't
know what he thought about the subject. He opposed the extension of slavery
in the Northwest Ordinance but in a letter to Massachusetts Congressman John
Holmes during the Missouri Compromise debates argued that slavery had the
right to expand. He blocked internal improvements as unconstitutional but approved of the Cumberland Road. He declared the purchase of Louisiana to be
outside of the national government's powers but negotiated and approved the
treaty of annexation. In the Burr trial his interference "was wholly unauthorized
and officious" because as president he had power to pardon Burr, and his "suggestion . . . in his letter to Hay, that Luther Martin, the counsel of Burr, should
be indicted as an accomplice . . . is a fearful commentary upon all the texts
that Jefferson preached of the jealousy and vigilance with which men in power
should be regarded. There is no other commentary so strong in the annals of
the government."[20] Baldwin's list has a modern ring to it because it sounds like
recent accounts that are critical of Jefferson's contradictions (or his hypocrisy),
especially as president.

The second reason we should pay attention to Baldwin's book concerns the
fact that for all of the faults that Baldwin highlighted concerning Randolph's
poor editing of Jefferson's papers and concerning Tucker's biography, he agreed
with the two men that Jefferson's ideas stemmed from his wide readings and
his nationalistic attitudes, not his life as a Virginian. Indeed, Baldwin singled
out Virginian John Randolph as a person motivated exclusively by local attach-

ments. Baldwin emphasized Randolph's obstructionist position on national projects, and, writing as a Unionist fearful of civil war, Baldwin portrayed Randolph as the sectionalist, not Jefferson. For example, Baldwin concluded that Jefferson based his suspicion of strong government "on his dislike of power, wherever lodged, or by whomsoever wielded" rather than Randolph's views "and others of the Virginia school . . . [that were] founded in Virginia feeling and State pride." Randolph was, in Baldwin's words, "a Virginian and Southron of the old regime . . . [, a man who owed] his primary and only allegiance to that venerable Commonwealth, and acknowledging the Federal Government but as a limited agency, which she, with others, had established, for a few simple purposes." Baldwin expressed anger that Jefferson didn't abandon "the principles of 1798" earlier in his life, but he faulted Randolph for "adhering to the tenets . . . even when they were abandoned by the fathers of the church."[21]

Henry Randall was another Unionist, and his biography of Jefferson followed Baldwin's by two years. Whereas Baldwin was critical of many of Jefferson's policies, Randall shifted attention back to Tucker's perspective by emphasizing Jefferson's stature during his lifetime as a national leader. According to the editors of portions of Randall's letters, "[He] ardently desired to bring Jefferson by a meticulous examination of his record into a more national focus where he would stand side by side in historical literature as well as in fact with Washington as a founder of the Republic." In addition, Randall deplored the sectionalism that increasingly drove a wedge between North and South by the end of the 1850s and worried that his coverage of Jefferson's attitudes toward slavery would create problems for nationalists in the South. Neither did Randall identify with abolitionists in the North. "I have no sympathy with the mad & fanatical spirit which controls a portion of our people," he wrote Virginia historian Hugh B. Grigsby in 1856. "I can't please them if I try. I won't *try*. . . . I shall probably be denounced & hunted. Be it so."[22]

In his private correspondence, Randall found fault with Tucker's biography, but his criticisms of it primarily centered on his belief that Tucker did not go far enough to defend Jefferson's actions as a nationalist and, especially, as founder of the Democratic party. "[Tucker] did not understand the *inner* history of parties; the *spirit & soul of the times* . . . ," Randall wrote. "He did not enter into Jefferson's *feelings* any more than he occupied his stand point in the colder matters of opinion.—It was ice trying to represent fire!" Randall also believed that his biography was superior to Tucker's because Randall emphasized the problems that Jefferson faced as governor of Virginia during the American Revolution, "and that puts the whole South & Virginia especially in a position of honor in regard to the Revolutionary Contest, which is wormwood to our sectionalists."[23]

For his part, Tucker's reaction to Randall's *Life* focused on his belief that Randall had paid too close attention to the language of the prior study. Hugh Grigsby told Randall that Tucker was "especially . . . [critical] of your having got your views or facts from his book, and then of your roving abroad for authorities to conceal your obligations." In a letter of November 12, 1858, Grigsby discounted Tucker's "declaration of war" because of his age and "a spirit of pugnacity becoming earlier years. We must make great allowances for extreme old age, which is apt to excite certain minds on particular topics in an unwonted way." Fortunately for both men, Tucker's animosity was short-lived; by December, Randall and Tucker had reconciled.[24]

III

In summary, whereas Thomas Jefferson Randolph would certainly have been distressed that his edition of his grandfather's papers provided fodder for Joseph Baldwin's book, he might have taken some satisfaction in the fact that (with the help of George Tucker and Henry S. Randall) he succeeded in shifting attention concerning Jefferson's legacy from his country to his nation. And whatever doubts the man himself expressed privately in 1800 concerning whether his life had benefited his country were swept away in the 1826 celebrations of the nation's founding, as documented in his letter to Weightman (Introduction).

Recent historians emphasize this view. Merrill Peterson similarly shows in his book on changing images of Jefferson through time how partisans of both slavery and abolition claimed Jefferson as speaking for them in the years prior to the Civil War and that this malleability persists into modern times. "Jefferson, unlike Hamilton," Peterson writes, "was protean, capable of infinite reinterpretation within the shared faith of the American people." John Boles continues this theme by referring to the South during the colonial and early national periods as "the normative region of the nation," and of these eras as "the age of Jefferson." "In Thomas Jefferson, Patrick Henry, and George Washington," Boles writes, "Virginia produced the Pen, the Voice, and the Sword of the Revolution; [and] Madison was the Father of the Constitution." Boles emphasizes how southerners throughout the period of Manifest Destiny "set the national agenda. . . . This was the high point of the national South, when southerners were at the liberal forefront of the nation and sought to protect the Republic from foreign threats and internal intrigue." As for Jefferson, Boles describes him as possessing contradictions due to his Virginian roots, but "for all his localism, for his attachment to Monticello with its vista to the West and his love affair with Albemarle County, Jefferson was a nationalist of the highest order."[25]

6. The Jefferson Memorial at Night. Modern lighting spotlights the Memorial at its best view-ing. If they have the time, visitors should visit Monticello and Poplar Forest in order to take the true measure of the man. Courtesy of Terry Adams, National Park Service.

Like historians, Americans today also accept Jefferson as a member of the pantheon of notables. Millions annually visit the newly refurbished Jefferson Memorial in Washington, D.C., in order to get the measure of the man who was instrumental in founding the nation and defining its ideals. Standing on the steps of the Memorial, one can believe that the spirit of Jefferson's life has been captured perfectly. The Memorial is especially impressive at night, as modern lighting illumines his statue and the writings that surround him. But his words are toned for modern ears. When they read the excerpt from his Declaration of Independence, few visitors probably notice that the right of rebellion has been removed and that someone changed his spelling at the end of the document from "honor" to "honour."[26]

Instead of trying to navigate their way to the Jefferson Memorial, those Amer-icans who want "to remember" Thomas Jefferson should stay in the left lane as they approach the tidal basin—thereby avoiding others who are sharply turn-ing right into the very difficult access—and cross the George Mason Memorial Bridge into Virginia. Today, as in Jefferson's time, both the meaning of his life and his contributions to his country are best viewed from that perspective.

Notes

Introduction

1. TJ to Roger C. Weightman, June 24, 1826, in Jefferson, *Portable Jefferson*, 584–85.
2. Bailyn, "Jefferson and the Ambiguities of Freedom," 59.
3. Appleby, "Thomas Jefferson and the Psychology of Democracy," 155, 171.
4. Foster, "Jefferson Fathered Slave's Last Child."
5. Peterson, *Jefferson Image*, 457.
6. Jordan, review of *Thomas Jefferson*, 510.
7. Malone, *Jefferson and His Time*, 6:xiii.
8. Jefferson, *Notes*, 160.
9. Lockridge, "Robert Bolling and Thomas Jefferson."
10. Egerton, *Gabriel's Rebellion*, esp. 154–62; see also Egerton, "The Empire of Liberty Reconsidered," 309–30.
11. Egerton, "Comment on Papers."
12. Hatzenbuehler, "'Growing Weary in Well-Doing,'" 36.
13. Fowler, "Mythologies of a Founder," 127.

Chapter 1. "Sowed a Bed of Peas": Observing and Criticizing Virginia's Gentry Culture

1. Peterson, *Thomas Jefferson and the New Nation*, 28.
2. TJ to John Adams, May 12, 1820, in Cappon, ed., *Adams-Jefferson Letters*, 2:567–68.
3. Ibid., 2:568.
4. Koch, *Philosophy*, 190. Catherine L. Albanese makes the same point in "Whither the Sons (and Daughters)?" 378–79.
5. Breen, *Tobacco Culture*.
6. Jefferson, *Notes*, 177–78.
7. Jefferson does not mention Small in his letters until 1769, seven years after leaving college. As for the specific training he received from Small, he did not write about it until 1811. TJ to John Walker, Sept. 3, 1769, in Jefferson, *Papers*, 1:32; TJ to William Small,

May 7, 1775, in Jefferson, *Papers*, 1:165; TJ to Thomas Jefferson Randolph, Nov. 24, 1808, in Jefferson, *Portable Thomas Jefferson*, 511; Jefferson, *Autobiography of Thomas Jefferson*, 20. See also Ganter, "William Small."

8. TJ to John Harvie, Jan. 14, 1760, in Jefferson, *Papers*, 1:3.

9. See, as examples, TJ to John Page, Jan. 20, 1763, TJ to William Fleming, [ca. Oct. 1763], TJ to John Page, Jan. 19, 23, 1764, TJ to John Page, May 25, 1766, in Jefferson, *Papers*, 1:7, 1:12–13, 1:13–15, 1:18–20. In the *Autobiography*, Jefferson wrote: "[Dr. Small] returned to Europe in 1762, having previously filled up the measure of his goodness to me, by procuring for me, from his most intimate friend, George Wythe, a reception as a student of law, under his direction, and introduced me to the acquaintance and familiar table of Governor Fauquier, the ablest man who had ever filled that office. With him, and at his table Dr. Small and Mr. Wythe . . . on these occasions I owed much instruction." Jefferson, *Autobiography*, 20–21.

10. TJ to John Page, Dec. 25, 1762, in Jefferson, *Papers*, 1:5.

11. TJ to John Page, May 25, 1766, in Jefferson, *Papers*, 1:18–20.

12. Jefferson, *Garden Book*, 4.

13. Although later in his life Jefferson cultivated the image of his father as a frontiersman, recent archaeological excavations document the fact that Peter Jefferson's house was patterned on those of tidewater planters.

14. Barbara McEwan emphasizes that he kept his elaborate charts of his garden because he was an experimental gardener, "not only for his personal tastes, but for what might be suitable for his countrymen at large. It is doubtful that any other contemporary American grower had in his home garden more types than did Jefferson." McEwan, *Thomas Jefferson: Farmer*, 160–61.

15. Jefferson, *Notes*, 73–80; Jefferson, *Garden Book*, 622–24.

16. Jefferson, *Notes*, 80; Jefferson, *Garden Book*, 622.

17. Jefferson, *Garden Book*, 623–24.

18. Jefferson, *Farm Book*, 46, 54, 58.

19. See, for example, Jefferson, *Farm Book*, 72–75 (animals), and 84–97 (plants). See also Jefferson, *Garden Book*, 6–23.

20. Jefferson, *Garden Book*, 302, 362, 403, 507; Martin, *Thomas Jefferson: Scientist*, 57–58.

21. TJ to Charles W. Peale, Apr. 17, 1813, in Jefferson, *Garden Book*, 509.

22. Jefferson, *Garden Book*, 5, 302.

23. Ibid., 619.

24. Ibid., 362.

25. TJ to Martha Jefferson, Mar. 28, 1787, Betts and Bear, eds., *Family Letters*, 34.

26. TJ to Ellen Randolph Coolidge, Aug. 27, 1825, Betts and Bear, eds., *Family Letters*, 458.

27. Jefferson, *Garden Book*, 55, 66, 86.

28. Ibid., 252, 393, 536, 564, 589, 593.

29. Malone, *Jefferson and His Time*, 6:48.

30. See TJ to George Divers, May 24, 1807, Divers to TJ, June 6, 1807, Divers to TJ, Apr. 30, 1815, in Jefferson, *Garden Book*, 348, 544.

31. Malone, *Jefferson and His Time*, 1:128–31, 156–60. Jefferson's father had also married into the most prominent tidewater family, the Randolphs, and Jefferson spent several of his earliest years at the family's mansion, Tuckahoe.

32. Malone, *Jefferson and His Time*, 1:162–63, 439–41.

33. TJ to John Adams, Oct. 28, 1813, in Cappon, ed., *Adams-Jefferson Letters*, 2:388–89. As will be seen, the word "intestate" limits the effect of the reform, since if there was a will a great estate could remain undivided. Jefferson, therefore, overstates his claim that he had "laid the axe" to aristocracy, although several of his friends railed against these reforms (Chapter 3).

34. Adams to TJ, Nov. 15, 1813, in Cappon, ed., *Adams-Jefferson Letters*, 2:400–401.

35. TJ to Adams, Jan. 24, 1814, in Cappon, ed., *Adams-Jefferson Letters*, 2:424.

36. For differing views of the beginnings of the gentry class in Virginia, see Quitt, "Immigrant Origins," 629–55; Breen, *Tobacco Culture*, 34–39; Greene, *Political Life*, 6–22, 26–27, 38–46; and Greene, *Pursuits of Happiness*, 9–18, 82–100. In opposition to the emphasis that scholars place on the indigenous factors promoting the rise of a gentry class in Virginia, Garrett Ward Sheldon writes that English aristocratic emigrants to Virginia in the seventeenth century transplanted into Virginia "the forms and manners of landed society—mansion houses, ancestral pretensions, English architectural gardens, upper-class education and sports." Sheldon, *Political Philosophy*, 114.

37. See Tate and Ammerman, eds., *Chesapeake in the Seventeenth Century*, esp. Earle, "Environment, Disease and Mortality," 96–125; and Galenson, *White Servitude*.

38. Rutman and Rutman, "Now-Wives and Sons-in-Law," 153–82.

39. McCusker and Menard, *Economy of British America*, 118–25, 138; Galenson and Menard, "Approaches to the Analysis of Economic Growth," 9–10.

40. Galenson and Menard, "Approaches to the Analysis of Economic Growth"; Herndon, *Tobacco in Colonial Virginia*. Herndon also points out that increased labor output due to experience and the invention of new plows also explains part of this increase. Also, the differing nature of the soils (sandy loam in the tidewater area versus the heavier soils of the Piedmont) ushered in a shift from "sweet scented" to Oronoco tobacco.

41. McCusker and Menard, *Economy of British America*, 135–37, and Galenson, *White Servitude*, 151–54.

42. Breen, *Puritans and Adventurers*, 126. See also Lockridge, *Settlement and Unsettlement*.

43. Lockridge, *Settlement and Unsettlement*, 90–91.

44. Galenson and Menard, "Approaches to the Analysis of Economic Growth," 6. See also Billings, *Colonial Virginia*, 134–35.

45. Sobel, *World They Made Together*, 54.

46. Greene, "Foundations of Political Power," 485–506. This profile remained valid for another century but changed dramatically after the 1820s. See Jordan, *Political Leadership*, 34–35; 71–72; 209–13.

47. Kern, "The Material World of the Jeffersons at Shadwell," 217, 242. For evidence of the importance of the Piedmont area in expanding tobacco culture, see Herndon, "Tobacco in Colonial Virginia," 9.

48. National Park Service, *Jamestown* (film).

49. Breen, *Tobacco Culture*, 22, 31, 161–87. See also Greene, "Society, Ideology, and Politics."

50. Jefferson, *Notes*, 166–68.

51. Royster, *Fabulous History of the Dismal Swamp Company*, 27–28, 90, 146, 217, 423.

52. Jefferson, *Farm Book*, 124–25.

53. Ibid., 271, 255–310; TJ to James Maury, Jan. 16, 1815, in Jefferson, *Writings*, ed. Lipscomb and Bergh, 14:319; TJ to Leroy and Bayard, July 5, 8, 1822, in Jefferson, *Works*, 12:245–46. That Jefferson was an experienced tobacco grower may be confirmed by his "I. On Tobacco Culture [1784/5?]" in Jefferson, *Papers*, 7:209–12. See also McEwan, *Thomas Jefferson: Farmer*, esp. 46–47.

54. See Table 5.1.

55. TJ to Robert Skipwith, Aug. 3, 1771, in Jefferson, *Portable Jefferson*, 349–50.

56. TJ to Samuel Kercheval, July 12, 1816, in Jefferson, *Portable Jefferson*, 558–59. Jefferson repeats to Kercheval his belief that "the earth belongs to the living" that he first developed in his letter to James Madison of Sept. 6, 1789, in ibid., 444–51. See also his letter to John Adams, Aug. 15, 1820: "I am a friend to *neology*. It is the only way to give to a language copiousness and euphony. Without it we should be held to the vocabulary of Alfred or of Ulphilas; and held to their state of science also." Cappon, ed., *Adams-Jefferson Letters*, 2:567.

57. Jefferson, *Notes*, 177–78. Judy Jo Small summarizes scholarly views of Beverley's *History* as "a naive or cavalier hodge-podge, lively but scarcely coherent in any aesthetic sense." Billings, Selby, and Tate characterize Stith's *History* as "good history. . . . The interpretation it propounded of the early years of the colony remained standard until well into the twentieth century." Small, "Robert Beverley and the New World Garden," 526; Billings, Selby, and Tate, *Colonial Virginia*, 248.

58. Hariot, *Briefe and true report*, 16.

59. Smith, *Generall Historie*, 52.

60. Ibid., 94.

61. Ibid., 165, 139, 143. See also 119: "This deare bought Land with so much bloud and cost, hath onely made some few rich, and all the rest losers."

62. Deetz has modified his earliest conclusions about the existence of earthfast construction in New England based upon the discovery of an earthfast house in Duxbury dating from the late 1620s and one in Kingston from the 1630s. "It is virtually certain that further archaeological research in New England will produce evidence of additional earthfast buildings, and a far more widespread tradition than has been believed to have been the case up to now." Deetz and Deetz, *Times of Their Lives*, 258.

63. Deetz, *In Small Things Forgotten*, 20–22, 146, 33; Deetz and Deetz, *Times of Their Lives*, 258–59; Deetz, *Flowerdew Hundred*, 15–18, 54. See also Hume, *Martin's Hundred*, 138–40; 248–49. One of the chief allegations that was raised against the Virginia Company that led to the revocation of its charter was "That their Houses were generally the worst, that . . . had ever [been] seen; the meanest Cottages in *England* being every way equal, if not superior, to the best Houses in *Virginia*." Hamor, *True Discourse*, 56.

64. Billings, Selby, and Tate, *Colonial Virginia*, 167.

65. Ibid., 59, 81, 101.

66. Beverley, *History*, 57, 59.

67. Ibid., 92. In fact, Beverley's father was likely one of the ring-leaders of the plant-cutting scheme and escaped prosecution only due to lack of evidence against him. Billings, Selby, and Tate, *Colonial Virginia*, 108.

68. Smith, *Generall Historie*, 147, 152, 158–59.

69. Beverley, *History*, 59, 64–65. Beverley might have gone even further in blaming Charles I for Virginia's problems had he used the account of Hamor, who wrote that in August 1641 Charles I had instructed Sir William Berkeley that Virginians, instead of "remov[ing] from place to place only to Plant Tobacco, That Tradesmen and Handycrafts men be compelled to follow their Severall Trades and occupations and that you draw them into Towns—To raise Staple Commodities Hemp Flax etc. Plant Vines and Mulberry Trees. Wee require you to use the best endeavor to cause the people there to apply themselves to the raising of more Staple Comodities as Hemp and Flax, Rope Seed and Madder Pitch Tarr for Tanning of Hydes, and leather, likewise every Plantation to Plant a Proportion of Vines answerable to their Numbers, and to Plant White Mulbery Trees, and to attend Silk Worms—Tobacco not to be raised at any certaine Prizes but left free." Hamor also noted that Charles I had begun the restrictions on trade that the Parliament later enacted into law: "Bond to be taken of all ships to bring their goods into His Majesties Domminions, that his Majesty may have his Customes. . . . Not to Trade with any Foraine Ships but upon great necessity." Hamor, *True Discourse*, 56–57.

70. Beverley, *History*, 92.

71. Keith, *History*, 130–68.

72. Interestingly, Beverley was also critical of Virginians for not settling in towns, primarily because his father had introduced legislation to that effect in 1680 and 1684 (see Beverley, *History*, 57, 318) but he eliminated such criticisms from the 1722 edition of his book because by that time his own family "was too much a beneficiary of the pattern of large landholding that resulted." The legislation to which Keith referred was introduced in 1691. Billings, Selby, and Tate, *Colonial Virginia*, 133, 136.

73. Keith, *History*, 169–73. This legislation, failing finally in 1706, was due to fears in England that Virginians would develop manufacturing. Billings, Selby, and Tate indicate that in addition to the failed legislation, there were other government reports and "several publications by Virginia residents" between the 1680s and the 1720s that regretted the lack of diversification in Virginia's economy. *Colonial Virginia*, 133–34.

74. For background on Stith, see Morton, *Colonial Virginia*, 2:624–25, 769.

75. Stith, *History*, 182–83.

76. Ibid., 278. As late as 1786 Jefferson reported in *Notes* that most of the private dwellings of Virginians were "of scantling and boards, plaistered with lime." "It is impossible to devise," he wrote, "things more ugly, uncomfortable, and happily more perishable. . . . A country whose buildings are of wood, can never increase in its improvements to any considerable degree. . . . Whereas when buildings are of durable materials, every new edifice is an actual and permanent acquisition to the state, adding to its value as well as its ornament." Jefferson, *Notes*, 152–55.

77. Beverley, *History*, xiii–xiv. See also Billings, Selby, and Tate, *Colonial Virginia*, 81.

78. For an alternative reading of early Virginia texts relating to the Garden of Eden metaphor, see Adams, *Best & Worst Country*, 116–23.

79. Smith, *Generall Historie*, 106.

80. Beverley, *History*, 296; Stith, *History*, 45. George Percy, one of the first Englishmen to explore the Virginia mainland, noted "faire meddowes and goodly tall Trees, with such Fresh-waters running through the woods, as I was almost ravished at the first sight thereof," and another early settler, William Simmonds, recorded that "we chanced in[to] a lande, even as God made it." Quoted in Billings, *Old Dominion*, 22, 27.

81. Beverley, *History*, 296–318. Seelye notes this "Jeremian emphasis" in Beverley's *History* and uses it to link southern and New England literature—"the laziness of Virginian planters being a southern counterpart to Puritan backsliding." *Prophetic Waters*, 344. Douglas Anderson writes that Beverley describes Virginians as "a morally and physically unpromising people planted in a natural paradise." Anderson, "Subterraneous Virginia," 234.

82. Small, "Robert Beverley," 527–33. Small believes that Beverley borrowed from (without acknowledging his reliance on) Baron de Lahontan, whose two-volume *New Voyages to North-America* appeared in London in 1703 and perhaps stimulated Beverley to write his *History*. She does not, however, discuss how much borrowing Beverley did from Smith.

83. Greene, "Intellectual Reconstruction of Virginia," 226. See also Sobel, *World They Made Together*, 85–90.

84. Beverley, *History*, 272. In later editions of the book, Beverley increased his attempts to stop slavery in order to increase the chance of developing a yeoman society. See Billings, Selby, and Tate, *Colonial Virginia*, 136.

85. Jefferson, *Notes*, 162–63.

86. TJ to Martha Jefferson Randolph, May 31, 1791, in Betts and Bear, eds., *Family Letters*, 84–85.

87. Ellen Randolph Coolidge to TJ, Aug. 1, 1825, TJ to Ellen Randolph Coolidge, Aug. 27, 1825, in Betts and Bear, eds., *Family Letters*, 454–58.

88. Jack Greene also makes this point and discusses how later commentators like Edmund Randolph, St. George Tucker, and John Daly Burk further developed the theme between 1780 and 1815. "Intellectual Reconstruction of Virginia," 232ff.

Chapter 2. "The God Who Gave Us Life, Gave Us Liberty at the Same Time":
A Summary View of the Rights of British America

1. Jefferson, *Papers*, 1:121–37. For an excellent historiographical overview of scholarly writing about *Summary View*, see Conrad, "Putting Rights Talk in Its Place," 260–65. However, Conrad's argument (that the Boston Port Bill specifically and the Intolerable Acts generally formed the "immediate provocation" for *Summary View* and that Jefferson's "controlling aim" in the document was to help create "an early, if still inchoate, feeling of national identity") stands in contrast to the central thesis of this chapter. Ibid., 257, 269, 271.

2. Greene, "Society, Ideology, and Politics," 43, 54–55. See also Greene, *Political Life*.

3. Billings, Selby, and Tate, *Colonial Virginia*, 303–9.

4. Jefferson, *Papers*, 1:27–30. See also "Virginia Nonimportation Resolutions, 1770," in ibid., 1:43–46.

5. Ibid., 1:328–31.

6. Malone, *Jefferson and His Time*, 1:180–81; Jefferson, *Papers*, 1:670.

7. Jefferson, *Papers*, 1:121, 134.

8. Ibid., 1:122.

9. Ibid., 1:129.

10. Ibid., 1:124–25.

11. Ibid., 1:131.

12. Ibid., 1:133.

13. Ibid., 1:131–32.

14. Ibid., 1:134–35.

15. The only contemporaneous text of Mason's included in *The Papers of Thomas Jefferson* is labeled "Petition of George Mason for Warrants for Lands in Fincastle County," dated June 1774. Indeed, from volume 1 of the *Papers*, one would reasonably conclude that Thomas Jefferson, not George Mason, was one of the chief architects of the policy of nonimportation in 1769. Jefferson, *Papers*, 1:112–15.

16. Wallenstein, "Flawed Keepers," 234.

17. Rutland, introduction to Mason, *Papers*, 1:cxii.

18. See, for example, Mason to Robert Dinwiddie, Sept. 9, 1761, in Mason, *Papers*, 1:46–47, and "Petition to King George III [from a Committee of the Ohio Company]," [Sept. 9, 1761], in ibid., 1:47–48.

19. Selby, *Revolution in Virginia*, 24.

20. Mason, "Scheme for Replevying Goods and Distress for Rent," [Dec. 23, 1765], in Mason, *Papers*, 1:61–62. Mason used similar language at the Constitutional Convention in 1787; see Miller, *George Mason*, 253, 294.

21. Mason, "To the Committee of Merchants in London," June 6, 1766, Mason, *Papers*, 1:68–72.

22. Mason to George Washington, Apr. 5, 1769, in Mason, *Papers*, 1:99. See also "The Nonimportation Association as Corrected by Mason," Apr. 23, 1769, and "The Letter of 'Atticus,'" May 11, 1769, in Mason, *Papers*, 1:101–9.

23. Mason, *Papers*, 1:109–110; see also "Virginia Nonimportation Association," June 22, 1770, in Mason, *Papers*, 1:120–24.

24. Billings, Selby, and Tate, *Colonial Virginia*, 319.

25. TJ to Thomas Adams, June 1, 1771, in Jefferson, *Papers*, 1:71–72.

26. Mason to [George Brent?], Dec. 6, 1770, in Mason, *Papers*, 1:127–28. Although nonimportation efforts failed throughout the colonies, T. H. Breen argues that they were successful in many northern colonies in mobilizing ordinary people—including women and college students—to political action. See Breen, "Baubles of Britain," 243–52. Because Mason's efforts were aimed almost exclusively at the upper class, however, it is doubtful that the nonimportation efforts of Mason and others had a similar effect in Virginia.

27. Mason, "Fairfax County Resolves," in Mason, *Papers*, 1:202–3.

28. Mason, *Papers*, 1:203

29. Jefferson, *Papers*, 1:125.

30. Mason, *Papers*, 1:208–9. See also "Fairfax County Militia Association," Sept. 21, 1774: "that we will always hold ourselves in Readiness, in Case of Necessity, hostile Invasion, or real Danger of the Community of which we are Members, to defend to the utmost of our Power, the legal prerogatives of our Sovereign King George the third, and the just Rights & Privileges of our Country, our Posterity & ourselves upon the Principles of the British Constitution." Ibid., 211.

31. Jefferson, *Papers*, 1:117–19.

32. Mason, *Papers*, 1:208–9.

33. Beverley, *History*, 64–92.

34. Keith, *History*, 2.

35. Ibid., 3. For a concise comparison of mercantilism and capitalism, see Williams, *Contours*, introduction.

36. Keith, *History*, 10.

37. Ibid., 11.

38. Ibid., 12–14.

39. Ibid., 148–52.

40. Ibid., 155.

41. Ibid., 169, 180.

42. Ibid., 177, 186.

43. Stith, *History*, vi (italics in the original).

44. Ibid., 41.

45. Ibid., 160.

46. Ibid., 160, 200, 197.

47. Ibid., 200.

48. Ibid., 223–24.

49. Bailyn, "Jefferson and the Ambiguities of Freedom," 32.

50. Murrin, "1787," 22–24. See also Ubbelohde, *American Colonies and the British Empire*, and Greene, *Quest for Power*.

51. Williams, "Small Farmer in Eighteenth-Century Virginia Politics," 91–101.

52. Murrin, "1787," 26.

53. Editor's note, in Mason, *Papers*, 1:65n; Wallenstein, "Flawed Keepers," 252–53; Schwartz, "George Mason," 146, 153.

54. Murrin, "Can Liberals Be Patriots?" 41–48.

55. Jefferson, *Papers*, 1:121, 135.

56. Darnton, *Great Cat Massacre*, 202.

57. Ibid., 202, 204.

Chapter 3. "Rights Inherent and Inalienable": The American Revolution in Virginia

1. Jefferson, *Papers*, 1:423.

2. Ibid., 1:423–24. B. L. Rayner, Jefferson's first biographer, emphasized the importance of the *Summary View* for the Declaration of Independence when he wrote that the former "was indeed the genuine precursor for boldness and originality of sentiment

and felicity of composition. . . . [It is] a more learned and elaborate production than the Declaration of Independence, to which it is inferior as a literary performance." Rayner, *Life of Jefferson*, Chap. 4.

3. For an extended discussion of these possible influences, see Hatzenbuehler, "'Growing Weary in Well-Doing.'" Since this article was published, Michael P. Zuckert has strengthened the case for Locke's influence—see Zuckert, *Natural Rights Republic*, and Zuckert, "Founder of the Natural Rights Republic."

4. Julian Boyd, *Declaration of Independence*, 14–15.

5. Malone, *Jefferson and His Time*, 1:221. See also Peterson, *Jefferson and the New Nation*, 89–91.

6. Maier, *American Scripture*, 135, xvii. See also p. 137: "Jefferson's point was more important than the sources of his language."

7. Maier, *American Scripture*, 126–27, 133–34. See also Richard Beeman's conclusion: "It seems certain that the preamble of the Virginia Declaration of Rights, drafted by George Mason and in circulation in Philadelphia in mid-June, had some influence on [Jefferson's] own preamble for the Declaration of Independence. . . . [T]o call [the similarity of phrasing] a coincidence strains the laws of probability." Beeman, "The American Revolution," 35.

8. Maier, *American Scripture*, 107–9, 126, 131–33, 98–99. For the specific way she believes that the English Declaration of Rights influenced Mason's, Jefferson's, and state declarations of independence and bills of rights, see her chart, 166.

9. Rowland, *Life of George Mason*, 250.

10. Fitzpatrick, *Spirit of the Revolution*, 6. Most recently, in commenting on the near identity of Mason's work and Jefferson's, Gore Vidal writes that the Declaration of Independence "mak[es] literature of Mason's somewhat desultory laundry list, consisting of John Locke's garments." Vidal, *Inventing a Nation*, 28.

11. Chinard, *Thomas Jefferson*, 74.

12. Boyd cites the June 6, 1776, edition of the *Pennsylvania Evening Post* in *Declaration of Independence*, 14–15.

13. Edmund Pendleton to TJ, May 24, 1776, in Jefferson, *Papers*, 1:297; Mason, *Papers*, 1:279, editorial note. Helen Hill Miller says a draft of the Declaration of Rights in Mason's hands arrived in the May 25 post in a letter from Thomas Ludwell Lee to his brother. Miller, *George Mason*, 142. John E. Selby and Pauline Maier agree that Jefferson worked from Mason's draft copy but do not specify how he received the draft version. See Selby, *Revolution in Virginia*, 103, 354 n. 8; Maier, *American Scripture*, 126–27, 268.

14. Mason, *Papers*, 1:277; see also Sutton, *Revolution to Secession*, 235 n. 19.

15. Jefferson, *Papers*, 1:423–24; Sutton, *Revolution to Secession*, 31.

16. Wilson, *Works*, 2:723, 727.

17. Becker, *Declaration of Independence*, 106, 109–16. See also Chinard, introduction to *Commonplace Book of Thomas Jefferson*, 41–45.

18. Wills, *Inventing America*, 251.

19. Wilson, *Works*, 2:745.

20. Considerable disagreement persists over whether the word "pursue" in 1776 meant "to chase" or "to acquire." Herbert Lawrence Ganter and Arthur M. Schlesinger

favor the latter position (i.e., a person has a right to "be happy") whereas Allen Jayne argues that Mason's phrase "pursuing and obtaining happiness" was inconsistent with Locke's idea of the elusive nature of happiness. Therefore, Jayne believes that Jefferson was more Lockean than Mason and "the fact that [Jefferson] did not include 'obtaining happiness' as a right indicates that he was not influenced by Mason's Virginia Declaration of Rights when drafting the Declaration of Independence." Ganter, "Jefferson's 'Pursuit of Happiness'"; Schlesinger, "Lost Meaning of 'The Pursuit of Happiness'"; Jayne, *Jefferson's Declaration of Independence*, 132.

21. Jefferson, *Papers*, 1:329–40, 417–20; Boyd, *Declaration of Independence*, 14; Maier, *American Scripture*, 104–23.

22. Editor's note, in Jefferson, *Papers*, 1:329–30n; TJ to Thomas Nelson, May 16, 1776, in ibid., 1:292.

23. Edmund Randolph to TJ, June 23, 1776, in Jefferson, *Papers*, 1:407, 408; TJ to William Fleming, July 1, 1776, in ibid., 1:412–13; William Fleming to TJ, July 27, 1776, in ibid., 1:475; TJ to Richard Henry Lee, July 8, 1776, in ibid., 1:455–56. Maier notes that Jefferson sent several copies of the Declaration as he had drafted it to friends but emphasizes that the changes that the Convention made had improved the document. Maier, *American Scripture*, 147–50.

24. Jefferson, *Papers*, 1:193.

25. Selby, *Revolution in Virginia*, 62–68. For background on Dunmore, see 14–22.

26. TJ to John Randolph, Nov. 29, 1775, in Jefferson, *Papers*, 1:269.

27. The king said, "The object is too important, the spirit of the British nation too high, the resources with which God hath blessed her too numerous, to give up so many colonies which she has planted with great industry, nursed with great tenderness, encouraged with many commercial advantages, and protected and defended with such expence and treasure." Jefferson had already disputed each of these points in *Summary View*. Jefferson, *Papers*, 1:283–84.

28. Fliegelman, *Declaring Independence*, 144–47.

29. TJ to Henry Lee, May 8, 1825, in Jefferson, *Works*, 12:409. Hans E. Eicholz supports this interpretation by emphasizing that the Declaration of Independence "was not *his* composition, so much as it was an expression of the American mind at the time, as he himself was keen to point out." Eicholz, *Harmonizing Sentiments*, 106.

30. Jordan, *Political Leadership*, 13–15; Sutton, *Revolution to Secession*, 50–51.

31. Jefferson, *Papers*, 1:560–76; Malone, *Jefferson and His Time*, 1:235–85; Jefferson, *Notes*, 137, 209–22. Jefferson boasted that the abolition of entail and primogeniture destroyed aristocratic privilege in Virginia, but wills still protected a person's ability to leave entire estates to single individuals. Only if a person died without a will was the inheritance partible. His successes in this area, which he later touted and exaggerated in his *Autobiography* and private letters, were limited by the fact that the legislation applied only to estates without wills. Jefferson, *Autobiography*, 57, 62; TJ to John Adams, Oct. 28, 1813, in Cappon, ed., *Adams-Jefferson Letters*, 2:388–89. Sutton, *Revolution to Secession*, 65.

32. Isaac, *Transformation of Virginia*, Chap. 8; Jan Lewis, *Pursuit of Happiness*, 48–56.

33. Miller, *George Mason*, 16–18.

34. Greene, "Society, Ideology, and Politics," 14–76; Breen, *Tobacco Culture*, 142ff., 193; Lewis, *Pursuit of Happiness*, 108–55; Isaac, *Transformation of Virginia*, 174–77; Billings, et al., *Colonial Virginia*, 323–26.

35. Isaac, *Transformation of Virginia*, 280–93; Isaac, "'Rage of Malice,'" 146–47. For Mason's role in getting the Statute for Religious Freedom adopted, see Daniel L. Dreisbach, "George Mason's Pursuit of Religious Liberty."

36. Jefferson, *Papers*, 2:545; see also "Notes and Proceedings on Discontinuing the Establishment of the Church of England," Jefferson, *Papers*, 1:525–58.

37. Jefferson, *Papers*, 1:132; Jefferson, *Notes*, 84, 159–61.

38. Jefferson, *Papers*, 2:546–47.

39. Isaac, "'Rage of Malice,'" 147, 162. See also Selby, *Revolution in Virginia*, 161: "Virginians gradually heeded his teaching on the constitutional intricacies of republicanism, but shunned his proposals that would have fundamentally altered class relationships."

40. Irons, "Spiritual Fruits of Revolution." See also Najar, "'Meddling with Emancipation,'" esp. 166–70.

41. See, primarily, Selby, *Revolution in Virginia*, Chaps. 9–12.

42. Horatio Gates to TJ, Oct. 6, 1780, in Jefferson, *Papers*, 4:16.

43. Nathanael Greene to TJ, Dec. 6, 1780, in ibid., 4:183–84.

44. Steuben to TJ, Jan. 12, 1781, in ibid., 4:345.

45. TJ to Richard H. Lee, July 17, 1779, in ibid., 3:39–40; "Notes and Plans for Western Defense," [July 23, 1779, and after], in ibid., 3:52–56.

46. George Washington to TJ, Feb. 6, 1781, in ibid., 4:543.

47. Steuben to TJ, Feb. 11, 1781, in ibid., 4:584. See also Steuben to TJ, Mar. 5, 1781, in ibid., 5:66–70.

48. TJ to George Nicholas, July 28, 1781, in ibid., 5:104–5; George Nicholas to TJ, July 31, 1781, in ibid., 105–6; "Charges Advanced by George Nicholas with Jefferson's Answers," [after July 31, 1781], in ibid., 106–8.

49. See TJ to George Washington, Nov. 28, 1779, in ibid., 3:204–6; TJ to Samuel Huntington, Dec. 16, 1779, in ibid., 3:224–27; "Advice of Council respecting Reinforcements of Militia," [ca. Sept. 4, 1780], in ibid., 3:597–601.

50. See TJ to George Washington, Mar. 19, 1780, in ibid., 3:321.

51. TJ to Samuel Huntington, Sept. 3, 1780, in ibid., 3:589–90.

52. See TJ to James Madison, Mar. 27, 1780, in ibid., 3:335–36; TJ to Steuben, Jan. 9, 1781, in ibid., 4:327; and TJ to John Walker, Jan. 18, 1781, in ibid., 4:400.

53. TJ to John Adams, August 1777, in ibid., 2:28; TJ to George Washington, June 11, 1780, in ibid., 3:433.

54. See Boyd's notes in Jefferson, *Papers*, 4:257–58.

55. TJ to Thomas McKean, Aug. 4, 1781, in Jefferson, *Papers*, 6:113.

56. Jefferson, *Papers*, 6:174–75; Chastellux, "Philosophical Encounter," 12.

57. Malone says that Jefferson declined due to his wife's ill health, following the birth of a daughter. Chastellux wrote in his travel journal on April 17 that Jefferson would have accompanied him to visit the Natural Bridge "but his wife was expecting her confinement at any moment, and [Jefferson] is as good a husband as he is a philosopher

and citizen." Malone, *Jefferson and His Time*, 1:394–95; Chastellux, "Philosophical Encounter," 17.

58. Editor's notes, in Jefferson, *Papers*, 6:175n; John Tyler to TJ, May 16, 1782, in ibid., 6:179.

59. TJ to James Monroe, May 20, 1782, in ibid., 6:184–87.

Chapter 4. Of Manna, Mouse, and Mammoth: *Notes on the State of Virginia* as Jefferson's Pentateuch

1. Miller, *Jefferson and Nature*, 17.

2. Malone, *Jefferson and His Time*, 1:377; Burstein, *Inner Jefferson*, 18; Ellis, *American Sphinx*, 85. From the opposite end of the spectrum, Douglas Anderson believes Jefferson intended for *Notes* to be incomprehensible, especially Query 14 where Jefferson deals with Virginia's Constitution and slavery—"an inner topography stubbornly resistant to our keenest instruments of analysis." Anderson, "Subterraneous Virginia," 247.

3. TJ to Marquis de Chastellux, Jan. 16, 1784, in Jefferson, *Papers*, 6:487.

4. Jefferson, Jefferson Papers, Massachusetts Historical Society. See Wilson, "Jefferson Unbound," 48–53.

5. TJ to Charles Francois D'Anmours, Nov. 30, 1780, in Jefferson, *Papers*, 4:168.

6. TJ to Charles Francois D'Anmours, Nov. 30, 1780, in Jefferson, *Papers*, 4:168.

7. TJ to John Fitzgerald, Feb. 27, 1781, Fitzgerald to TJ, Apr. 1, 1781, in Jefferson, *Papers*, 5:15, 311. See Robert L. Darnton, *Business of Enlightenment*, 34–35, for the various versions of the *Encyclopédie* and their publishing histories.

8. TJ to James Hunter, May 28, 1781, in Jefferson, *Papers*, 6:25. Finally, in 1783 he was asked to return it. Editorial note following TJ to David S. Franks [Mar. or Apr. 1783], in Jefferson, *Papers*, 6:258.

9. Peterson, *Thomas Jefferson and the New Nation*, 249.

10. Wilson, "Jefferson and the Republic of Letters," 57. See also Hatzenbuehler, "Of Manna, Mouse, and Mammoth."

11. Peterson, *Thomas Jefferson and the New Nation*, 250.

12. Concerning the focus of *Notes*, David Waldstreicher writes, "[Jefferson's] historic role in the events of the American Revolution makes sense only in the light of the peculiar anxieties of his generation of Virginia planters. . . . This background . . . can [also] help us understand the particular passion he brought to reforming Virginia from within. It also helps us to make sense of his attitude toward slavery, which he pronounced unjust, continued to profit from and yet blamed on the British as the epitome of everything that was wrong with the empire his generation had inherited." Waldstreicher, introduction to *Notes*, 21, 3, 10. But in the preface, Waldstreicher insists that *Notes* is a document "about Virginia and America simultaneously. . . . [A]t every turn the *Notes* reveals itself as a quintessentially American document." Waldstreicher, preface to *Notes*, iv–v.

13. "Marbois Queries concerning Virginia" [before Nov. 30, 1780], in Jefferson, *Papers*, 4:166–67. Silvio A. Bedini suggests that Jefferson rearranged Marbois's queries "according to what he visualized a guide book would include." Bedini, *Jefferson: Statesman of Science*, 94.

14. Jefferson, *Notes*, 108–9.

15. Ibid., 164–65.

16. Ibid., 166. The table (167) downplays the importance of wheat and, especially, corn because it does not attempt to estimate the amount of these products consumed on Virginia's plantations and farms.

17. Fowler, "Mythologies of a Founder," 131.

18. Darnton, *Business of Enlightenment*, 7.

19. Darnton, *Great Cat Massacre*, 192–93.

20. Ibid., 205.

21. Darnton, *Business of Enlightenment*, 7–8. Cynthia Koepp makes a similar point, that the *Encyclopédie* "often purport[ed] to be comprehensive and systematic" but instead fascinates and frustrates because of "omissions and lack of predictability." Koepp, "Alphabetical Order," 234.

22. Jefferson, *Notes*, 4.

23. Paine, *Common Sense*, 34–35.

24. Jefferson, *Notes*, 16.

25. Ibid., 43–47.

26. Ibid., 55.

27. Ibid., 58.

28. Ibid., 59.

29. Ibid., 65.

30. TJ to Madison, May 11, 1785, in Jefferson, *Papers*, 8:148.

31. TJ to Chastellux, June 7, 1785, in Jefferson, *Papers*, 8:184.

32. TJ to John Stockdale, Feb. 27, 1787, in Jefferson, *Papers*, 11:183.

33. Jefferson, *Notes*, xvii.

34. Ibid., 19.

35. Peden, note 1, in Jefferson, *Notes*, 296.

36. Jefferson, *Notes*, 197.

37. Ibid., 198–99.

38. Ibid., 31–32.

39. Ibid., 32–33.

40. Ibid., 33. For attacks on Jefferson as a heretic for undermining the possibility of a worldwide flood, see Martin, *Thomas Jefferson: Scientist*, esp. 239ff.

41. Jefferson, *Notes*, 47.

42. TJ to Chastellux, June 7, 1785, in Jefferson, *Papers*, 8:184.

43. Sheridan, *Jefferson and Religion*, 16–18.

44. Jefferson, *Notes*, 46. These conclusions are at odds with those of James A. Caesar that Jefferson did not take sides in the "monogenesis" (differences among humans resulted from environment and, therefore, might be overcome) or "polygenesis" (different human species were permanently different due to genetic differences) debates that raged during his time. Caesar, "Natural Rights and Scientific Racism," 170–71.

45. Jefferson, *Notes*, 137–43.

46. Jordan, *White over Black*, esp. Chaps. 1, 12, and 13. See also Jack N. Rakove, who points out that however offensive we find these views today, we must recall that Jefferson

used these arguments not to support but rather to oppose slavery. Rakove, "Our Jefferson," 222.

47. Jefferson, *Papers*, 1:495.

48. Jefferson, "Thomas Jefferson: Second Inaugural Address," 22. See also Sanford, "Religious Beliefs of Thomas Jefferson," 70–71.

49. Buckley, "Political Theology," 80.

50. TJ to David Rittenhouse, July 19, 1778, in Jefferson, *Papers*, 2:202–3.

51. Jefferson, *Notes*; seven of the ten appear on 137; the eighth begins on p. 143; the ninth starts on 146; and the tenth, 149.

52. Jefferson, *Notes*, 148.

53. See, for example, TJ to Edward Carrington, Jan. 16, 1787, in Jefferson, *Papers*, 11:49

54. Jefferson, *Notes*, 161.

55. Ibid., 162.

56. Ibid., 163. For a discussion of fears among Virginians by the mid-1700s that they were becoming lazy and indolent, see Sobel, *World They Made Together*, 61–62.

57. Jefferson, *Notes*, 163; Deuteronomy 8:17–20 (King James Version). It is also interesting to contemplate possible connections with Deuteronomy 18:18–19: "I will raise them up a Prophet from among their brethren like unto thee, and will put my words in his mouth; and he shall speak unto them all that I shall command him. And it shall come to pass, *that* whosoever will not harken unto my words which he shall speak in my name, I will require *it* of him."

58. Malone, *Jefferson and His Time*, 1:235–85. See also Hatzenbuehler, "'Growing Weary in Well-Doing,'" 20–21, and Jefferson, *Notes*, 137ff.

59. TJ to George Wythe, Nov. 1, 1778, in Jefferson, *Papers*, 2:229–30.

60. Jefferson, *Notes*, xix–xxi.

61. Jack P. Greene makes a similar point—"No inhabitant at any time during the period [1780–1815] . . . provided a more powerful social and cultural critique of [Virginia] than did Jefferson in his *Notes on the State of Virginia*." Greene also emphasizes, however, that *Notes* also celebrated Virginia's and Virginians' achievements—"No matter how urgent his pleas, in the *Notes* and elsewhere, for the reformation of many aspects of Virginian society, his relationship to his state was ever defined by an abiding Virginia patriotism"—a point later amplified by Edmund Randolph and others. Greene, "Intellectual Reconstruction of Virginia," 231, 249–50.

62. Jefferson, "Jefferson's Extracts from the Gospels," *Papers*.

Chapter 5. Refreshing the Tree of Liberty with the Blood of Patriots and Tyrants: Defending Virginia with Extremist Language in the 1780s and 1790s

1. Fiske, *The Critical Period*.

2. TJ to John Adams, Nov. 13, 1787, in Jefferson, *Papers*, 12:351.

3. TJ to William S. Smith, Nov. 13, 1787, in Jefferson, *Papers*, 12:356.

4. For a discussion of this historiography, see Hatzenbuehler, "Refreshing the Tree of Liberty," 89–91. Since this article was published, several additional books have empha-

sized the point that, while Jefferson's radicalism may have been nurtured by his years in France, he would have held his views whether the French Revolution occurred or not. See O'Brien, *Long Affair*; Ellis, *American Sphinx*, 99–105; and Adams, *Paris Years of Thomas Jefferson*, 5, 37, 294–97. In his most recent book, Ellis puts it most colorfully: "Like Voltaire, Jefferson longed for the day when the last king would be strangled with the entrails of the last priest." Ellis, *Founding Brothers*, 139.

5. TJ to James Monroe, June 17, 1785, in Jefferson, *Papers*, 8:233.

6. TJ to John Barrister, Jr., Oct. 15, 1785, in ibid., 636–37.

7. TJ to William S. Smith, June 22, 1785, in ibid., 8:249; TJ to James Monroe, Nov. 11, 1784, in ibid., 7:512; TJ to John Adams, May 25, 1785, in ibid., 8:164.

8. William S. Smith to TJ, Dec. 5, 1786, in ibid., 8:249.

9. John Jay to TJ, Oct. 27, 1786, in ibid., 8:488–89.

10. TJ to William S. Smith, Dec. 5, 1786, in ibid., 8:578; John Adams to TJ, Nov. 30, 1786, in ibid., 8:619; TJ to Abigail Adams, Dec. 21, 1785, in ibid., 8:621.

11. TJ to William S. Smith, Dec. 5, 1786, in ibid., 8:578; John Adams to TJ, Nov. 30, 1786, in ibid., 8:619; TJ to Abigail Adams, Dec. 21, 1785, in ibid., 8:621; TJ to Ezra Stiles, Dec. 24, 1786, in ibid., 8:629.

12. TJ to John Adams, Oct. 18, 1813, in Cappon, ed., *The Adams-Jefferson Letters*, 2:388–89. For Jefferson's ruminations about anti-republican tendencies in Massachusetts during the War of 1812 and the Missouri Crisis of the 1820s, see Onuf, *Jefferson's Empire*, 123–29.

13. TJ to C. W. F. Dumas, Dec. 25, 1788, in Jefferson, *Papers*, 10:631; TJ to William Carmichael, Dec. 26, 1786, in ibid., 10:633–34; TJ to Edward Carrington, Jan. 16, 1787, in ibid., 11:48–50.

14. Evans, "Private Indebtedness and the Revolution in Virginia"; David Ramsay to TJ, Nov. 8, 1786, in Jefferson, *Papers*, 10:513, and Apr. 7, 1787, in ibid., 11:279; Alexander Donald to TJ, Mar. 1, 1787, in ibid., 11:194.

15. Szatmary, *Shays' Rebellion*, 1–33. A more recent interpretation of Shays's Rebellion downplays the importance of the debts and emphasizes sectional differences between the western farmers and the eastern merchants and speculators who feared that they would lose their investments. Richards, *Shays's Rebellion*, 62–79. Richards also emphasizes that kinship ties best explain who turned out to support Shays as well as those who wanted new churches in their western towns. Ibid., 91–113, 164.

16. TJ to Nathaniel Tracy, Aug. 17, 1785, in Jefferson, *Papers*, 8:398.

17. TJ to Abigail Adams, Aug. 30, 1787, in ibid., 12:65.

18. TJ to Edward Carrington, Jan. 16, 1787, in ibid., 11:49.

19. John Jay to TJ, Dec. 14, 1786, in ibid., 10:596–99. The Jay-Gardoqui Treaty would have opened trade with Spain in return for Americans renouncing the right to trade on the Mississippi River for twenty years.

20. Abigail Adams to TJ, Jan. 29, 1787, in ibid., 11:86; TJ to Abigail Adams, Feb. 22, 1787, in ibid., 11:174–75.

21. John Adams to TJ, Nov. 30, 1786, in ibid., 10:557.

22. William Short to TJ, Mar. 26, 1787, in ibid., 11:239–42; James Madison to TJ, Apr. 23, 1787, in ibid., 11:307; Benjamin Franklin to TJ, Apr. 19, 1787, in ibid., 11:301–2.

23. TJ to David Hartley, July 2, 1787, in ibid., 11:526.

24. James Madison to TJ, June 6, 1787, in ibid., 11:400–402.

25. TJ to Benjamin Hawkins, Aug. 4, 1787, in ibid., 11:684. See also letters to David Ramsay, William Hay, John Blair, and George Washington written between Aug. 4 and 14, 1787, in ibid., 11:685–87, 12:28–36.

26. John Adams to TJ, Nov. 10 1787, in ibid., 12:335.

27. TJ to William S. Smith, Nov. 13, 1787, in ibid., 12:356. He later wrote in his *Anas* that the monarchists had been so scared by Shays's Rebellion that they wanted a Constitution. Jefferson, *Complete Anas*, 187.

28. McCoy, "James Madison and Visions of American Nationality"; Banning, "Hamiltonian Madison: A Reconsideration"; and Banning, *Sacred Fire of Liberty*.

29. Banning, *Jefferson and Madison*, 193, 77. See also Banning, "Hamiltonian Madison" and *Sacred Fire of Liberty*, Chap. 10.

30. Banning, *Sacred Fire of Liberty*, 298–303.

31. Banning, *Sacred Fire of Liberty*, 320; Yazawa, "Republican Expectations"; Kaplan, *Alexander Hamilton*, 96.

32. Yazawa, "Republican Expectations," 35, 3. See also Freeman, "Slander, Poison, Whispers and Fame," and Jefferson, *Complete Anas*.

33. Risjord, "The Compromise of 1790," 312. I am borrowing the phrase from Higginbotham, *Keystone in the Democratic Arch*.

34. Banning, *Sacred Fire of Liberty*, 321.

35. I am borrowing this phrase from Koch, *Jefferson and Madison*. See also Banning, *Jefferson and Madison*, xii, where he states that the two men formed "a long and intimate political collaboration"; and Ellis, *Founding Brothers*, 80, that Jefferson and Madison "would not abandon the government, but capture it."

36. Jefferson, *Complete Anas*, 39.

37. Jefferson, *Papers*, 18:611–88. The appendix also includes a discussion of the involvement of Hamilton with James Reynolds and his alleged affair with Reynolds's wife to mask accusations that he had abused his office as secretary of treasury to speculate in government securities.

38. TJ to George Mason, Feb. 4, 1791, in Jefferson, *Papers*, 19:241. See also TJ to Thomas Paine, June 19, 1792 [out of sequence in the *Papers*], in ibid., 20:312; TJ to Lafayette, June 16, 1792, in ibid., 24:85, where he refers to the monarchical sect as "preachers without followers"; and "Notes of a Conversation with George Washington," Oct. 1, 1792, in ibid., 24:428.

39. TJ to Jonathan B. Smith, Apr. 26, 1791, in ibid., 20:290.

40. TJ to George Washington, May 8, 1791, in ibid., 20:291.

41. TJ to James Madison, May 9, 1791, in ibid., 20:293. See also TJ to John Adams, July 17, 1791, in ibid., 20:302. In fact, Adams wrote only the *Discourses on Davila*, published between April 1790 and April 1791, not the letters of Publicola, which were written by his son John Quincy Adams. Editor's note, in Jefferson, *Papers*, 22:38.

42. "Opinion on the Constitutionality of the Bill for Establishing a National Bank," Feb. 15, 1791, in Jefferson, *Papers*, 19:276–79.

43. TJ to James Sullivan, July 31, 1791, in ibid., 21:709.

44. TJ to James Madison, June 29, 1792, in ibid., 24:133. For a full measure of this

change in nomenclature, see esp. TJ to Volney, Dec. 9, 1795, in ibid., 28:551, where Jefferson referred to the existence in the United States of "two political sects[, o]ne which fears the people most, the other the government."

45. Hofstadter, *Idea of a Party System*, 12.

46. TJ to James Madison, Dec. 28, 1794, in Jefferson, *Papers*, 28:228; TJ to James Madison, Mar. 27, 1796, in ibid., 29:51; TJ to Philip Mazzei, Apr. 24, 1796, in ibid., 29:81.

47. "Memoranda of Conversations with the President," Mar. 1, 1792, in ibid., 23:284ff.; "Notes of a Conversation with George Washington," July 10, 1792, in ibid., 24:210.

48. "Notes of a Conversation with George Washington," May 23, 1793, in ibid., 26:101–2.

49. TJ to James Madison, Aug. 11, 1793, in ibid., 26:652. For Washington's response to these and other charges, see GW to TJ, July 16, 1796, in ibid., 29:142.

50. See, for example, Banning, *Sacred Fire of Liberty*, 390–91.

51. Koch, *Jefferson and Madison*, 182–84; "Petition on the Election of Jurors," [Oct. 1798], in Jefferson, *Republic of Letters*, 2:1076–78.

52. TJ to Monroe, Sept. 7, 1797, in Jefferson, *Papers*, 29:526. See also TJ to Madison, Oct. 26, 1798, in Jefferson, *Republic of Letters*, 2:1075.

53. TJ to Monroe, Sept. 7, 1797, in Jefferson, *Papers*, 29:527.

54. TJ to Madison, Oct. 26, 1798, in Jefferson, *Republic of Letters*, 2:1077–78.

55. Koch, *Jefferson and Madison*, 184.

56. For Jefferson's draft of the Kentucky Resolutions and Madison's responses, see Jefferson, *Republic of Letters*, quotes on 2:1080 and 2:1082.

57. Jefferson, *Republic of Letters*, 2:1082–85.

58. TJ to James Madison, Jan. 30, 1799, in Jefferson, *Republic of Letters*, 2:1091. See also Tucker, *Life of Jefferson*, 63: "Mr. Jefferson . . . spoke of the doctrine as, of all others which had been broached by the federal government, the most formidable . . . that the common law could become a part of the law of the general government only by positive adoption; and being neither adopted, nor capable of being adopted, by reason of the limited powers of the federal government, it could constitute no part of the law."

59. TJ to Edmund Randolph, Aug. 18, 1799, in Jefferson, *Writings*, ed. Lipscomb and Bergh, 10:125–29.

60. Ellis, *Founding Brothers*, 200. Forrest McDonald, among others, has touted this same position, that the people in the states, not the people of the United States as a whole, ratified the Constitution. See, for example, McDonald and McDonald, *Requiem*.

61. TJ to John Taylor, June 1 1798, in Jefferson, *Writings*, ed. Lipscomb and Bergh, 10:44–47.

Chapter 6. "Pursu[ing] Federal and Republican Principles": The Unfulfilled Revolution of Jefferson's Presidency

1. TJ to Spencer Roane, Sept. 6, 1819, in Jefferson, *Portable Jefferson*, 562. According to Stephen Howard Browne, the inaugural address was notable because it "[gave] to principle the force of artistic expression" and melded "partisan, theoretical and rhetorical" perspectives on republican government. Browne, *Jefferson's Call for Nationhood*, 131.

2. All of the quotes from Jefferson's first inaugural address are taken from Jefferson, "Thomas Jefferson: First Inaugural Address."

3. TJ to Elbridge Gerry, Jan. 26, 1799, in Jefferson, *Writings*, ed. Lipscomb and Bergh, 10:74–86; Brown, *Redeeming the Republic*, 206, 241.

4. TJ to Elbridge Gerry, Jan. 26, 1799, in Jefferson, *Writings*, ed. Lipscomb and Bergh, 10:77. In the inaugural address, Jefferson promised to "support . . . state governments in all their rights, as the most competent administrations for our domestic concerns and the surest bulwarks against anti-republican tendencies."

5. Jefferson, "Opinion on the Constitutionality of a National Bank," in Jefferson, *Papers*, 19:276, 279–80.

6. TJ to George Mason, Feb. 4, 1791, in ibid., 19:242.

7. TJ to George Washington, May 23, 1792, in ibid., 23:537.

8. TJ to George Washington, Sept. 9, 1792, in ibid., 24:353.

9. TJ to Elbridge Gerry, Jan. 26, 1799, in Jefferson, *Writings*, ed. Lipscomb and Bergh, 10:77. In the inaugural address, Jefferson advocated "a wise and frugal government, which shall . . . not take from the mouth of labor the bread it has earned" and "economy in the public expense, that labor may be lightly burdened."

10. TJ to George Washington, Sept. 9, 1792, in Jefferson, *Papers*, 24:355.

11. TJ to William Short, Jan. 3, 1793, in Jefferson, *Portable Jefferson*, 456.

12. TJ to Elbridge Gerry, Jan. 26, 1799, in Jefferson, *Writings*, ed. Lipscomb and Bergh, 10:77. He said in the inaugural address that he favored "a well-disciplined militia—our best reliance in peace and for the first moments of war, till regulars may relieve them."

13. Jefferson, *Notes*, 175–76.

14. See esp. Combs, *Jay Treaty*.

15. TJ to Elbridge Gerry, Jan. 26, 1799, in Jefferson, *Writings*, ed. Lipscomb and Bergh, 10:77–78; Kaplan, *Colonies into Nation*, Chap. 10.

16. Kaplan, "Jefferson and the Constitution" and "Thomas Jefferson."

17. "Washington's Final Manuscript of the Farewell Address," in Gilbert, *To the Farewell Address*, 145; Kaplan, "Consensus of 1789."

18. TJ to Elbridge Gerry, Jan. 26, 1799, in Jefferson, *Writings*, ed. Lipscomb and Bergh, 10:78.

19. The (Hartford) *Connecticut Courant* demeaned this passage with the words: "If by that power you mean the Supreme God, I heartily unite with you, for we have great and pressing occasion for his assistance." Nov. 9, 1801, no. 4.

20. Jefferson, "Bill for Establishing Religious Freedom," in Jefferson, *Portable Jefferson*, 252.

21. Jefferson, *Notes*, 159.

22. TJ to Nehemiah Dodge and Others, A Committee of the Danbury Baptist Association, in the State of Connecticut, in Jefferson, *Portable Jefferson*, 303; Sheridan, *Jefferson and Religion*, 68.

23. Jefferson, *Notes*, 175.

24. McCoy, *Elusive Republic*, esp. Chap. 8.

25. Jefferson, *Papers*, 1:122.

26. Jefferson, *Notes*, 164–65.

27. Sloan, *Principle and Interest*, 194–95.

28. Risjord, *Thomas Jefferson*, 130–34.

29. Johnstone, *Jefferson and the Presidency*, 14.

30. Ibid., esp. Chap. 5.

31. Cunningham, *Process of Government*, 322–23. See also Cunningham, *Jeffersonian Republicans* and *Jeffersonian Republicans in Power*.

32. TJ to Robert R. Livingston, Apr. 18, 1802, in Jefferson, *Portable Jefferson*, 486.

33. DeConde, *This Affair of Louisiana*; Paquette, "Revolutionary Saint Domingue," 209–11 (Hamilton quotation on 211).

34. Quoted in Cooke, *Alexander Hamilton*, 234.

35. TJ to John Breckinridge, Aug. 12, 1803, in Jefferson, *Portable Jefferson*, 497.

36. Cunningham, *Process of Government*, 275.

37. All of the quotes from Jefferson's second inaugural address are taken from "Thomas Jefferson: Second Inaugural Address."

38. Peterson, *Thomas Jefferson and the New Nation*, 851–54, 865–74; Kennedy, *Burr, Hamilton, and Jefferson*, 360. See also TJ to George Hay, May 20, 26, 28, 1807, and Sept. 4 and 7, 1807, in Jefferson, *Writings*, ed. Lipscomb and Bergh, 11:205–6, 209, 210, 360–61, 365.

39. TJ to Henry Dearborn and Albert Gallatin, June 25, 1807, in Jefferson, *Writings*, ed. Lipscomb and Bergh, 11:255.

40. TJ to J. W. Eppes, July 12, 1807, in Jefferson, *Works*, 9:457.

41. Onuf, *Jefferson's Empire*, 122–23.

42. Ibid., 135, 132.

43. TJ to George Hay, Sept. 4, 1807, in Jefferson, *Works*, 9:360–61; TJ to Thomas Paine, Sept. 6, 1807, in ibid., 9:362–63; TJ to James Wilkinson, Sept. 20, 1807, in ibid., 9:375.

44. Spivak, *Jefferson's English Crisis*, 73–74.

45. Jefferson, *Writings*, ed. Lipscomb and Bergh, 11:165, 170, 172.

46. TJ to James Bowdoin, July 10, 1807, in ibid., 11:269; TJ to Craven Peyton, Aug. 10, 1807, quoted in Spivak, *Jefferson's English Crisis*, 71.

47. TJ to William H. Cabell, July 16, 1807, Jefferson Papers, Library of Congress; Spivak, 78–83.

48. See, for example, TJ to William H. Cabell, Aug. 7, 11, 17, 1807, in Jefferson, *Writings*, ed. Lipscomb and Bergh, 11:307–10, 318–23, 331–32, and, more generally, Thomas Jefferson Papers, Library of Congress.

49. TJ to William H. Cabell, Aug. 11, 1807, in Jefferson, *Writings*, ed. Lipscomb and Bergh, 11:323.

50. TJ to James Madison, Aug. 20, 1807, in ibid., 11:341.

51. TJ to Henry Dearborn, Aug. 28, 1807, Jefferson Papers, Library of Congress.

52. TJ to Robert Smith, Sept. 3, 1807, Jefferson Papers, Library of Congress.

53. TJ to Thomas Paine, Oct. 9, 1807, TJ to Caesar Rodney, Oct. 8, 1807, Smith to TJ, Oct. 19, 1807, quoted in Spivak, *Jefferson's English Crisis*, 74, 85, 87.

54. Spivak, *Jefferson's English Crisis*, 75–77; 84.

55. Ibid., 83. Joseph Wheelan reaches the opposite conclusion—that the cabinet was ready for war but Jefferson wasn't. Wheelan, *Jefferson's War*, 335.

56. Gallatin to TJ, Oct. 21, 1807, quoted in Spivak, *Jefferson's English Crisis*, 89; Spivak, *Jefferson's English Crisis*, 96; TJ to William H. Cabell, Nov. 1, 1807, in Jefferson, *Writings*, ed. Lipscomb and Bergh, 11:388–89.

57. Hatzenbuehler and Ivie, *Congress Declares War*, 82–91.

58. TJ to William H. Cabell, Nov. 1, 1787, in *Writings*, ed. Lipscomb and Bergh, 11:388–89; Mannix, "Gallatin, Jefferson and the Embargo of 1808." Spivak says Madison was most likely the author of the embargo. Spivak, *Jefferson's English Crisis*, 109.

59. Spivak, *Jefferson's English Crisis*; McCoy, *Elusive Republic*.

60. Cunningham, *Process of Government*, 119. David Mayer sees no contradiction in the Louisiana Purchase and the implementation of the embargo by arguing that in both cases Jefferson stayed within the broad confines of law. In Mayer's view, both were properly the responsibility of the national government because they concerned foreign, not domestic, affairs. Mayer, *Constitutional Thought of Thomas Jefferson*, 220–21, 256.

61. Hatzenbuehler and Ivie, *Congress Declares War*, Chap. 7.

62. TJ to Benjamin Austin, Jan. 9, 1816, in Jefferson, *Portable Jefferson*, 549–50.

63. John Murrin portrays the situation differently based upon his belief that Madison's changes in Hamilton's plans were temporary—Andrew Jackson later killed the Second National Bank and just prior to the Panic of 1837 the national debt had been erased—and that the army had largely been purged of Federalists by the end of Jefferson's administration. Murrin, "Jeffersonian Triumph and American Exceptionalism."

64. (Hartford) *Connecticut Courant*, Oct. 26, Nov. 2, 9, 1801.

65. Quoted in Egerton, "Thomas Jefferson and the Hemings Family," 328.

66. Foster et al., "Jefferson Fathered Slave's Last Child," 27–28.

67. Neiman, "Coincidence or Causal Connection?" 198–210; Gordon-Reed, "Memories," 236 and *Thomas Jefferson and Sally Hemings*. For Dan Jordan's statement accepting the consensus position, see *http://www.monticello.org/plantation/hemingscontro/appendixd.html*.

In 1981, the University Press of Virginia published a slim volume entitled *Thomas Jefferson and His Unknown Brother* that contains a transcript of thirty-two of at least fifty letters between the famous Jefferson and "his 'unknown' brother Randolph between 1789 and 1815." In his preface to this volume, James A. Bear, Jr., offers this opinion: "This brief correspondence contains little of real historical significance" (Bear, preface to *Thomas Jefferson and His Unknown Brother*, 12). He was wrong. Jefferson's visit to Monticello lasted from the afternoon or evening of August 5 through September 30. Jefferson, *Jefferson's Memorandum Books*, 2:1208–12. A letter that he wrote to Randolph inviting him to Monticello becomes the focal point for a rebuttal to the consensus position. See Scholars Report at http://www.tjheritage.org/documents/screport.pdf.

68. See Rahe's dissent from the Scholars Report at http://www.tjheritage.org/documents/screport.pdf.

69. Rothman, "James Callender and Social Knowledge," 103. See also Rothman, "Can the 'Character Defense' Survive?" and *Notorious in the Neighborhood*.

70. Douglas Adair made a similar point forty years before Rothman by indicating that in order to refute Callender's accusations Jefferson would have had to admit that

Sally Hemings was the daughter of his father-in-law, John Wayles. Adair, "The Jefferson Scandals," 174.

71. Rothman, "James Callender and Social Knowledge," 105–6.

72. Clinton, *Plantation Mistress*, 218–19.

73. Wyatt-Brown, *Southern Honor*, 307–10. See also John Emilio and Estelle Free-man, *Intimate Matters*, 36: "Male planters, by virtue of their class, were not bound by the prohibitions against interracial sex. Thus relationships between white planters and black women often formed."

74. Rothman, "James Callender and Social Knowledge," 106.

75. Randall, *Life of Jefferson*, 3:18–20.

76. Randall to Hugh B. Grigsby, Feb. 15, Dec. 4, 1856, July 26, 1857, in Klingberg and Klingberg, eds., *Correspondence*, 29–30, 71–72, 95. Dr. Robley Dunglison also mentions that not everyone in Jefferson's neighborhood revered him. "[H]e had more personal detractors there—partly owing to the differences in political sentiments . . . but still more perhaps . . . on the subject of religion." Dunglison, *Autobiographical Ana*, 33.

77. Henry S. Randall to James Parton, June 1, 1868, in Flower, *James Parton*, 236.

78. Randall to Parton, June 1, 1868, in ibid., 237.

79. Leary, "Sally Hemings's Children," 205–6.

80. McLaughlin, *Jefferson and Monticello*, 29, and *http://www.monticello.org/planta-tion/Sally_Hemings.html* (accessed Mar. 10, 2005).

81. Randall to Parton, June 1, 1868, in Flower, *James Parton*, 239.

Chapter 7. "[My] Country and It's Unfortunate Condition": Continuing and Reversing Commitment to Change in Later Years

1. TJ to Pierre Samuel du Pont de Nemours, Mar. 2, 1809, TJ to General John Arm-strong, Mar. 5, 1809, in Jefferson, *Writings*, ed. Lipscomb and Bergh, 12:259–60, 262.

2. "To the Inhabitants of Albemarle County, in Virginia," Apr. 3, 1809, in ibid., 12:269–70.

3. Patton, *Jefferson, Cabell and the University of Virginia*, 18.

4. TJ to John Adams, Oct. 28, 1813, in Cappon, ed., *Adams-Jefferson Letters*, 2:390.

5. Jefferson, *Notes*, 148.

6. Ibid., 146–47.

7. Ibid., 161.

8. TJ to John Adams, Oct. 18, 1813, in Cappon, ed., *Adams-Jefferson Letters*, 2:390.

9. TJ to Wilson Cary Nicholas, Apr. 2, 1816, in Jefferson, *Writings*, ed. Lipscomb and Bergh, 14:451–54.

10. TJ to Joseph Carrington Cabell, Jan. 24, 1816, Feb. 2, 1816, in ibid., 14:414, 420–23.

11. TJ to Joseph Carrington Cabell, Jan. 24, 1816, Feb. 2, 1816, in ibid., 14:422–23.

12. Patton, *Jefferson, Cabell and the University of Virginia*, 18–22.

13. TJ to Joseph C. Cabell, Jan. 5, 1815, in Jefferson, *Writings*, ed. Ford, 9:500–501.

14. TJ to Samuel Kercheval, July 12, 1816, in Jefferson, *Works*, 12:13; TJ to Spencer Roane, Sept. 6, 1819, in ibid., 139; TJ to John Hampden Pleasants, Apr. 19, 1924, in Jef-ferson, *Writings*, ed. Lipscomb and Bergh, 16:29.

15.TJ to David Barrow, May 1, 1815, in Jefferson, *Works*, 11:470–71. For a discussion emphasizing the ambiguities in Jefferson's religious beliefs, see Little, "Religion and Civil Virtue in America."

16. TJ to Edward Coles, Aug. 25, 1814, in Jefferson, *Writings*, ed. Ford, 11:418–19. Coles described Jefferson's answer as "in perfect accordance with his character, in fine harmony with his philanthropic republicanism, & in every way worthy of the renown[ed] author of the Declaration of Independence." Quoted in McCoy, *Last of the Fathers*, 310–12.

17. Langhorne, "Edward Coles, Thomas Jefferson, and the Rights of Man"; McCoy, *Last of the Fathers*, 313–15.

18. *Interpreter's Bible*, 10:337.

19. TJ to Horatio G. Spafford, Mar. 17, 1814, in Jefferson, *Writings*, ed. Lipscomb and Bergh, 14:20.

20. TJ to James Madison, Feb. 17, 1826, in Jefferson, *Works*, 12:456.

21. Mayer, *Constitutional Thought of Thomas Jefferson*, 2–16, 327. Mayer argues that this emphasis on Whig ideals continued through 1776, at which time Jefferson turned his attention more to developing ideas of republicanism (popular participation in government) and federalism (separation of powers). The first inaugural, in Mayer's views, successfully melded Whig, republican, and federal ideas.

22. Jefferson, *Writings*, ed. Lipscomb and Bergh, 19:407, 416.

23. TJ to Charles Clay, Jan. 29, 1815, in ibid., 19:14, 234; TJ to William B. Giles, Dec. 26, 1825, in ibid., 16:151.

24. Egerton, *Charles Fenton Mercer*, 119–26; Addis, *Jefferson's Vision*, 52.

25. Patton, *Jefferson, Cabell and the University of Virginia*, 43, 57–62; Dabney, *Mr. Jefferson's University*, 4–6; Wills, *Mr. Jefferson's University*, 30–31.

26. TJ to Albert Gallatin, Feb. 15, 1818, in Jefferson, *Writings*, ed. Lipscomb and Bergh, 16:258.

27. TJ to Joseph Carrington Cabell, Jan. 24, 1816, in ibid., 14:413; TJ to Joseph Carrington Cabell, Jan. 14, 1818, in Jefferson, *Works*, 12:85.

28. TJ to Joseph Carrington Cabell, Feb. 7, 1826, in ibid., 14:452.

29. McCoy, *Last of the Fathers*, 241.

30. Chambers, *Poplar Forest and Thomas Jefferson*, 8.

31. Jefferson, *Jefferson's Memorandum Books*, 2:1163.

32. Chambers, *Poplar Forest and Thomas Jefferson*, 80–84; 106.

33. Ibid., 36.

34. Heath, *Hidden Lives*, 46, 50. He also paid slaves, chiefly Phil Hubbard, to haul dirt from the rear of the house to create a sunken lawn—see Chambers, *Poplar Forest and Thomas Jefferson*, 53–55 (spelling "Phill" or "fill").

35. Chambers, *Poplar Forest and Thomas Jefferson*, 121.

36. Kimball, *Thomas Jefferson: Architect*, 72.

37. Ibid.; Chambers, *Poplar Forest and Thomas Jefferson*, 98.

38. Heath, *Hidden Lives*, 4, 5, 58–59.

39. Chambers, *Poplar Forest and Thomas Jefferson*, 87; 145–47.

40. Ibid., 57, 71, 104, 110–11, 117, 120–21, 128, 135–36, 142–43; [Ellen Randolph Coolidge] to Henry S. Randall, ca. 1856, in Randall, *Life of Thomas Jefferson*, 3:342.

41. Wells, "Accommodation and Appropriation." I am grateful to Professor Wells for sharing this manuscript with me.

42. Chambers, *Thomas Jefferson and Poplar Forest*, 37.

43. Ibid., 37, 110–11.

44. It is interesting to note that after the house passed from Jefferson's family, the new owners changed the configuration of Poplar Forest to bring it into line with other Virginia houses of the time period by separating slaves and masters. By 1845, the new owners had built a new kitchen away from the main house and following a major fire in 1845 added a new stairwell to the center room, which they transformed into an access room to the upper and to the lower floors of the house. The octagonal room on the main floor under Jefferson's bedroom on the eastern side of the house now became the dining room, and the family moved into the other rooms on that level. This rearrangement moved the slaves, who once lived on that floor, to a new house removed some distance from the mansion. Chambers, *Thomas Jefferson and Poplar Forest*, 189–92.

45. *Interpreter's Bible*, 10:582.

46. Francis Eppes to Nicholas P. Trist, Nov. 7, 1826, Mar. 2, 1828, quoted in Chambers, *Thomas Jefferson and Poplar Forest*, 169, 172. Thomas Jefferson Randolph recalled a similar situation in his memoirs: "Farming on high lands at that time in Virginia was not profitable. . . . Tobacco was made exclusively on virgin soils the first and second years after clearing; leaving the land in the best condition to raise corn for the support of the plantation. . . . Then corn was planted every year on these virgin soils, turned fresh from tobacco, until the washing of rains had impoverished it. It was then abandoned to gullies, broom straw, and briers. In 1804 nine tenths of the cleared land in my neighborhood was in this condition. Their owners having sold at low rates and moved westward. After every dry year the roads would be thronged with emigrants west. In 1825 these lands were restored to cultivation but not to a remunerating fertility." Quoted in Vance, *Thomas Jefferson Randolph*, 51.

47. Although more Virginians of Ellen's and Francis's generation moved to Kentucky, Tennessee, and Ohio than the Deep South, the net effect of the emigration on Virginia was huge. David Hackett Fischer and James C. Kelley report that more than one-third of children born in Virginia about 1800 left the state. Fischer and Kelley, *Bound Away*, 137–40, 203–4. See also Jordan, *Political Leadership*, 3–6.

48. Jefferson [design and instructions for his burial marker], Thomas Jefferson Papers, Library of Congress, Washington, D.C.

**Conclusion: "Whether My Country Is the Better for My Having Lived at All?":
Changing the Meaning of Jefferson's Life**

1. "A Memorandum (Services to My Country)," [ca. 1800], in Jefferson *Writings*, ed. Peterson, 702–4.

2. Vance, *Thomas Jefferson Randolph*, 45; quotation on 110.

3. Ibid., 126–28.

4. Jefferson, *Memoir*, v–viii.

5. Quoted in Vance, *Thomas Jefferson Randolph*, 131.

6. Quoted in ibid., 131, 141.

7. Ibid., 142. Aside from Tucker's own comments, his book relies primarily on the sources contained in Jefferson's *Memoir*. So did an earlier biography by B. L. Rayner, who wrote it, he said, because the *Memoir* was "too voluminous, and consequently too expensive, to admit of a general circulation; nor is the mode of arrangement the best adapted to its reception into ordinary use as a work of reference. These considerations have suggested the plan of the present undertaking, which aspires to no higher claims than that of an analytic and, it is hoped, a well-asserted generalization of the original publication." Rayner, *Life of Jefferson*, preface.

8. Tucker, *Life of Jefferson*, 1:iii–x. Rayner's biography, published two years before Tucker's, also emphasizes Jefferson's nationalism but extends his influence to Europe and "the general amelioration of associated man throughout the world." Rayner also interprets Jefferson's decision to leave the Second Continental Congress to serve in the Virginia Assembly as based upon a desire to put into effect "the great work of political regeneration which he had sketched for his country and for mankind." Rayner, *Life of Jefferson*, Chaps. 2, 8.

9. Tucker, *Life of Jefferson*, 1:2–11. Tucker was an antislavery Virginian; later in *Life of Jefferson* he wrote: "His views of the future difficulties arising from domestic slavery, are yet in a state of probation. . . . But on all these great questions there are more and more converts to his opinions, among intelligent minds." Ibid., 2:563.

10. Ibid., 1:372–73.

11. Ibid., 2:127–28. Tucker's anger and attempts to sully Callender's name notwithstanding, it should be noted that he did not disavow Callender's charges (Chapter 7).

12. Ibid., 2:253. See also 255: "The [Burr trial] tended to confirm him in an opinion which he had long since entertained; that the judiciary, as well as every other branch of the government, should not be beyond the reach of the public disapprobation." Ibid., 261.

13. Ibid., 2:441–45, 562–63.

14. Ibid., 2:562–64. For a contemporary expression of this same point, see Mary Jo Salter: "He'd have the men / who come to his university / understand this: originality / is knowing what to copy, and when. / And why to amend." Salter, "The Hand of Thomas Jefferson," 90–91.

15. TJ to Roger C. Weightman, June 24, 1826, in Jefferson, *Writings*, ed. Peterson, 1516–17. See also TJ to Henry Lee, May 8, 1825, in ibid., 1501.

16. Baldwin, *Flush Times*, 72–77. Baldwin rose to prominence in Alabama as a lawyer and also briefly pursued a political career, having been elected in 1844 as a Whig to the Alabama legislature. In California, he continued to practice law, served for four years as associate justice of the California Supreme Court, and died unexpectedly in September 1864.

17. Ibid., 82–105; quotation on 86.

18. Baldwin, *Party Leaders*, 54–61; quotation on 61.

19. Ibid., 99. Later in the book he wrote, "Jefferson, while his state-papers convey an idea of great philanthropy of character and a philosophic serenity of temper, yet discloses in his correspondence an apparent vindictiveness and prejudice which are unequalled

[*sic*] among his contemporaries. . . . Indeed, the whole tone of his mind was partisan, and though his intellect was large enough to originate and resolve great ideas and principles, they were usually the ideas and principles of his own side." For a recent account of the *Anas*, see Freeman, "Slanders, Poison, Whispers, and Fame."

20. Baldwin, *Party Leaders*, 102–33; quotations on 109 and 115.

21. Ibid., 73, 139–40, 148, 170, 260. Baldwin's antithesis to Randolph is Henry Clay, whom he labeled "an American" (260). One additional, important area where Baldwin drew a major difference between Randolph and Jefferson is the War of 1812, which Randolph opposed because he saw it would increase the power of the national government, whereas Jefferson did not follow through with war during the *Chesapeake* crisis because he did not have the emotional temperament war requires. Baldwin was critical of both men, however, for not supporting a powerful navy for the United States (172, 218, 189).

22. Klingberg and Klingberg, *Correspondence*, 9; Randall to Hugh B. Grigsby, June 18, 1856, Randall to Grigsby, July 26, 1857, in ibid., 58–60, 95.

23. Randall to Hugh B. Grigsby, Dec. 24, 1857, Dec. 4, 1858, in ibid., 76–77. For Grigsby's opinion of Tucker's *Life*, see Grigsby to Randall, Dec. 8, 1856, in ibid., 75.

24. Hugh B. Grigsby to Randall, Nov. 12, 1858, in ibid., 147–49. A comparison of the language Randall and Tucker used suggests that there may be something to Tucker's charges. See Randall, *Life*, 3:18–20, and Tucker, *Life*, 2:126–27.

25. Boles, *South through Time*, 160–61; Peterson, *Jefferson Image*, 226.

26. For the changes in the wording of Jefferson's writings on the walls of the Memorial, see Fetter, "Revision of the Declaration of Independence," 137 and Fowler, "Mythologies of a Founder," 124.

Bibliography

Adair, Douglass. "The Jefferson Scandals." In *Fame and the Founding Fathers: Essays by Douglass Adair*. 1960; New York: W. W. Norton, 1974.

Adams, Stephen. *The Best and Worst Country in the World: Perspectives on the Early Virginia Landscape*. Charlottesville: University Press of Virginia, 2001.

Adams, William Howard. *The Paris Years of Thomas Jefferson*. New Haven: Yale University Press, 1997.

Addis, Cameron. *Jefferson's Vision for Education, 1760–1845*. New York: Peter Lang, 2003.

Albanese, Catherine L. "Whither the Sons (and Daughters)?" In *The American Revolution: Its Character and Limits*, ed. Jack P. Greene, 362–87. New York: New York University Press, 1987.

Anderson, Douglas. "Subterraneous Virginia: The Ethical Poetics of Thomas Jefferson." *Eighteenth-Century Studies* 33 (1999–2000): 233–49.

Appleby, Joyce. "Thomas Jefferson and the Psychology of Democracy." In *The Revolution of 1800: Democracy, Race, and the New Republic*, ed. James Horn, Jan Ellen Lewis, and Peter Onuf, 155–72. Charlottesville: University of Virginia Press, 2002.

Bailyn, Bernard. "Jefferson and the Ambiguities of Freedom." In *To Begin the World Anew: The Genius and Ambiguities of the American Founders*. New York: Alfred A. Knopf, 2003.

Baldwin, Joseph G. *The Flush Times of Alabama and Mississippi: A Series of Sketches*. New York: D. Appleton, 1853.

———. *Party Leaders,—Sketches of Thomas Jefferson, Alexander Hamilton, Andrew Jackson, Henry Clay, and John Randolph of Roanoke* . . . 1855; New York: D. Appleton, 1868.

Banning, Lance. "The Hamiltonian Madison: A Reconsideration." *Virginia Magazine of History and Biography* 92 (1984): 3–28.

———. *Jefferson and Madison : Three Conversations from the Founding*. Madison, Wisc.: Madison House, 1995.

———. *The Sacred Fire of Liberty: James Madison and the Founding of the Federal Republic*. Ithaca: Cornell University Press, 1995.

Bear, James A., Jr. Preface to *Thomas Jefferson and His Unknown Brother*. Ed. Bernard Mayo. Charlottesville: University Press of Virginia, 1981.

Becker, Carl L. *The Declaration of Independence: A Study in the History of Political Ideas.* 1922; New York: Vintage Books, 1970.

Bedini, Silvio A. *Thomas Jefferson: Statesman of Science.* New York: Macmillan, 1990.

Beeman, Richard. "The American Revolution." In *Thomas Jefferson: A Reference Biography*, ed. Merrill D. Peterson. New York: Charles Scribner's Sons, 1986.

Beverley, Robert. *The History and Present State of Virginia, in Four Parts.* 1705; Chapel Hill: University of North Carolina Press, 1947.

Billings, Warren M., ed. *The Old Dominion in the Seventeenth Century: A Documentary History.* Chapel Hill: University of North Carolina Press, 1975.

Billings, Warren M., John E. Selby, and Thad W. Tate. *Colonial Virginia: A History.* White Plains, N.Y.: KTO Press, 1986.

Boles, John B. *The South through Time: A History of an American Region.* Englewood Cliffs, N.J.: Prentice Hall, 1995.

Boyd, Julian. *The Declaration of Independence: The Evolution of the Text as Shown in Facsimiles of Various Drafts by Its Author, Thomas Jefferson.* Princeton: Princeton University Press, 1945.

Breen, T. H. "'Baubles of Britain': The American and Consumer Revolutions of the Eighteenth Century." In *Diversity and Unity in Early North America*, ed. Philip D. Morgan, 227–56. London and New York: Routledge, 1993.

———. *Puritans and Adventurers: Change and Persistence in Early America.* New York: Oxford University Press, 1980.

———. *Tobacco Culture: The Mentality of the Great Tidewater Planters on the Eve of Revolution.* Princeton: Princeton University Press, 1985.

Brown, Roger H. *Redeeming the Republic: Federalists, Taxation, and the Origins of the Constitution.* Baltimore: Johns Hopkins University Press, 1993.

Brown, Stuart Gerry. *Thomas Jefferson.* New York: Washington Square Press, 1966.

Browne, Stephen Howard. *Jefferson's Call for Nationhood.* College Station, Tex.: Texas A&M University Press, 2003.

Buckley, Thomas E. "The Political Theology of Thomas Jefferson." In *The Virginia Statute for Religious Freedom: Its Evolution and Consequences in American History*, ed. Merrill D. Peterson and Robert C. Vaughan, 75–107. Cambridge: Cambridge University Press, 1988.

Burstein, Andrew. *The Inner Jefferson: Portrait of a Grieving Optimist.* Charlottesville: University Press of Virginia, 1995.

———. "Jefferson's Rationalizations." *William and Mary Quarterly*, 3rd ser., 57 (2000): 183–97.

Bush, George W. "President George W. Bush's Inaugural Address." *http://www.whitehouse.gov/news/inaugural.html.*

Caesar, James A. "Natural Rights and Scientific Racism." In *Thomas Jefferson and the Politics of Nature*, ed. Thomas S. Engeman, 165–89. Notre Dame, Ind.: University of Notre Dame Press, 2000.

Cappon, Lester J., ed. *The Adams-Jefferson Letters: The Complete Correspondence between Thomas Jefferson and Abigail and John Adams.* 2 vols. Chapel Hill: University of North Carolina Press, 1959.

Cerami, Charles A. *Jefferson's Great Gamble: The Remarkable Story of Jefferson, Napoleon and the Men behind the Louisiana Purchase*. Naperville, Ill.: Sourcebooks, 2003.

Chambers, S. Allen, Jr. *Poplar Forest and Thomas Jefferson*. Forest, Va.: Corporation for Jefferson's Poplar Forest, 1993.

Chastellux, Chevalier de. "A Philosophical Encounter." In *Visitors to Monticello*, ed. Merrill D. Peterson, 10–17. Charlottesville: University Press of Virginia, 1989.

Chinard, Gilbert. Introduction to *The Commonplace Book of Thomas Jefferson: A Repertory of His Ideas on Government*, by Thomas Jefferson. Ed. Gilbert Chinard. Baltimore: Johns Hopkins University Press, 1926.

———. *Thomas Jefferson: The Apostle of Americanism*. Boston: Little, Brown, 1939.

Clinton, Catherine. *The Plantation Mistress: Woman's World in the Old South*. New York: Pantheon Books, 1982.

Clinton, William Jefferson. "American Renewal: We Must Care for One Another [First Inaugural Address]." *Vital Speeches of the Day* 59 (Feb. 15, 1993).

Combs, Jerald A. *The Jay Treaty: Political Battleground of the Founding Fathers*. Berkeley and Los Angeles: University of California Press, 1970.

Conrad, Stephen A. "Putting Rights Talk in Its Place: *The Summary View* Revisited." In *Jeffersonian Legacies*, ed. Peter S. Onuf, 254–80. Charlottesville: University Press of Virginia, 1993.

Cooke, Jacob E. *Alexander Hamilton*. New York: Charles Scribner's Sons, 1982.

Cunningham, Noble E., Jr. *The Jeffersonian Republicans in Power: Party Operations, 1801–1809*. Chapel Hill: University of North Carolina Press, 1963.

———. *The Jeffersonian Republicans: The Formation of Party Organization*. Chapel Hill: University of North Carolina Press, 1957.

———. *The Process of Government under Jefferson*. Princeton: Princeton University Press, 1978.

Curtis, William Eleroy. *The True Thomas Jefferson*. Philadelphia: J. B. Lippincott, 1901.

Dabney, Virginius. *Mr. Jefferson's University: A History*. Charlottesville: University Press of Virginia, 1981.

Darnton, Robert. *The Business of Enlightenment: A Publishing History of the Encyclopédie, 1775–1800*. Cambridge, Mass.: Belknap Press, 1979.

———. *The Great Cat Massacre and Other Episodes in French Cultural History*. New York: Basic Books, 1984.

DeConde, Alexander. *This Affair of Louisiana*. New York: Scribner, 1976.

Deetz, James. *Flowerdew Hundred: The Archaeology of a Virginia Plantation, 1619–1864*. Charlottesville: University Press of Virginia, 1993.

———. *In Small Things Forgotten: An Archaeology of Early American Life*. Exp. and rev. ed. New York: Anchor Books, 1996.

Deetz, James, and Patricia Scott Deetz. *The Times of Their Lives: Life, Love, and Death in Plymouth Colony*. New York: W. H. Freeman, 2000.

Dershowitz, Alan. *America Declares Independence*. Hoboken, N.J.: John Wiley and Sons, 2003.

Dodd, William E. *Statesmen of the Old South or From Radicalism to Conservative Revolt*. 1911; New York: Macmillan, 1926.

Dorsey, John M., ed. *The Jefferson-Dunglison Letters*. Charlottesville: University Press of Virginia, 1960.

Dreisbach, Daniel L. "George Mason's Pursuit of Religious Liberty in Revolutionary Virginia." *Virginia Magazine of History and Biography* 108 (2000): 5–44.

Duberman, Martin. "'Writhing Bedfellows' in Antebellum South Carolina: Historical Interpretations and the Politics of Evidence." In *Carryin' on in the Lesbian and Gay South*, ed. John Howard, 15–33. New York: New York University Press, 1997.

Dunglison, Robley. *The Autobiographical Ana of Robley Dunglison, M.D.* Ed. Samuel X. Rodbill. Philadelphia: American Philosophical Society, 1963.

Earle, Carville. "Environment, Disease and Mortality in Early Virginia." In *The Chesapeake in the Seventeenth Century: Essays on Anglo-American Society*, ed. Thad W. Tate and David L. Ammerman, 96–125. Chapel Hill: University of North Carolina Press, 1979.

Egerton, Douglas R. *Charles Fenton Mercer and the Trial of National Conservatism*. Jackson and London: University Press of Mississippi, 1989.

———. "Comment on Papers." Unpublished remarks, annual meeting of the Society for Historians of the Early American Republic, University of Virginia, 1989.

———. "The Empire of Liberty Reconsidered." In *The Revolution of 1800: Democracy, Race, and the New Republic*, ed. James Horn, Jan Ellen Lewis, and Peter Onuf, 309–30. Charlottesville: University of Virginia Press, 2002.

———. *Gabriel's Rebellion: The Virginia Slave Conspiracies of 1800 and 1802*. Chapel Hill: University of North Carolina Press, 1993.

———. "Thomas Jefferson and the Hemings Family: A Matter of Blood." *Historian* 59 (1997): 327–45.

Eicholz, Hans L. *Harmonizing Sentiments: The Declaration of Independence and the Jeffersonian Ideal of Self-Government*. New York: Peter Lang, 2001.

Ellis, Joseph J. *American Sphinx: The Character of Thomas Jefferson*. New York: Alfred A. Knopf, 1997.

———. *Founding Brothers: The Revolutionary Generation*. New York: Alfred A. Knopf, 2001.

———. "Jefferson: Post-DNA." *William and Mary Quarterly*, 3rd ser., 57 (2000): 125–38.

Emilio, John B., and Estelle B. Freeman. *Intimate Matters: A History of Sexuality in America*. New York: Harper and Row, 1988.

Engeman, Thomas S., ed. *Thomas Jefferson and the Politics of Nature*. Notre Dame, Ind.: University of Notre Dame Press, 2000.

Evans, Emory G. "Private Indebtedness and the Revolution in Virginia." *William and Mary Quarterly*, 3rd ser., 19 (1962): 511–33.

Fetter, Frank W. "The Revision of the Declaration of Independence in 1941." *William and Mary Quarterly*, 3rd ser., 31 (1974): 133-38.

Fischer, David H. *Growing Old in America*. New York: Oxford University Press, 1977.

Fischer, David H., and James C. Kelly. *Bound Away: Virginia and the Westward Movement*. Charlottesville: University Press of Virginia, 2000.

Fiske, John. *The Critical Period of American History: 1783–1789*. Boston: Houghton Mifflin, 1888.

Fitzpatrick, John C. *The Spirit of the Revolution: New Light from Some of the Original Sources of American History*. Boston and New York: Houghton Mifflin, 1924.

Fliegelman, Jay. *Declaring Independence: Jefferson, Natural Language, and the Culture of Performance*. Stanford: Stanford University Press, 1993.

Flower, Milton Embick. *James Parton: The Father of Modern Biography*. Durham: Duke University Press, 1951.

Ford, Worthington Chauncey, ed. *Thomas Jefferson and James Thomson Callender, 1798–1802*. Brooklyn, N.Y.: Historical Printing Club, 1897.

Foster, E. A., et al. "Jefferson Fathered Slave's Last Child." *Nature* 196 (Nov. 5, 1998): 27–28.

Fowler, Robert Booth. "Mythologies of a Founder." In *Thomas Jefferson and the Politics of Nature*, ed. Thomas S. Engeman, 123–41. Notre Dame, Ind.: University of Notre Dame Press, 2000.

Freeman, Joanne B. "Slander, Poison, Whispers, and Fame: Jefferson's 'Anas' and Political Gossip in the Early Republic." *Journal of the Early Republic* 15 (1995): 25–57.

Galenson, David W. *White Servitude in Colonial America: An Economic Analysis*. Cambridge: Cambridge University Press, 1981.

Galenson, David W., and Russell R. Menard. "Approaches to the Analysis of Economic Growth in Colonial British America." *Historical Methods* 13 (1980): 3–18.

Ganter, Herbert L. "Jefferson's 'Pursuit of Happiness' and Some Forgotten Men." *William and Mary Quarterly*, 2nd ser., 16 (1936): 422–34, 559–85.

———. "William Small, Jefferson's Beloved Teacher." *William and Mary Quarterly*, 3rd ser., 4 (1947): 505–11.

Gilbert, Felix. *To the Farewell Address: Ideas of Early American Foreign Policy*. Princeton: Princeton University Press, 1961.

Gordon-Reed, Annette. "'The Memories of a Few Negroes': Rescuing America's Future at Monticello." In *Sally Hemings and Thomas Jefferson: History, Memory, and Civic Culture*, ed. Jan Ellen Lewis and Peter S. Onuf, 236–52. Charlottesville: University Press of Virginia, 1999.

———. *Thomas Jefferson and Sally Hemings: An American Controversy*. Charlottesville: University Press of Virginia, 1997.

Greene, Jack P. "Foundations of Political Power in the Virginia House of Burgesses." *William and Mary Quarterly*, 3rd ser., 16 (1959): 485–506.

———. "The Intellectual Reconstruction of Virginia in the Age of Jefferson." *Jeffersonian Legacies*, ed. Peter S. Onuf, 225–53. Charlottesville: University Press of Virginia, 1993.

———. *Political Life in Eighteenth-Century Virginia*. Williamsburg: Colonial Williamsburg Foundation, 1986.

———. *Pursuits of Happiness: The Social Development of Early Modern British Colonies and the Formation of American Culture*. Chapel Hill: University of North Carolina Press, 1988.

———. *The Quest for Power: The Lower Houses of Assembly in the Southern Royal Colonies, 1689–1776*. Chapel Hill: University of North Carolina Press, 1963.

———. "Society, Ideology, and Politics: An Analysis of the Political Culture of Mid-

Eighteenth Century Virginia." In *Society, Freedom, and Conscience: The American Revolution in Virginia, Massachusetts, and New York*, ed. Richard M. Jellison. New York: W. W. Norton, 1976.

Griggs, Edward Howard. *American Statesmen: An Interpretation of Our History and Heritage*. Croton-on-Hudson, N.Y.: Orchard Hill Press, 1927.

Halliday, E. M. *Understanding Thomas Jefferson*. New York: HarperCollins, 2001.

Hamor, Ra[l]phe. *A True Discourse of the Present State of Virginia . . .* In *The Old Dominion in the Seventeenth Century: A Documentary History of Virginia, 1606-1689*, ed. Warren M. Billings, 36–57. Chapel Hill: University of North Carolina Press, 1975.

Hamowy, Ronald. "Jefferson and the Scottish Enlightenment: A Critique of Garry Wills's *Inventing America: Jefferson's Declaration of Independence*." *William and Mary Quarterly*, 3rd ser., 36 (1979): 503–23.

Hariot, Thomas. *A Briefe and True Report of the New Found Land of Virginia*. 1588; Ann Arbor, Mich.: University Microfilms, 1966.

Hatzenbuehler, Ronald L. "'Answering the Call': The First Inaugural Addresses of Thomas Jefferson and William Jefferson Clinton." In *The Romance of History: Essays in Honor of Lawrence S. Kaplan*, ed. Scott L. Bills and E. Timothy Smith, 53–67. Kent: Kent State University Press, 1997.

———. "'Growing Weary in Well-Doing': Thomas Jefferson's Life among the Virginia Gentry." *Virginia Magazine of History and Biography* 101 (1993): 5–36.

———. "Of Manna, Mouse, and Mammoth: Notes on Jefferson's Empiricism." Unpublished paper presented at the annual meeting of the Southern Historical Association, November 1985.

———. "Refreshing the Tree of Liberty with the Blood of Patriots and Tyrants: Thomas Jefferson and the Origins of the U.S. Constitution." In *Essays on Liberty and Federalism: The Shaping of the U.S. Constitution*, ed. David E. Narrett and Joyce S. Goldberg, 88–104. College Station, Tex.: Texas A&M University Press, 1988.

———. "Thomas Jefferson." In *Popular Images of American Presidents*, ed. William C. Spragens, 27–45. Westport, Conn.: Greenwood Press, 1988.

———. "Thomas Jefferson and the American Revolution." In *The American Revolution, 1775-1783: An Encyclopedia*, ed. Richard L. Blanco, 1: 821–25. 2 vols. New York and London: Garland Publishing, 1993.

Hatzenbuehler, Ronald L., and Robert L. Ivie. *Congress Declares War: Rhetoric, Leadership, and Partisanship in the Early Republic*. Kent: Kent State University Press, 1983.

Heath, Barbara J. *Hidden Lives: The Archaeology of Slave Life at Thomas Jefferson's Poplar Forest*. Charlottesville: University Press of Virginia, 1999.

Hellenbrand, Harold. *The Unfinished Revolution: Education and Politics in the Thought of Thomas Jefferson*. Newark: University of Delaware Press, 1990.

Herndon, Melvin G. *Tobacco in Colonial Virginia: "The Sovereign Remedy."* 1957; Williamsburg, Va.: 350th Anniversary Celebration Corp., 1968.

Higginbotham, Sanford W. *The Keystone in the Democratic Arch: Pennsylvania Politics, 1800-1816*. Harrisburg, Pa.: Pennsylvania Historical and Museum Commission, 1952.

Hofstadter, Richard. *The Idea of a Party System: The Rise of Legitimate Opposition in the*

United States, 1780–1840. Berkeley, Los Angeles, and London: University of California Press, 1970.

Howell, Wilbur Samuel. "The Declaration of Independence and Eighteenth-Century Logic." *William and Mary Quarterly*, 3rd ser., 18 (1961): 470–84.

Hume, Ivor Noel. *Martin's Hundred*. Charlottesville: University Press of Virginia, 1979.

The Interpreter's Bible: The Holy Scriptures in the King James and Revised Standard Versions with General Articles and Introduction, Exegesis, Exposition for Each Book of the Bible. 12 vols. New York: Abingdon, Cokesbury Press, 1951–57.

Irons, Charles F. "The Spiritual Fruits of Revolution: Disestablishment and the Rise of the Virginia Baptists." *Virginia Magazine of History and Biography* 109 (2001): 158–86.

Isaac, Rhys. "'The Rage of Malice of the Old Serpent Devil': The Dissenters and the Making and Remaking of the Virginia Statute for Religious Freedom." In *The Virginia Statute for Religious Freedom: Its Evolution and Consequences in American History*, ed. Merrill D. Peterson and Robert C. Vaughan. Cambridge: Cambridge University Press, 1988.

———. *The Transformation of Virginia, 1740–1790*. Chapel Hill: University of North Carolina Press, 1982.

Jayne, Allen. *Jefferson's Declaration of Independence: Origins, Philosophy and Theology*. Lexington: University Press of Kentucky, 1998.

Jefferson, Thomas. *Autobiography of Thomas Jefferson*. 1853; New York: Capricorn Books, 1959.

———. *The Commonplace Book of Thomas Jefferson: A Repertory of His Ideas on Government*. Ed. Gilbert Chinard. Baltimore: Johns Hopkins University Press, 1926.

———. *The Complete Anas of Thomas Jefferson*. Ed. Franklin B. Sawvel. 1903; New York: Da Capo Press, 1970.

———. *The Family Letters of Thomas Jefferson*. Ed. Edwin Morris Betts and James Adam Bear, Jr. Columbia, Mo.: University of Missouri Press, 1966.

———. "Jefferson's Extracts from the Gospels." In *The Papers of Thomas Jefferson*, ed. Dickinson W. Adams. 2nd ser. Princeton: Princeton University Press, 1983.

———. *Jefferson's Memorandum Books: Accounts, with Legal Records and Miscellany, 1767–1826*. Ed. James A. Bear, Jr. and Lucia C. Stanton. 2 vols. Princeton: Princeton University Press, 1997.

———. *Memoir, Correspondence, and Miscellanies, from the Papers of Thomas Jefferson*. Ed. Thomas Jefferson Randolph. 3 vols. 1829; Boston: Gray and Bowen, 1830.

———. *Notes on the State of Virginia*. Ed. William Peden. 1787; Chapel Hill: University of North Carolina Press, 1954.

———. *The Papers of Thomas Jefferson*. Ed. Julian P. Boyd et al. 28 vols. to date; Princeton: Princeton University Press, 1950–.

———. *The Portable Thomas Jefferson*. Ed. Merrill D. Peterson. New York: Viking Press, 1975.

———. *The Republic of Letters: The Correspondence between Thomas Jefferson and James Madison, 1776–1826*. Ed. James Morton Smith. 3 vols. New York: Norton, 1995.

———. The Thomas Jefferson Papers, Library of Congress, Washington, D.C.

——. "Thomas Jefferson: First Inaugural Address in Washington, D.C., Wednesday, March 4, 1801." In *Inaugural Addresses of the Presidents of the United States from George Washington, 1789, to George Bush, 1989.* Washington, D.C.: Government Printing Office, 1989.

——. Thomas Jefferson Papers, Massachusetts Historical Society, Boston, Mass.

——. "Thomas Jefferson: Second Inaugural Address, Monday, March 4, 1805." In *Inaugural Addresses of the Presidents of the United States from George Washington, 1789, to George Bush, 1989.* Washington, D.C.: Government Printing Office, 1989.

——. *Thomas Jefferson's Farm Book, with Commentary and Relevant Extracts from Other Writings.* Ed. Edwin Morris Betts. Princeton: Princeton University Press, 1953.

——. *Thomas Jefferson's Garden Book, 1766–1824, with Relevant Extracts from His Other Writings.* Ed. Edwin Morris Betts. Philadelphia: American Philosophical Society, 1944.

——. *The Works of Thomas Jefferson.* Ed. Paul Leicester Ford. 12 vols. New York: G. P. Putnam's Sons, 1904–5.

——. *The Writings of Thomas Jefferson.* Ed. Paul Leicester Ford. 10 vols. New York: G. P. Putnam's Sons, 1892–99.

——. *The Writings of Thomas Jefferson.* Ed. Andrew A. Lipscomb and Albert E. Bergh. 20 vols. Washington, D.C.: Thomas Jefferson Memorial Association, 1903–5.

——. *Writings.* Ed. Merrill D. Peterson. New York: Library of America, 1984.

Johnson, Allen. *Jefferson and His Colleagues: A Chronicle of the Virginia Dynasty.* New Haven: Yale University Press, 1921.

Johnson, George R., Jr. *The Will of the People: The Legacy of George Mason.* Fairfax, Va.: George Mason University Press, 1991.

Johnstone, Robert M., Jr. *Jefferson and the Presidency: Leadership in the Young Republic.* Ithaca: Cornell University Press, 1978.

Jordan, Daniel P. *Political Leadership in Jefferson's Virginia.* Charlottesville: University Press of Virginia, 1983.

Jordan, Winthrop. Review of *Thomas Jefferson: An Intimate Biography,* by Fawn Brodie. *William and Mary Quarterly,* 3rd ser., 32 (1975): 510–12.

——. *White over Black: American Attitudes toward the Negro, 1550–1812.* Chapel Hill: University of North Carolina Press, 1968.

Kaplan, Lawrence S. *Alexander Hamilton: Ambivalent Anglophile.* Wilmington, Del.: Scholarly Resources, 2002.

——. *Colonies into Nation: American Diplomacy, 1763–1801.* New York: Macmillan, 1972.

——. "The Consensus of 1789: Jefferson and Hamilton on American Foreign Policy." In *Entangling Alliances with None: American Foreign Policy in the Age of Jefferson,* 67–78. Kent: Kent State University Press, 1987.

——. "The Idealist as Realist." In *Entangling Alliances with None: American Foreign Policy in the Age of Jefferson,* 3–23. Kent: Kent State University Press, 1987.

——. *Jefferson and France: An Essay on Politics and Political Ideas.* New Haven: Yale University Press, 1967.

——. "Jefferson and the Constitution: The View from Paris, 1786–89." *Diplomatic History* 11 (1987): 321–35.

————. *Thomas Jefferson: Westward the Course of Empire.* Wilmington, Del.: Scholarly Resources, 1999.

Keith, William. *The History of the British Plantations in America.* . . . 1738; New York: Arno Press, 1972.

Kennedy, Roger G. *Burr, Hamilton, and Jefferson: A Study in Character.* New York: Oxford University Press, 2000.

————. *Mr. Jefferson's Lost Cause: Land, Farmers, and the Louisiana Purchase.* New York: Oxford University Press, 2003.

Kern, Susan. "The Material World of the Jeffersons at Shadwell." *William and Mary Quarterly*, 3rd ser., 62 (2005): 213–42.

Kimball, Fiske. *Thomas Jefferson: Architect.* 1916; New York: Da Capo Press, 1968.

Klingberg, Frank J., and Frank W. Klingberg, eds. *The Correspondence between Henry Stephens Randall and Hugh Blair Grigsby, 1856–1861.* Berkeley and Los Angeles: University of California Press, 1952.

Koch, Adrienne. *Jefferson and Madison: The Great Collaboration.* New York: Knopf, 1950.

————. *The Philosophy of Thomas Jefferson.* 1943; Gloucester, Mass.: Peter Smith, 1957.

Koepp, Cynthia J. "The Alphabetical Order: Work in Diderot's *Encyclopédie.*" In *Work in France: Representations, Meaning, Organization, and Practice,* ed. Steven Laurence Kaplan and Cynthia J. Koepp, 229–57. Ithaca: Cornell University Press, 1986.

Langhorne, Elizabeth. "Edward Coles, Thomas Jefferson, and the Rights of Man." *Virginia Cavalcade* 23 (1973–74): 30–37.

Lanier, Shannon, and Jane Feldman. *Jefferson's Children: The Story of One American Family.* New York: Random House, 2000.

Leary, Helen F. M. "Sally Hemings's Children: A Genealogical Analysis of the Evidence." *National Genealogical Society Quarterly* 89 (2001): 165–207.

Lewis, Jan. *The Pursuit of Happiness: Family and Values in Jefferson's Virginia.* Cambridge: Cambridge University Press, 1983.

————. "The White Jeffersons." In *Sally Hemings and Thomas Jefferson: History, Memory, and Civic Culture,* ed. Jan Ellen Lewis and Peter S. Onuf, 127–60. Charlottesville: University Press of Virginia, 1999.

Lind, Michael. *The Next American Nation: The New Nationalism and the Fourth American Revolution.* New York: Free Press, 1995.

Little, David. "Religion and Civil Virtue in America: Jefferson's Religious Statute Reconsidered." In *The Virginia Statute for Religious Freedom: Its Evolution and Consequences in American History,* ed. Merrill D. Peterson and Robert C. Vaughan, 237–55. Cambridge: Cambridge University Press, 1988.

Lockridge, Kenneth A. *On the Sources of Patriarchal Rage: The Commonplace Books of William Byrd and Thomas Jefferson and the Gendering of Power in the Eighteenth Century.* New York: New York University Press, 1992.

————. "Robert Bolling and Thomas Jefferson: Gemini Rising." *Journal of Family History* 28 (2003): 465–89.

————. *Settlement and Unsettlement in Early America: The Crisis of Political Legitimacy before the Revolution.* Cambridge: Cambridge University Press, 1981.

Maier, Pauline. *American Scripture: Making the Declaration of Independence*. New York: Alfred A. Knopf, 1997.

Malone, Dumas. *Jefferson and His Time*. 6 vols. Boston: Little, Brown, 1948–81.

Mannix, Richard. "Gallatin, Jefferson and the Embargo of 1808." *Diplomatic History* 3 (1979): 151–72.

Martin, Edwin Thomas. *Thomas Jefferson: Scientist*. New York: H. Schuman, 1952.

Mason, George. *The Papers of George Mason, 1725–1792*. 3 vols. Ed. Robert A. Rutland. Chapel Hill: University of North Carolina Press, 1970.

Matthews, Richard K. *The Radical Politics of Thomas Jefferson: A Revisionist View*. Lawrence, Kans.: University Press of Kansas, 1984.

Mayer, David N. *The Constitutional Thought of Thomas Jefferson*. Charlottesville: University Press of Virginia, 1994.

Mayo, Bernard, ed. *Thomas Jefferson and His Unknown Brother*. Charlottesville: University Press of Virginia, 1981.

McCoy, Drew R. *The Elusive Republic: Political Economy in Jeffersonian America*. Chapel Hill: University of North Carolina Press, 1980.

———. "James Madison and Visions of American Nationality in the Confederation Period." In *Beyond Confederation: Origins of the Constitution and American National Identity*, ed. Richard Beeman, Stephen Botein, and Edward C. Carter II, 226–58. Chapel Hill: University of North Carolina Press, 1987.

———. *The Last of the Fathers: James Madison and the Republican Legacy*. Cambridge: Cambridge University Press, 1989.

McCusker, John J., and Russell R. Menard. *The Economy of British America, 1607–1789*. Chapel Hill: University of North Carolina Press, 1985.

McDonald, Forrest, and Ellen Shapiro McDonald. *Requiem: Variations on Eighteenth-Century Themes*. Lawrence, Kans.: University Press of Kansas, 1988.

McDonald, Robert M. S. "Was There a Religious Revolution in 1800?" In *The Revolution of 1800: Democracy, Race, and the New Republic*, ed. James Horn, Jan Ellen Lewis, and Peter Onuf, 173–97. Charlottesville: University of Virginia Press, 2002.

McEwan, Barbara. *Thomas Jefferson: Farmer*. Jefferson, N.C.: McFarland, 1991.

McLaughlin, Jack. *Jefferson and Monticello: The Biography of a Builder*. New York: Henry Holt, 1988.

Miller, Charles A. *Jefferson and Nature: An Interpretation*. Baltimore: Johns Hopkins University Press, 1988.

Miller, Helen Hill. *George Mason: Gentleman Revolutionary*. Chapel Hill: University of North Carolina Press, 1975.

Morse, John T. *Thomas Jefferson*. 1883; Boston and New York: Houghton Mifflin, 1911.

Morton, Richard L. *Colonial Virginia*. 2 vols. Chapel Hill: University of North Carolina Press, 1960.

Murrin, John M. "Can Liberals Be Patriots? Natural Right, Virtue, and Moral Sense in the America of George Mason and Thomas Jefferson." In *Natural Rights and Natural Law: The Legacy of George Mason*, ed. Robert P. Davidow, 35–65. Fairfax, Va.: George Mason University Press, 1986.

————. "The Jeffersonian Triumph and American Exceptionalism." *Journal of the Early Republic* 20 (2000): 1–25.

————. "1787: The Invention of American Federalism." In *Essays on Liberty and Federalism: The Shaping of the U.S. Constitution,* ed. David E. Narrett and Joyce S. Goldberg, 20–47. College Station, Tex.: Texas A&M University Press, 1988.

Muzzey, David Saville. *Thomas Jefferson.* New York: Charles Scribner's Sons, 1918.

Najar, Monica. "'Meddling with Emancipation': Baptists, Authority, and the Rift over Slavery in the Upper South." *Journal of the Early Republic* 25 (2005): 157–86.

National Park Service. *Jamestown.* Film. Washington, D.C.: U.S. Department of the Interior, 1981.

Neiman, Fraser D. "Coincidence or Causal Connection? The Relationship between Thomas Jefferson's Visits to Monticello and Sally Hemings's Conceptions." *William and Mary Quarterly,* 3rd ser., 57 (2000): 198–210.

O'Brien, Conor Cruise. *The Long Affair: Thomas Jefferson and the French Revolution, 1785–1800.* Chicago: University of Chicago Press, 1996.

Onuf, Peter S., ed. *Jeffersonian Legacies.* Charlottesville: University Press of Virginia, 1993.

————. *Jefferson's Empire: The Language of American Nationhood.* Charlottesville: University Press of Virginia, 2000.

Onuf, Peter S., and Leonard J. Sadosky. *Jeffersonian America.* Walden, Mass.: Blackwell Publishers, 2002.

Paine, Thomas. *Common Sense and The Crisis.* Garden City, N.Y.: Doubleday Dolphin Book, 1960.

Paquette, Robert L. "Revolutionary Saint Domingue in the Making of Territorial Louisiana." In *A Turbulent Time: The French Revolution and the Greater Caribbean,* ed. David Barry Gaspar and David Patrick Geggus, 204–25. Bloomington, Ind.: Indiana University Press, 1997.

Patton, John Shelton. *Jefferson, Cabell and the University of Virginia.* New York and Washington, D.C.: Neale, 1906.

Peterson, Merrill D. *The Jefferson Image in the American Mind.* New York: Oxford University Press, 1960.

————. *Thomas Jefferson and the New Nation: A Biography.* New York: Oxford University Press, 1970.

Quitt, Martin H. "Immigrant Origins of the Virginia Gentry: A Study of Cultural Transmission and Innovation." *William and Mary Quarterly,* 3rd ser., 45 (1988): 629–55.

Rakove, Jack N. "Our Jefferson." In *Sally Hemings and Thomas Jefferson: History, Memory, and Civic Culture,* ed. Jan Ellen Lewis and Peter S. Onuf. Charlottesville: University Press of Virginia, 1999.

Randall, Henry S. *The Life of Thomas Jefferson.* 3 vols. New York: Derby and Jackson, 1858.

Rayner, B. L. *Life of Thomas Jefferson.* Ed. Eyler Robert Coates, Sr. 1834; 2005: *http://etext.lib.virginia.edu/jefferson/biog/.*

Richards, Leonard L. *Shays's Rebellion: The American Revolution's Final Battle.* Philadelphia: University of Pennsylvania Press, 2002.

Risjord, Norman K. "The Compromise of 1790: New Evidence on the Dinner Table Bargain." *William and Mary Quarterly*, 3rd ser., 33 (1976): 309–14.

———. *Thomas Jefferson*. Madison, Wisc.: Madison House, 1994.

Rothman, Joshua D. "Can the 'Character Defense' Survive? Measuring Polar Positions in the Jefferson-Hemings Controversy by the Standards of History." *National Genealogical Society Quarterly* 89 (2001): 219–33.

———. "James Callender and Social Knowledge of Interracial Sex in Antebellum Virginia." In *Sally Hemings and Thomas Jefferson: History, Memory, and Civic Culture*, ed. Jan Ellen Lewis and Peter S. Onuf, 87–113. Charlottesville: University Press of Virginia, 1999.

———. *Notorious in the Neighborhood: Sex and Families across the Color Lines in Virginia, 1787–1861*. Chapel Hill: University of North Carolina Press, 2003.

Rowland, Kate Mason. *The Life of George Mason, 1725–1792*. 2 vols. 1892; New York: Russell and Russell, 1964.

Royster, Charles. *The Fabulous History of the Dismal Swamp Company: A Story of George Washington's Times*. New York: Alfred A. Knopf, 1999.

Rutland, Robert A. Introduction to *The Papers of George Mason, 1725–1792*, by George Mason. Ed. Robert A. Rutland. 3 vols. Chapel Hill: University of North Carolina Press, 1970.

Rutman, Darrett B., and Anita H. Rutman. "'Now-Wives and Sons-in-Law': Parental Death in a Seventeenth-Century Virginia County." In *The Chesapeake in the Seventeenth Century: Essays on Anglo-American Society*, ed. Thad W. Tate and David L. Ammerman, 153–82. Chapel Hill: University of North Carolina Press, 1979.Salter, Mary Jo. "The Hand of Thomas Jefferson." In *Sunday Skaters: Poems by Mary Jo Salter*. New York: Knopf, 1994.

Sanford, Charles B. "The Religious Beliefs of Thomas Jefferson." In *Religion and Political Culture in Jefferson's Virginia*, ed. Garrett Ward Sheldon and Daniel L. Dreisbach, 61–91. Lanham, Md.: Rowman and Littlefield, 2000.

Schachner, Nathan. *Thomas Jefferson: A Biography*. New York: Thomas Yoseloff, 1957.

Schlesinger, Arthur M. "The Lost Meaning of 'The Pursuit of Happiness.'" *William and Mary Quarterly*, 3rd ser., 21 (1964): 325–27.

Schouler, James. *Thomas Jefferson*. New York: Dodd, Mead, 1893.

Schwartz, Stephen A. "George Mason: Forgotten Founder, He Conceived the Bill of Rights." *Smithsonian* 31 (2000): 142–54.

Seelye, John D. *Prophetic Waters: The River in Early American Life and Literature*. New York: Oxford University Press, 1977.

Selby, John E. *The Revolution in Virginia, 1775–1783*. Williamsburg, Va.: Colonial Williamsburg Foundation, 1988.

Sheldon, Garrett Ward. *The Political Philosophy of Thomas Jefferson*. Baltimore: Johns Hopkins University Press, 1991.

Sheldon, Garrett Ward, and Daniel L. Dreisbach. *Religion and Political Culture in Jefferson's Virginia*. Lanham, Md.: Rowman and Littlefield, 2000.

Sheridan, Eugene R. *Jefferson and Religion*. Charlottesville: Thomas Jefferson Memorial Foundation, 1998.

———. "Thomas Jefferson and the Giles Resolutions." *William and Mary Quarterly*, 3rd ser., 49 (1992): 589–608.

Simms, Henry H. *The Rise of the Whigs in Virginia, 1824–1840*. Richmond, Va.: William Byrd Press, 1929.

Simpson, Stephen. *The Lives of George Washington and Thomas Jefferson, with a Parallel*. Philadelphia: Henry Young, 1833.

Sloan, Herbert E. *Principle and Interest: Thomas Jefferson and the Problem of Debt*. New York: Oxford University Press, 1995.

Small, Judy Jo. "Robert Beverley and the New World Garden." *American Literature* 55 (1983): 525–40.

Smith, John. *The General Historie of Virginia, New England, and the Summer Isles*. 1624; Ann Arbor, Mich.: University Microfilms, 1966.

Sobel, Mechal. *The World They Made Together: Black and White Values in Eighteenth Century Virginia*. Princeton: Princeton University Press, 1987.

Spivak, Burton. *Jefferson's English Crisis: Commerce, Embargo, and the Republican Revolution*. Charlottesville: University Press of Virginia, 1979.

Stith, William. *The History of the First Discovery and Settlement of Virginia . . .* 1747; Spartanburg, S.C.: Reprint Company, 1965.

Sutton, Robert P. *Revolution to Secession: Constitution Making in the Old Dominion*. Charlottesville: University Press of Virginia, 1989.

Szatmary, David P. *Shays' Rebellion: The Making of an Agrarian Insurrection*. Amherst, Mass.: University of Massachusetts Press, 1980.

Tate, Thad W., and David L. Ammerman, eds. *The Chesapeake in the Seventeenth Century: Essays on Anglo-American Society*. Chapel Hill: University of North Carolina Press, 1979.

Trent, William P. *Southern Statesmen of the Old Regime*. New York: Thomas Y. Crowell, 1897.

Tucker, George. *The Life of Thomas Jefferson. . . .* 2 vols. London: Charles Knight, 1837.

Ubbelohde, Carl. *The American Colonies and the British Empire, 1607–1763*. New York: Thomas Y. Crowell, 1968.

Vance, Joseph Carroll. "Thomas Jefferson Randolph." Ph.D. diss., University of Virginia, 1957.

Vidal, Gore. *Inventing a Nation: Washington, Adams, Jefferson*. New Haven: Yale University Press, 2003.

Waldstreicher, David. Preface and introduction to *Notes on the State of Virginia by Thomas Jefferson with Related Documents*, iv–vi, 1–38. Boston: Bedford/St. Martin's, 2002.

Wallenstein, Peter. "Flawed Keepers of the Flame: The Interpreters of George Mason." *Virginia Magazine of History and Biography* 102 (1994): 229–70.

Warren, Robert Penn. *Brother to Dragons: A Tale in Verse and Voice*. 1953; New York: Random House, 1977.

Watson, Thomas E. *The Life and Times of Thomas Jefferson*. New York: D. Appleton, 1903.

Weisberger, Bernard A. *America Afire: Jefferson, Adams, and the Revolutionary Election of 1800*. New York: HarperCollins, 2000.

Wells, Camille. "Accommodation and Appropriation: White and Black Domestic Landscapes in Early 19th-Century Virginia." Unpublished paper presented at the annual conference of the Omohondro Institute of Early American History and Culture, 1996.

Wheelan, Joseph. *Jefferson's War: America's First War on Terror, 1801–1805.* New York: Carroll and Graf, 2003.

Williams, David Alan. "The Small Farmer in Eighteenth-Century Virginia Politics." *Agricultural History* 43 (1969): 91–101.

Williams, William Appleman. *The Contours of American History.* 1961; Chicago: Quadrangle Books, 1966.

Wills, Garry. *Inventing America: Jefferson's Declaration of Independence.* Garden City, N.Y.: Doubleday, 1978.

———. *Mr. Jefferson's University.* Washington, D.C.: National Geographic, 2002.

Wilson, Douglas L. "Jefferson and the Republic of Letters." In *Jeffersonian Legacies,* ed. Peter S. Onuf. Charlottesville: University Press of Virginia, 1993.

———. "Jefferson Unbound." *Virginia Cavalcade* 50 (2001): 48–53.

Wilson, James. *The Works of James Wilson.* Ed. Robert Green McCloskey. 2 vols. Cambridge, Mass.: Harvard University Press, 1967.

Wyatt-Brown, Bertram. *Southern Honor: Ethics and Behavior in the Old South.* New York: Oxford University Press, 1982.

Yarbrough, Jean M. *American Virtues: Thomas Jefferson on the Character of a Free People.* Lawrence: University Press of Kansas, 1998.

Yazawa, Melvin. "Republican Expectations: Revolutionary Ideology and the Compromise of 1790." In *A Republic for the Ages: The United States Capitol and the Political Culture of the Early Republic,* ed. Donald R. Kennon, 3–35. Charlottesville: University Press of Virginia for the United States Capitol History Society, 1999.

Zuckert, Michael P. "Founder of the Natural Rights Republic." In *Thomas Jefferson and the Politics of Nature,* ed. Thomas S. Engeman, 11–58. Notre Dame, Ind.: University of Notre Dame Press, 2000.

———. *The Natural Rights Republic: Studies in the Foundation of the American Political Tradition.* Notre Dame, Ind.: University of Notre Dame Press, 1996.

Index

Ronald L. Hatzenbuehler is professor of history at Idaho State University in Pocatello. He is the author (with Robert L. Ivie) of *Congress Declares War: Rhetoric, Leadership, and Partisanship in the Early Republic* (1983) and numerous articles on Thomas Jefferson and the early republic.